Feminism & Foucault

Reflections on Resistance

Edited by

Irene Diamond and Lee Quinby

Northeastern University Press

Boston

Northeastern University Press 1988

Library of Congress Cataloging in Publication Data

Feminism & Foucault.

  Bibliography: p.
  Includes index.
  1. Power (Social sciences). 2. Foucault, Michel.
3. Feminism—Philosophy. 4. Patriarchy. 5. Sex role.
I. Diamond, Irene, 1947– . II. Quinby, Lee, 1946–
III. Title: Feminism and Foucault.
HM136F43   1988   305.4'2'01   87-34874
ISBN 1-55553-032-X (alk. paper)
ISBN 1-55553-033-8 (pbk. : alk. paper)

Designed by Jennie Ray Bush

Composed in Plantin Light by David E. Seham Associates, Metuchen, New Jersey. Printed and bound by Halliday Lithograph, West Hanover, Massachusetts. The paper is Sebago Antique, an acid-free sheet.

MANUFACTURED IN THE UNITED STATES OF AMERICA
98 97 96 95   8 7 6 5

Acknowledgments

Irene Diamond thanks Jeff Land and Lee Quinby thanks Tom Hayes for their willingness to read, listen, and make thoughtful suggestions. Lee Quinby also thanks Hobart and William Smith Colleges for a grant that facilitated their East Coast–West Coast collaboration. And both are deeply grateful to Andrew Mandel of Northeastern University Press, whose enthusiasm, patience, and incisive analyses were especially helpful at critical stages in the preparation of this volume.

Appreciation is extended to the following authors and publishers for permission to include these works in this volume.

Biddy Martin, "Feminism, Criticism, and Foucault"; an expanded version of this essay appeared in *New German Critique* 27 (Fall 1982). Reprinted with permission.

Meaghan Morris, "The Pirate's Fiancée: Feminists and Philosophers, or maybe tonight it'll happen," from *Foucault: Power, Truth, Strategy*, edited by M. Morris and P. Patten. Copyright © 1979 by Feral Publications. Reprinted with permission.

Susan Bordo, "Anorexia Nervosa: Psychopathology as the Crystallization of Culture"; an earlier version of this essay was published in the *Philosophical Forum* 17, no. 2 (Winter 1985–86).

Kathleen B. Jones, "On Authority: Or, Why Women Are Not Entitled to Speak." Reprinted by permission of New York University Press, from *Authority Revisited: Nomos XXIX*, edited by J. Roland Pennock and John W. Chapman. Copyright © 1987 by New York University.

Mary Lydon, "Foucault and Feminism: A Romance of Many Dimensions"; first published in *Humanities in Society* 5, nos. 3 and 4 (Summer and Fall 1982). Reprinted with permission.

Peggy Kamuf, "Penelope at Work: Interruptions in *A Room of One's Own*"; first published in *Novel: A Forum on Fiction* 16, no. 1 (Fall 1982). Copyright © 1982 by Novel Corp. Reprinted with permission.

Irene Diamond and Lee Quinby, "American Feminism and the Language of Control"; this essay is based in part on "American Feminism in the Age of the Body," *Signs* 10 (Fall 1984), pp. 119–25.

Sharon Welch, "The Truth of Liberation Theology: Particulars of a Relative Sublime," from *Communities of Resistance and Solidarity* by Sharon Welch. Copyright © 1985 by Orbis Books. Reprinted with permission.

Contents

Introduction

Irene Diamond and Lee Quinby

Why this volume? Is this yet another attempt to authorize feminism by marrying it into respectability? Are we trying to arrange a final divorce from Marxism—or Freudianism or Lacanian analysis—for a happier union with Foucauldian genealogy? At one point, the thought that we might be construed as calling for a new orthodoxy led us to put this project aside.[1] We put that particular concern to rest because at this historical juncture, when feminism is on the defensive politically, the contributions of feminists who have drawn on Foucault's analyses of power in the contemporary world are particularly helpful in combating this threat. By delineating the different cultural and political realms where masculinist power is eviscerating feminist gains, such contributions also uncover a multiplicity of points of resistance without appealing to a monolithic "politically correct" position. Indeed, the essays here are notable for challenging tendencies toward either feminist or Foucauldian orthodoxy precisely because of the new views of empowerment and resistance gained from working with the two approaches.

Thus, rather than a new marriage or political school, we would say that the convergences of feminism and Foucault suggest the possibility of a friendship grounded in political and ethical commitment. This friendship is not without tensions of course, but, as we will indicate, such tensions are healthy insofar as they check closure and sustain reflexivity. Both Foucault and feminists have pointed to the ways in which friendship provides a model for nonhierarchical, reciprocal relations that run counter to the hierarchical modes that have dominated Western society.[2] In oral and written discussion, friendship's reciprocity takes the form of dialogue, what Foucault has called "the work of reciprocal elucidation" in which "the rights of each person are in some sense immanent in the discussion."[3] By respecting differences without seeking absorption or dialectical synthesis, feminist and Foucauldian analyses can interact with each other to create dialogical rather than monological descriptions. Such an enterprise is admittedly difficult, but, as the following essays suggest, not inherently impossible because of the ways in which these two otherwise rather different approaches to cultural analysis converge.

Four convergences of feminism and Foucault are especially striking. Both identify the body as the site of power, that is, as the locus of domination through which docility is accomplished and subjectivity constituted. Both point to the local and intimate operations of power rather than focusing exclusively on the supreme power of the state. Both bring to the fore the crucial role of discourse in its capacity to produce and sustain hegemonic power and emphasize the challenges contained within marginalized and/or unrecognized discourses. And both criticize the ways in which Western humanism has privileged the experience of the Western masculine elite as it proclaims universals about truth, freedom, and human nature. Despite their seemingly different objectives, then, feminist and Foucauldian analyses come together in the ways they have attempted to dismantle existing but heretofore unrecognized modes of domination. In short, these convergences comprise some of the most powerful forms of resistance available to us as we approach the last decade of the twentieth century. This is not to insist that feminist and Foucauldian analyses really mirror one another, but, on the contrary, to suggest that each approach asks different questions and offers distinctive insights that the other has ignored or missed and to suggest further that these questions and insights can be mutually corrective.

Certainly one of Foucault's most notable contributions to contemporary social criticism generally and feminist concerns specifically is his explication of power/knowledge. According to Foucault, power's relation to knowledge is never separable, because within each society there is a "regime of truth" with its own particular mechanisms for producing truth. He describes contemporary societies as having a " 'political economy' of truth" characterized by five traits:

> "Truth" is centered on the form of scientific discourse and the institutions which produce it; it is subject to constant economic and political incitement (the demand for truth, as much for economic production as for political power); it is the object, under diverse forms, of immense diffusion and consumption (circulating through apparatuses of education and information whose extent is relatively broad in the social body, not withstanding certain strict limitations); it is produced and transmitted under the control, dominant if not exclusive, of a few great political and economic

apparatuses (university, army, writing, media); lastly, it is the issue of a whole political debate and social confrontation ("ideological" struggles).[4]

Despite similarities with sociology-of-knowledge contentions regarding the conditions of knowledge creation, Foucault's notion of power/knowledge challenges assumptions that ideology can be demystified and, hence, that undistorted truth can be attained. He insists that truth is never "outside power, or lacking in power."[5] In rejecting the idea that power functions only through "Thou shalt nots" or forms of restrictive commandments and laws, Foucault brings to our attention the complex network of disciplinary systems and prescriptive technologies through which power operates in the modern era, particularly since the normalizing disciplines of medicine, education, and psychology have gained ascendancy. Sexuality, in his view, emerged in this historical period as a mechanism of new ways of organizing knowledge.

Since feminism also arose in this era, it is important for us to consider the ways in which it might be implicated in the "technologies of sex," even as it emerged as a form of resistance to them. Significantly, the formation of nineteenth-century feminism coincided with medical and scientific treatments of women's hysteria, invalidism, and capacity for reproduction. The writings of Margaret Fuller, Elizabeth Cady Stanton, and Charlotte Perkins Gilman challenged scientific and medical expertise in these areas. In this sense, feminism may be thought of as what Foucault called a "reverse" discourse that, as he states about homosexuality, "began to speak in its own behalf, to demand that its legitimacy or 'naturality' be acknowledged, often in the same vocabulary, using the same categories by which it was medically disqualified."[6] As a reverse discourse, the first wave of feminism challenged the normalizing powers of medicine, science, and education at the very time that the deployment of sexuality, with its "disciplines of the body" and "regulations of the population," took command over the power of sovereignty. We should also recall, however, that the power of a reverse discourse is precarious. As the eruption of the second wave of feminism in our period suggests, over the course of the century many of the tenets of nineteenth-century feminism have been appropriated into operations of disciplinary power—hence the need for a new wave.

A second area in which Foucault's methodology is especially relevant for feminism involves the theory of the subject. For Foucault, "there is no subject," and much of his last work explicitly attempts to dethrone the sovereignty of the illusory subject that he argues is a product of the particular disciplinary practices and rationalizing discourses of the modern era. This subject is marked by a proclivity not only to find its source of meaning and identity within what is seen to be an individual's deepest recesses but also—in keeping with its Christian legacy—to renounce the truth it discovers as the product of a sinful being. *The History of Sexuality,* vol. 1, demonstrates how the Christian imperatives toward confession and self-renunciation are transformed into secular injunctions to investigate sexuality and its secrets. Volume two of *The History of Sexuality* helps further refute assumptions of an unchanging or universal selfhood by contrasting our society's notion of a deep self with classical Greek society's notion of the individual, which constitutes itself "as its own master." "What was missing in classical antiquity," Foucault argues, "was the problematization of the institution of the self as subject." In our time, such problematization has taken precedence and renders us particularly susceptible to the operations of normalizing power, for the theory of the subject carries with it a demand for a unitary morality. Foucault urges a "search for styles of existence as different from each other as possible" in resistance to that demand.[7]

The women's movement has certainly been involved in the search for alternative styles of existence, but at times these "alternatives" have been founded on the prevailing theory of the subject and hence contribute to, rather than resist, normalizing power. Feminist works that uphold an eternal femininity or a natural sexuality are deeply implicated in the deep-self notion of the modern era. The second half of the nineteenth century in particular was a period in which the idea of a "true self" and a singular identity based on one's "innate" femininity or masculinity took hold in Western society. Foucault's publication of the memoirs of Herculine Barbin, a nineteenth-century hermaphrodite who was forced by legal and medical authorities to "choose" a sexual identity as male or female and thereafter remain within that classification, dramatically captures the historical moment when science, law, and bureaucracy formalized sexual essentialism.

Feminist writings of the nineteenth and twentieth centuries have frequently subscribed to such essentialism, either by casting femininity as morally superior to masculinity or by arguing that people are "truly" androgynous but that culture suppresses their other half. From within feminism, a powerful critique of essentialism has come from Marxist and materialist feminists, but that critique remains problematic because, to the extent that their definitions of power grant primacy to the category of labor, their arguments about the social construction of self retain a centering that may be understood as a type of cultural essentialism. A similar point may be made regarding feminist works that draw on semiotic theory and/or Lacanian analysis: they challenge assumptions of innate femininity and masculinity, yet their focus on the site of the linguistic subject often employs an all-too-familiar binary opposition between masculinity and femininity, albeit one in which the traditional hierarchy is reversed.[8]

Foucault's methodology is valuable not only as it pertains to discourse's relation to power/knowledge and practices of self, but also because of the way in which its epistemological tenets acknowledge uncertainty and indeterminacy. For Foucault, explanation is necessarily partial, blending with interpretation's capacity to illuminate, clarify, and decipher. He warns against the seduction of totalizing theory, which appears to resolve all differences and contradictions through unified and cohesive explanation. In place of history's search for "origins," with its corresponding teleological spirit-of-the-age arguments, he proposes genealogy, which, with "patience and a knowledge of details," "operates on a field of entangled and confused parchments, on documents that have been scratched over and recopied many times." What is at stake in replacing history with genealogy is nothing less than the "destruction of the subject who seeks knowledge in the endless deployment of the will to knowledge."[9] These arguments, which call for caution and reflexivity, need not lead to paralysis, as is sometimes claimed, either in the search for greater understanding of historical change or in political efforts to effect change.

Foucault's challenge to our society's will to knowledge and his assessment of the mechanisms of power/knowledge are consonant with his ethics, one of his most frequently overlooked contributions to contemporary social criticism. In his later interviews and analyses in particular, he proposes that ethics should be grounded in resistance to whatever form totalitarian power might take, whether it stem from religion, science, or political oppression. In Western societies, he adds, religion and law have lost their viability for grounding ethical practices. An ethics based on the "so-called scientific knowledge of what the self is," moreover, is also a dead end. One direction he does point to for contemporary society is some version of an aesthetics of daily life. But because his intellectual stance is to reject the role of the prophet or the legislator of morality, Foucault refuses to draw up a blueprint for contemporary ethics and, indeed, assaults the notion of a single ethic. As he puts it, "The search for a form of morality acceptable to everybody in the sense that everyone should submit to it strikes me as catastrophic."[10] In place of a unitary morality, he upholds the "philosophical ethos" found in "the very specific transformations that have proved to be possible in the last twenty years in a certain number of areas that concern our ways of being and thinking, relations to authority, relations between the sexes, the way in which we perceive insanity or illness."[11]

The value of Foucault is not that he puts forward a set of ethical mandates but that he refuses to do so, offering instead a method that exposes the totalizing proclivities of conventional ethical visions. John Rajchman has argued that Foucault's work is an unfamiliar "modern" ethic, "which, instead of attempting to determine what we should do on the basis of what we essentially are, attempts by analyzing who we have been constituted to be, to ask what we might become. . . . Its principle is freedom, but a freedom which does not follow from any postulation of our nature or essence."[12] Such an ethics supplants human-nature arguments with genealogical investigation; it requires, in Foucault's words, "a patient labor giving form to our impatience for liberty."[13]

Foucault's own labors in explicating how disciplinary power molds through localized mechanisms of enticement, regulation, surveillance, and classification are invaluable for demonstrating how specific historical and cultural practices constitute distinct forms of selfhood. Yet it is also precisely this feature of Foucault's methodology that has most to gain from the crucial contributions of feminists to social theory and action. For, although Foucault's descriptions of historical practices of self-help counter claims of an eternal, unified self, his discussions gloss over the gender configurations of power. As feminists have shown, power has long been masculinist, and a primary target of masculinist power has been the subjugation of women, most especially through their bodies.

Thus, in *The History of Sexuality*, vol. 1, Foucault is premature in claiming the deployment of sexuality as the predominant mode of power in the modern era. In arguing that Western societies have gone from "*a symbolics of blood* to *an analytics of sexuality,*" he is too quick to give precedence to a generative mode of power. Although his analyses remind us that in contemporary society power is not monolithically held by men, feminists have demonstrated that the kind of power that Foucault associates with the sovereign's right of death—a power operating primarily within kinship systems that is "essentially a right of seizure: of things, time, bodies, and ultimately life itself"—remains vested in individual men and men as a group. In short, feminist analyses should help Foucauldians see that these two regimes of power coexist and often intertwine in contemporary society.[14]

Both first- and second-wave feminists have documented the far-ranging, deeply structured forms of masculinist domination. The medicalization of women's bodies, for example, which made pregnancy into a disease and undermined women-centered healing institutions; the physical and sexual abuse of women, from witchburning to rape; and the mutilation of women's bodies for the sake of "beauty" are just some of the ways feminists have identified women's bodies as the locus of masculinist power. These analyses expose the gaps in Foucauldian genealogies that purport to detail disciplinary power's operations in the deployment of sexuality while overlooking women's writings on issues like pregnancy, abortion, birth control, anorexia, bulimia, cosmetic surgery, and treatments of breast and uterine cancer. Genealogies could benefit from feminist discussions of how masculinist domination has been supported and justified through a whole set of binary oppositions that grant superiority to the first term over the second—male/female, mind/body, spirit/matter. Many feminists have shown how the patriarchal arguments revolving around sexual difference conceal the cultural construction of both power and bodies by couching it in the name of the "natural."[15]

Like the Foucauldian analysis of "Man," the feminist critique of masculinist uses of the "natural" extends to the deconstruction of Western humanism. But for feminists, the problem with humanism is not merely that it derives from illusory assumptions about an autonomous and universal self, but that this particular self is the domain of privileged white men. The valuation of their narrowed and partial experiences and activities and the corresponding devaluation of women's and other subjugated groups' experiences and activities not only are central to Western humanism but are its way of maintaining subordination of the Other.[16] For example, women's arts and crafts have been ignored or dismissed as inferior, while their historical involvement in community matters is not even recognized as political activity. The very achievements of Western humanism have been built on the backs of women and people of color.

One of the major vehicles of the feminist critique of Western humanism involves the issue of authority and processes of authorization. Foucault might have given new status to discourse, but he fails to take into account the relations between masculinist authority and language, discourse, and reason. Language, feminists claim, is never gender-free. They have demonstrated the ways in which women have been subsumed by the generic masculine, trivialized and degraded through derogatory metaphors, deprived of access to sacred languages, or silenced altogether. As for written discourse, they have shown how women's lives have been constructed so as to deny them access to writing and how the canonization of men's works is an ideological process. While Foucault's works are certainly critical of the rationalizing process of power/knowledge, feminists have been far more astute in showing how reason has been constructed as a masculine domain that is divorced from and deemed superior to the senses, emotion, and imagination. Although Foucault points to the ways in which rationalizing discourses suppress discourses of marginalized groups, and claims that such discourses are sites of resistance, his work only rarely attends to such discourses and virtually ignores those by women.[17] His almost exclusive focus on works by men pushes women's discourses of resistance to the margins of his texts.

Women's political activities have also been marginalized, but feminist scholars have shown the strength and vitality of women's essential role in neighborhood and community politics. Foucault points to the importance of local struggles, but he himself fails to capture the gender component of such actions as bread riots, rent strikes, campaigns for alternative health clinics, and toxic-waste protests. Recalling feminism's insight that "the personal is political," this politics speaks to the ways that power operates at the most intimate levels of daily life. Most recently, ecofeminists have extended the meaning of this slogan by revealing how global toxic contamination is registered at the most local and personal level, from the contamination of women's breast milk to the death and disfigurement of living beings and cultures wrought by such disasters as Bhopal, Love Canal, and Chernobyl. Because so much of women's political activity occurs at the local level and stems from their involvement in the sustenance of life, they often manifest an ethic of activism that confronts domination without the smashing and terror so characteristic of masculinist revolutionary action.

Given this catalogue of feminist and Foucauldian contributions to the analysis of power, how might scholars and activists engaged by questions of historical change and ethics proceed? As many of the essays in this volume suggest, there are inevitable tensions between the two forms of analysis. But rather than bewailing inconsistency and incompatibility, these essays consider the energy that emerges from such tensions. For example, feminist analysis clearly illuminates the seeming ubiquitousness of masculinist power over women. Foucauldian analysis exposes the effects of normalizing power in the production of human subjects. Both are necessary for a fuller understanding of power and possible paths of resistance. Another mutually corrective tension resides in the space between feminism's tendency toward utopianism and essentialism (through claims for a higher truth derived from women's experience) and Foucault's skepticism about emancipatory politics and inclination toward relativism. We would suggest that within these tensions one finds the potential for an ethics of activism that is particularly appropriate for challenging the Faustian impulses of the contemporary era: one that fosters a mode of empowerment that is at the same time infused with an awareness of the limits to human agency.

This volume is divided into three parts. In the first, "On Initiating a Dialogue," Biddy Martin, Meaghan Morris, and Frances Bartkowski provide an introduction to, overview, and critique of the works by Foucault that have proven most relevant to feminists, namely, the volumes following *The Archaeology of Knowledge*. Hubert Dreyfus and Paul Rabinow have noted that "in Foucault's later works, practice, on all levels, is considered more fundamental than theory."[18] As Martin's essay indicates, Foucault's shift from archaeology to genealogy created a point of compatibility between his method of investigating social practices and the feminist goal of understanding and altering them. Martin employs Foucauldian insights to caution feminists about the perils of searches for *the* authentic female sexuality; she also suggests, however, as a point of departure from Foucault, that such theorizing has a certain political and historical necessity. Morris's essay takes up the discussion of the value of Foucault's work for feminists in her examination of two key areas of debate within contemporary feminism: the theory of the subject and the project of "feminine" writing. Foucault's analyses of the technologies of subjection and the possibilities of insurrectionary knowledges, she argues, displace "the problematics of humanism—and thus of 'anti-humanism' " and enable us to multiply sites of resistance.

In "Epistemic Drift in Foucault," Bartkowski reenacts some of the skepticism feminists expressed in regard to Foucault's works upon the publication of *The History of Sexuality*, vol. 1, yet she by no means dismisses his work entirely. She points to Foucault's failure to grapple with feminist concerns in his analysis of power; she then uses that absence to situate a feminist discourse within the Foucauldian analysis of sexuality in order to invoke and at times provoke a dialogue between the two.

The essays of Part II, "Discipline and the Female Subject," draw on Foucault's insights into the mechanisms of power/knowledge in order to illuminate how disciplinary power—whether it be power to produce a particular bodily configuration or to divide knowledge into academic disciplines—is always gendered. In "Foucault, Femininity, and the Modernization of Patriarchal Power," Sandra Lee Bartky argues that modern forms of femininity render women's bodies docile in a manner distinct from contemporary Western society's disciplinary practices for men. Susan Bordo employs the feminist/Foucauldian approach to demonstrate that anorexia nervosa is a crystallization of the production of femininity. Kathleen Jones, Mary Lydon, and Peggy Kamuf examine the ways in which traditional constructions of authority, knowledge, and truth produce a masculinist world that excludes women, excises ambiguity, and proclaims universal truth. Jones deconstructs the dominant discourse on authority in order to show that its dichotomy between public authority and private compassion not only denies authority to women but also cripples its conceptual capacity. Lydon pursues the question of what can occur when women do engage in authoritative discursive practices, specifically within the academy, and gives warning about the tendency to become the confessing animals Foucault describes in *The History of Sexuality*. Feminist practice, she argues, should instead appropriate Foucault's strategy of giving and denying identity "in the same breath." Picking up on the issue of identity, Peggy Kamuf reads Virginia Woolf's *A Room of One's Own* through the lens of Foucault's critique of the human subject in order to move the feminist project toward a recognition that the liberation of the female subject carries with it the potential for female subjection. By focusing on forms of "self-interruption" in Woolf's text, Kamuf reminds us of the danger of conceptualizing the female subject as singular and unified.

Part III, "The Uses of Foucault for Feminist Praxis," presents essays that draw on Foucault's warnings against totalizing theories and his insights regarding power/knowledge to reflect on contemporary feminism's political praxis. The diversity of opinions and strategies represented in these reflections underscores our contention that the employment of Foucault by feminists does not impose a new orthodoxy. Thus, for example, all of the authors who deal with sexuality make use of Foucault's notions of the production of sexual desire, yet there is no effort to force consensus here on the applicability of the desexualization strategy he suggests. Winifred Woodhull focuses specifically on the desexualization strategy and rape and argues that feminist efforts to redefine rape as a crime of power, rather than sex, unwittingly comply with the notion that sex exists in a hidden area outside prevailing power relations. She points to the problematics of women relying on the state for their safety and urges women to take up avenues of resistance that challenge the isolating routines of daily life. This question of effective resistance is also crucial to Jana Sawicki's examination of the heated politics surrounding contemporary discussions of sexual freedom and difference. Sawicki points to the questionable appeals to a repressed and innocent sexuality that are often made by sexual libertarians, yet she also contends that Foucault's desexualization strategy doesn't necessarily preclude support for radical sexual struggles. For Sawicki, difference is a resource that helps us multiply sources of resistance.

The last two essays of Part III address the issue of a visionary politics for feminism. In the first, which is our own, we draw on the desexualization strategy to question what is perhaps the most fundamental tenet of modern feminism, namely, the discourse of the right to control our bodies. We suggest that practices that "treat our bodies and the planet with care, concern, and lightness" may be particularly promising in the contemporary political context. Sharon Welch's closing essay asks how feminists can resist oppression and domination amidst such twentieth-century barbarisms as mass famine, El Salvador's civil war, and the threat of nuclear holocaust. Welch explores the possibilities of a feminist theology of liberation that does not regard itself as the definitive exposition of the structure of freedom and justice. Welch terms her theology a "poetics of revolution" that "emerges from an effort to live on the edge, accepting both the power and peril of discourse, engaging in a battle for truth with a conscious preference for the oppressed."

Notes

1. The use of Foucauldian methodology exclusive of feminist categories does risk imposing an orthodoxy, however. See, for instance, the collection entitled *Foucault: A Critical Reader*, ed. David Couzens Hoy (New York: Basil Blackwell, 1986), which, although otherwise a fine collection, is strikingly devoid of feminist issues or contributions.

2. Regarding friendship, see Foucault's remarks in Hubert Dreyfus and Paul Rabinow, *Michel Foucault: Beyond Structuralism and Hermeneutics* (Chicago: University of Chicago Press, 1983), p. 233; and Martha A. Ackelsberg, " 'Sisters' or 'Comrades'? The Politics of Friends and Families," in *Families, Politics, and Public Policy: A Feminist Dialogue on Women and the State*, ed. Irene Diamond (New York: Longman, 1983).

3. On the issue of dialogue versus polemics, see Foucault's comments in an interview conducted shortly before his death in *The Foucault Reader*, ed. Paul Rabinow (New York: Pantheon, 1984), pp. 381–82.

4. Michel Foucault, *Power/Knowledge*, ed. Colin Gordon (New York: Pantheon, 1980), pp. 131–32.

5. Ibid., p. 131.
6. Michel Foucault, *The History of Sexuality*, vol. 1, trans. Robert Hurley (New York: Vintage, 1980), p. 101.
7. "Michel Foucault: Final Interview," *Raritan Review* 5, no. 1 (Summer 1985): 12. For an extended example of Foucault's mode of genealogical exploration, see his demonstration of how moral-conduct books of ancient Greece enabled "[male] individuals to question their own conduct, to watch over and give shape to it, and to shape themselves as ethical subjects" in *The Use of Pleasure* (New York: Pantheon, 1985), p. 13.
8. For a more thorough discussion of the theory of the subject, see Meaghan Morris's "The Pirate's Fiancée" in this volume. Donna Haraway also deals with these issues in "A Manifesto for Cyborgs: Science, Technology, and Socialist Feminism in the 1980s," *Socialist Review* 15 (March-April 1985): 76.
9. Michel Foucault, "Nietzsche, Genealogy, History," in *The Foucault Reader*, p. 76 and p. 97, respectively.
10. "Michel Foucault: Final Interview,"*Raritan Review* 5, no. 1 (Summer 1985): 12.
11. Michel Foucault, "What is Enlightenment?" in *The Foucault Reader*, pp. 46–47
12. John Rajchman, "Ethics After Foucault," *Social Text* 13/14 (Winter/Spring 1986): 166–67.
13. Foucault, "What is Englightenment?" p. 50.
14. For Foucault's discussion of the shift from the symbolics of blood to the deployment of sexuality, see *History of Sexuality*, vol. 1, pp. 136–50.
15. The feminist debate about sexual difference is both extensive and complex, but the following provide useful overviews of the issues: *The Future of Difference: The Scholar and the Feminist*, ed. Hester Eisenstein and Alice Jardine (Boston: G. K. Hall, 1980); *Writing and Sexual Difference*, ed. Elizabeth Abel (Chicago: University of Chicago Press, 1982); Catharine R. Stimpson, "The Idea of Women's Studies, the Ideas of Women's Studies: An Assessment," in *Interpreting the Humanities*, vol. 2 (Princeton, N.J.: Woodrow Wilson National Fellowship Foundation, 1986), pp. 89–111.
16. In masculinist ideology, subordination of the Other includes, depending on the context, such categories as women, people of color, homosexuals, and nature.
17. Two of Foucault's edited works do focus on discourses of resistance, *I, Pierre Riviere* and *Herculine Barbin*.
18. Dreyfus and Rabinow, *Michel Foucault*, p. 131.

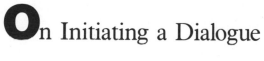

On Initiating a Dialogue

I

Biddy Martin

Feminism, Criticism, and Foucault

In a lecture given on January 6, 1976, and later published in a collection of interviews entitled *Power/Knowledge*, Michel Foucault discusses his own work in terms of the discovery over the past fifteen years of "a certain fragility in the bedrock of existence—even, and perhaps above all, in those aspects of it that are most familiar, most solid, and most intimately related to our bodies and our everyday behavior."[1] And he relates this "vulnerability to criticism" of aspects of knowledge and power that have long been obscured to a recognition of the inhibiting effects of "global, *totalitarian theories*."[2] His polemics against systematizing, universalizing theories and their will to truth are clearly directed in part at scientific Marxism and its economism as well as to the "laws" of psychoanalysis; and his *History of Sexuality* challenges various twentieth-century sexual liberationists' attempts to combine those two theories.[3] Certainly, both his polemics and his methodological breaks with traditional social theory make him interesting for feminists, whose political and theoretical projects converge at important points with the provocations of Foucault.

Feminist theory and political strategies have effected a profound shift in conceptions of "politics" and in assumptions about the location and exercise of power. Having identified the ideological construction of the sexed subject as a crucial place to situate the question of sexual difference and the struggle against women's oppression, radical and lesbian feminists in particular have consistently refused to privilege the economic over the ideological conditions of oppression and change; they have legitimized the struggle over the production, distribution, and transformation of meaning as a focus for political intervention and opposition. Of course, American radical and lesbian feminist literature and political strategies have been and continue to be criticized with varying degrees of legitimacy by Marxists and Marxist feminists as a cultural feminism that fails to take the material conditions of change into account. However, in spite of significant theoretical work by critical Marxists both here and abroad, feminists remain frustrated by the tendency even within the New Left to focus on what were once regarded as mere superstructural phenomena without acknowledging or incorporating feminist perspectives or challenges. In the third issue of the British journal *Politics and Power*, several women addressed this problem in an editorial in which they announced their resignation from the staff and noted that "a critique of existing Left priorities and practices does not necessarily lead to a positive commitment to new forms of political behavior and the awareness of new sites of struggle for which we had been hoping."[4] Male members of the editorial board responded in an attempt to acknowledge the limitations of their past commitments and to demonstrate their understanding of the issues and critique: "The sphere of the personal—ways of living, style, behavior, personal interaction, sexual relations, language and gesture—is seen by feminism *directly* as a political field. It is not *made* political by the intervention of 'outside' forces; it is political."[5] They conclude with the following challenge to themselves: "Our relationship to sexual politics cannot be subordinated to or exclusively defined by socialism, not the least because the meaning of 'socialism' is itself a matter of major and essential dispute."[6]

Clearly, sexual politics and socialist politics remain, at least to some extent, separate in the minds of many Marxists and Marxist feminists. And I would argue that American work in Marxist feminist theory suffers particularly from the limitations of a functionalist articulation of the relationship between patriarchy and capitalism, both conceived as monolithic and total systems of oppression. The obstacles to a materialist feminism (one might just as well say materialist Marxism) derive in part from the personal-political struggles between and among the men and women involved; however, the problems are also fundamentally methodological. The development of materialism necessitates approaches to sexuality, subjectivity, and power that go beyond both traditional Marxist and radical feminist analyses and can provide a way out of a theoretical and strategic impasse in all attempts to relate the abstractions patriarchy and capitalism. It requires that we suspend our commitment to our universal, explanatory categories at least long enough to get at the operations of power at their most material and concrete.

The debates documented in *Women and Revolution* expose the problems and challenges within American Marxist feminism. In her conclusion to the essays collected there, Heidi Hartmann writes of her own influential essay, "The Unhappy Marriage of Marxism and Feminism," that it "postulates the existence of two separate but interlocking sets of social relations, capitalism and patriarchy, each with a material base, each with its own dynamic."[7] Hartmann concedes to her critics that she has, in effect, left Marxism intact and has argued for the use of Marxist methods in the analysis of patriarchy. Her goal, she writes, "was to retrieve patriarchy from the realm of the purely ideological where it has been consigned by most Marxists and many Marxist feminists."[8] This retrieval involves arguing that gender is as central as class in the social formation and that patriarchy can be defined in terms of men's control over women's labor power in the home and the economy outside the home. Hartmann is quite legitimately criticized by other contributors to that volume, despite the importance of her analysis and the insights it has made possible, for reducing the dynamics of patriarchy to economic terms and for failing to incorporate the material effects of psychosexual conditions into her conception of patriarchy. Some critics challenge her dual-systems approach in favor of a single system that could explain a general intersection of sexual politics with the needs of capital. The choice between a dual or single system does not, I would suggest, get at the problem. Perhaps it is the systemic nature of current conceptions of capitalism and patriarchy that makes it impossible to get at the operations of power and the possibilities for resistance in modern Western societies, to comprehend the constitution and the transformation of power relations at the level of the local and everyday. Such total theories of a monolithic control or power held by a clearly identifiable and coherently sovereign group see power as originating outside of and independent of concrete social interactions and their material effects. Ultimately, all local and specific manifestations of power become the reflection of the prohibitive power of a system exterior to us, or interior only in the negative sense of our "socialization." Subjectivity and sexuality are conceived as secondary effects of an essentially negative, repressive exercise of power from above. Liberation, then, is articulated in terms of the demand for transgression of or end to external prohibitions—an essentially liberal line of thinking.

Foucault's deconstructions of traditional conceptions of power provoke questions about the history, the consequences, and the validity of this kind of theorizing. In an interview with J. L. Brochier, Foucault describes his focus in this way: "When I think of the mechanics of power, I think of its capillary form of existence, of the extent to which power seeps into the very grain of individuals, reaches right into their bodies, permeates their gestures, their posture, what they say, how they learn to live and work with other people."[9] According to Foucault, power comes from below; it is induced in the body and produced in every social interaction. It is not exercised negatively from the outside, though negation and repression may be one of its effects. Power in the modern world is the relation between pleasures, knowledge, and power as they are produced and disciplined. The state is not the origin, but an overall strategy and effect, "a composite result made up of a multiplicity of centers and mechanisms."[10] The same might be said of large-scale resistances or "revolution." Methodologically, then, the task set by Foucault could be described as his translator Alan Sheridan has described it: "It is the task of a political anatomy to analyze the operation of these 'micro-powers,' the relations that are made between them and their relations with the strategic aims of the state apparatus."[11]

Foucault's elaborations of the relationship between desire-knowledge-power have opened up exciting critiques of both liberal and traditional Marxist approaches to questions of ideology, sexuality, and power—approaches that we have taken over into our own work on feminist theory to varying degrees. His questions and hypotheses are part of a radical reevaluation in poststructuralist thought of the classical humanist conceptual split between ideology and economics, sexuality and politics, the individual and the social, the subversive and the repressive. As such, they open up a space for feminist questions that have been obscured, marginalized, and/or subsumed under the teleological projects of other theories. Of course, it is important to keep in mind that feminism has never assumed a place within "avant-garde" theory or practice automatically or unproblematically. There are surprisingly few references in Foucault's writings or in interviews with him to feminist analyses or to the women's movement in spite of the fact that he has identified sexuality as a privileged object of analysis. The work of asserting and articulating the significance of poststructuralist thought for feminist inquiries, as well as the importance of feminism for poststructuralism, must be done by those who are committed to demonstrating rather than assuming harmonies in the two projects. It is essential that feminist thinkers not be seduced by the work of Foucault, that we not attempt to apply the hypotheses he articulates to the situation of women without careful attention to the implications of his work.

What seems crucial about the work of Foucault, particularly in the American context, is his break with classical theories of representation and power. His *History of Sexuality* states very clearly that discourses on sexuality, not sexual acts and their histories, are the essential place to grasp the workings of power in modern Western societies. As Alan Sheridan explains, Foucault's "political anatomy—anatomy of the body politic in terms of an anatomy of the politicization of the body—is presented with Foucault's usual modesty as 'another grid for deciphering history.' "[12] In fact, Foucault's study is not really a history of sexuality in the conventional sense of that word, but a history of the discourses on sexuality and the various ways in which those discourses and the pleasures and powers they have produced have been deployed in the service of hierarchical relations in Western culture over the past three hundred years. Foucault describes the transformation in the nature of power in the seventeenth century in terms of a new power over life that evolved in two forms: "One of these poles . . . centered on the body as a machine: its disciplining, the optimization of its capabilities, the extortion of its forces, the parallel increase of its usefulness and its docility, its integration into systems of efficient and economic controls, all this was ensured by the procedures of power that characterized the *disciplines:* an *anatomo-politics of the human body*. The second . . . focused on the species body. Their supervision was effected through an entire series of interventions and *regulatory controls: a biopolitics of the population*."[13]

Foucault challenges the traditional notion of sex as an instinctual drive or force, intrinsically liberating for the individual when expressed, and apparently disruptive of a necessarily repressive state. His "history" not only questions the validity of Freudian and Marxist approaches to sexual liberation from Reich to Marcuse, but goes so far as to ask whether those arguments have not been formulated from within the same discursive and strategic limitations as the power they would like to attack. The repressive hypothesis—the argument that the past two to three hundred years have been characterized by sexual repression and negation—has held up well. Foucault suggests that the coincidence of the emergence of capitalism with the supposed advent of the age of repression has given the belief in repression "a solemn historical and political guarantee."[14] And he points out that this conception of sex as essentially repressed within capitalism is gratifying because of the opportunity it affords us to "speak out against the powers that be, to utter truths and promise bliss, to link together enlightenment, liberation, and manifold pleasures; to pronounce a discourse that combines the fervor of knowledge, the determination to change the laws, and the longing for the garden of earthly delights."[15]

In fact, Western culture, far from having repressed sexuality, has actually produced it, multiplied it, spread it out as a particularly privileged means of gaining access to the individual and the social bodies, as a way of "policing" society through procedures of normalization rather than prohibition. Repression becomes one effect among many of this larger phenomenon. According to Foucault, the bourgeois class, long regarded as the class that introduced repression in order to enhance the productivity of its working class, actually applied its techniques first to itself in the process of distinguishing itself from the aristocracy and the working classes. It made its sexuality and the health of its "bodies" a fundamental source of its own identity and its own discipline. As Sheridan points out, "the nineteenth-century bourgeoisie became obsessed with biological, medical, eugenic doctrines of all kinds. . . . The value placed on the body and its sexuality was bound up with establishment in society of bourgeois hegemony."[16]

What we have long accepted to be a natural but prohibited force constitutes, in fact, a construct, a systematization of pleasure in relation to the changing articulation and needs of power in our world. What we have believed to be the secret of ourselves and have felt compelled to tell in our search for redemption or liberation, or at the very least, health, amounts to our possible subjection to surveillance, to the intervention of experts in our lives, to discipline. The talk about sex, the obsession with it are part of the operations of power in contemporary society; they make normalization and control possible and invisible. To insist, then, on more and more sex and a greater freedom to speak it is to isolate sexuality and ourselves, to misunderstand "sexuality" in ways that allow for a systematization and regulation of desire toward particular social and political ends.

Foucault insists that our subjectivity, our identity, and our sexuality are intimately linked; they do not exist outside of or prior to language and representation, but are actually brought into play by discursive strategies and representational practices. The relationship between the body and discourse or power is not a negative one; power renders the body active and productive. Sexuality and identity can only be understood, then, in terms of the complicated and often paradoxical ways in which pleasures, knowledges, and power are produced and disciplined in language, and institutionalized across multiple social fields. For Foucault, representation and discourses are themselves acts of power, acts of division and exclusion, which give themselves as knowledge. The body does not give knowledge that is then merely transmitted by an essentially neutral language and allowed or disallowed by a centralized form of prohibition. Discourse makes the body an object of knowledge and invests it with power. Our task, then, is not to search for the truth about sex, but to ask what is at stake in the historical question, in the compulsion to speak about the unspeakable. Foucault states it this way: "This is the essential thing: that Western man has been drawn for three centuries to the task of telling everything concerning his sex; that since the classical age there has been a constant optimization and an increasing valorization of the discourse on sex; and that this carefully analytical discourse was meant to yield multiple effects of displacement, intensification, reorientation, and modification of desire itself."[17]

Foucault also challenges any easy division between a dominant and essentially repressive discourse and one oppositional, pure voice of liberation. He characterizes power as a multiplicity of force relations, the interplay of various discursive fields with their immanent necessities and developments. Power and authority are no longer vested in a central point, not in Foucault's analysis or in the actual workings of power in our world. Nor does resistance arise from a single point. For that reason, a very different form of political organization and struggle suggests itself, an alternative to the frontal attack on the state led by the One revolutionary subject, local struggles that undermine institutional power where it reveals itself in ideology under the mask of humanism, or as it operates in homes, schools, prisons, therapists' offices, and factories, wherever the work of normalization is carried on. What is crucial is the capacity to shift the terms of the struggle, the ability to see our position within existing structures but to respond from somewhere else. What Leftists have criticized in the women's movement as fragmentation, lack of organization, absence of a coherent and encompassing theory, and the inability to mount a frontal attack may very well represent fundamentally more radical and effective responses to the deployment of power in our society than the centralization and abstraction that continue to plague Leftist thinking and strategy.

Beginning, then, at the level of discourse and the operations of power involved in the acquisition and distribution of knowledge, Foucault is able to deconstruct some of the last vestiges of the self-evident and apparently natural, exposing the workings of power in any will to or pretense at truth, finality, or nature. All categories of the natural or the normal, as well as the unnatural or abnormal, are exposed as social constructs rather than distinctions given at the level of the body or individual psyche, categories that have been produced discursively and which function as mutually determining oppositions to normalize and to discipline. His methodological deconstructions explode the self-evidence of constituted meanings, defy the acceptance of received categories as exhaustive, and expose the cost at which such coherence and solidity are effected. The point from which Foucault deconstructs is off-center, out of line, apparently unaligned. It is not the point of an imagined absolute otherness, but an "alterity" that understands itself as an internal exclusion. From that perspective, it is possible to grasp and restructure the organization of our bodies, psyches, and lives through discourse.

There are obvious convergences between Foucault's work and the interests of feminists, in terms of focus and methodology. Certainly, feminist analyses of the medical, psychiatric, and educational institutions since the nineteenth century would support Foucault's suggestion that the intervention of experts and their knowledge of the female body have everything to do with the constitution of power in our world. Foucault has argued that the hysterization of the female body, a body now saturated with sex and inherently pathological, represented the production of knowledge and pleasures (in addition to the repression of those things) for the purpose of discipline and control of families and populations. "It is worth remembering that the first figure to be invested by the deployment of sexuality, one of the first to be 'sexualized,' was the 'idle' woman.

She inhabited the outer edge of the 'world,' in which she always had to appear as a value, and of the family, where she was assigned a new destiny charged with conjugal and parental obligations."[18]

Health-care systems continue to monopolize "scientific" knowledge and exercise control over individual bodies, families, and the social body. And their operations are not the reflections of the needs of capital and/or the state in any simple sense; they are producing and reproducing as well as transforming the relations that are immanent and essential to their hierarchies and to the perpetuation of the status of their knowledges in society. Feminists have also voiced objections to classical liberationist approaches to questions of sexuality and power. The conception of a natural but repressed and inherently subversive female sexuality does run through feminist literature and theory both here and in Europe, and I would suggest that there is a level of historical and political necessity to those arguments in spite of their limitations. There is a related tendency to condemn male sexuality as naturally or intrinsically aggressive among some feminist thinkers who emphasize women's passive victimization or internalization in relation to it. Again, this emphasis has its historical necessity as a response to the forms of violence against women that have been ignored or accepted by the society as self-evident for so long. However, the stress on victimization suffers strategic and theoretical limitations insofar as it reproduces, at least implicitly, the notion of women's passivity and suggests the presence of an essential and as yet undiscovered eroticism. It is an emphasis that does not get beyond the discursive limitations and manipulations of the object of its attacks.

In spite of the problems in certain formulations within feminist analyses and movement(s), it is legitimate to argue that feminist theorizing, taken as a whole, has gone beyond the male liberationists' focus on more and better sex to an understanding of sex as the structuring and regulating of desire toward socially and politically oppressive ends. Sexual expression, far from having liberated women, has historically often led to increased male access to women's bodies, allowing exploitation not just sexually but economically and politically as well. And feminists have long argued that to demand greater sexual freedom without formulating that demand in terms of a transformation of the social relations within which sexuality is organized and articulated is to invite an intensification of old constraints on women's desire. Traditionally, feminists have been labeled prudish by those liberationists who would force them into a position for or against sex; there is a sense of urgency within the women's movement now of the importance of developing our understanding of "sexuality" so that we can move beyond these false alternatives and shift the focus of attention to the relations that have produced "sexuality" as we know it.

Certainly, lesbian feminist theory has pushed the analysis of sexuality beyond the demand for the right to more sexual freedoms; the developing critique of the institutionalization of heterosexuality challenges the assumption of a natural sexual instinct and analyzes the social configurations through which and as a result of which the apparatus of sexuality is constructed. The initial impulse of Adrienne Rich's article "Compulsory Heterosexuality" demonstrates from the point of view of excluded lesbian experience that heterosexuality is itself a compulsory set of relations produced not at the level of the body, but at the level of discourse and social practice, a compulsory sexuality that enables male dominance and refuses autonomy or solidarity among women.[19] Turning the question back onto the discourse that has, in a sense, created "homosexuality" and "lesbianism" as we have come to know them effects what Foucault has called a methodological "desexualization of the question." According to Foucault, "the real strength of the women's liberation movements is not that of having laid claim to the specificity of their sexuality and the rights pertaining to it, but that they have actually departed from the discourse conducted within the apparatuses of sexuality. Ultimately, it is a veritable movement of desexualization, a displacement effected in relation to the sexual centering of the problem, formulating the demand for forms of culture, discourse, language and so on which are no longer part of that rigid assignation and pinning-down to their sex which they had initially in some sense been politically obliged to accept in order to make themselves heard."[20]

In a recent interview published in *Christopher Street*, Foucault makes similarly supportive statements about the implications of the gay (male) liberation movement, emphasizing its creation of supports for relationships other than those allowed within or by the heterosexual nuclear family structure. The creation of cultural and social supports for other relational forms goes far beyond the essentially liberal demand for homosexual or for women's rights. It has implications for the society as a whole as it facilitates different conceptions and possibilities for relating. Ultimately, such shifts threaten that "bedrock of existence" of which Foucault has spoken elsewhere and undermine the structures on which contemporary power alignments and their solidity depend. In spite of what his critics have charged, Foucault's work does not negate the pos-

sibility of concrete political struggle and resistance. It does insist that
we understand and take account of the ways in which we are implicated
in power relations and the fact that we are never outside of power. He
does not advocate *a* position; however, he is obviously aware of the necessity of taking position(s) and would insist that we remain aware of
the possibilities for new pleasures and new forms of resistance created
in every confrontation.

Desexualization and Cultural Criticism

In its most radical form, feminist criticism and practice can be a fundamentally deconstructive strategy that questions the possibility of universals or absolute meanings and exposes the constitution of power at
stake in their assertion. Of course, both our humanist heritage and obvious
historical and political necessities leave us with a conflict between a fundamentally deconstructive impulse and a need to construct the category
woman and to search for truths, authenticity, and universals. It is the
necessity of a doubled strategy with respect to the question of the unity
of woman and the value of "desexualization" that I would like to address
here.

Feminist criticism must be engaged in elaborating the extent to which
the phallocentric meanings and truths of our culture have necessarily
repressed multiplicity and the possibility of actual difference by appro-
priating difference, naming it opposition, and subsuming it under the
"Identity of Man." Feminism shares with poststructuralist criticism a
critique of the hegemony of the identical and the desire for other forms
of discourse. Unlike many of the male critics, feminists are quite consciously involved in systematically articulating the extent to which woman
has been situated very differently with respect to the "human," to "Man,"
than has man; and feminist analyses demonstrate ever more convincingly
that women's silence and exclusion from struggles over representation
have been the condition of possibility for humanist thought: the position
of woman has indeed been that of an internal exclusion within Western
culture, a particularly well-suited point from which to expose the workings
of power in the will to truth and identity.

If women have been marginal in the constitution of meaning and power
in Western culture, the question of woman has been central, crucial to
the discourse of man, situated as she is within the literary text, the critical
text, the psychoanalytic situation, and social texts of all kinds as the

riddle, the problem to be solved, the question to be answered. Foucault has not acknowledged the specificity of women's situation with respect to secrecy and truth; his analysis of the power struggles at stake in the humanist's pretense at truth makes it possible, however, to go beyond simply substituting new and more correct answers to the question of woman by insisting that we ask what is at stake in the question, what is involved in the articulation of the problem of sexual difference; how are discipline and power constituted at the moment at which woman is made the object of knowledge? Foucault's methodological work and our own insistence on a different approach to meaning and ideology allow us to question every text not so much in terms of what it presents, but in terms of what it does to obscure its own political bases. For Foucault, the question of the truth of one's sex, of one's self is not a self-evident question, and the answers that literature, medicine, psychiatry, and religion provide are, in fact, a matter of rendering our bodies and psyches subject to control. Having created sex and gender as problems of a particular kind, the experts must necessarily intervene in our lives to provide solutions and to bind us within a particular identity, a subjectivity. Woman, as a category of meaning, and women have been subject to the gaze, the interventions, and the control of medical, psychoanalytic, and aesthetic experts who do the work of limiting and regulating what it means to be a woman in line with the exigencies of their own discursive fields and legitimating truths.

Such an analysis of the question of woman as it has figured in male discourse allows and, in fact, insists that we examine our own formulations for potential reductions and prescriptions. The question for those of us engaged in the development of new forms of discourse is how to enter struggles over the meaning(s) of woman in ways that do not repress pluralities, without losing sight of the political necessity for fiction and unity. We are forced, when we ask the question of woman, to question the extent to which we make ourselves the riddle, establishing among us a new set of experts who will speak the truth of ourselves and our sex in categorical terms; we must question the extent to which our projects and our meanings subsume difference and possibility under the conceptual and strategic grasp of a unitary identity of woman, the extent to which we close our struggle around certain privileged meanings, naturalizing the construct woman once again. Is it possible to ask and not answer, or to avoid the certainties and limitations with which the question has been answered by those who would consolidate their power around their privileged position with respect to knowledge?

Some American radical feminist thought (the work, for example, of Mary Daly) is, for all its importance and contributions, particularly susceptible to a polemic against patriarchy that ultimately ontologizes woman in terms of an essential superiority and a privileged relationship to nature and truth. The tendency in such polemics is to counter what are considered to be male distortions of reality with what are held to be authentic female representations, and to correct male distortions with the authentic experience that can be read out of women's texts and lives. Unfortunately, this cultural criticism cannot go far beyond the assertion and documentation of a history of sexism, and our own cultural production is based on the premise that we as feminists can speak authentically, can speak the truth of ourselves for all women by virtue of our supposed exclusion from male culture and as a result of our rejection of their meanings. The tendency to place women outside culture, to define femininity in terms of an absolute exclusion and consequent innocence with respect to language and ideology reflects an overly simplistic understanding of the relationship between identity and discourse. It reproduces the classical split between the individual and the social formation, assuming that we can shed what is supposedly a false consciousness imposed and maintained from the outside, and begin to speak an authentic truth. The search for a more perfect self, for a truer, more natural sexuality, a more authentic "I" too often represents a refusal to account for the position from which we speak, to ground ourselves materially and historically, to acknowledge and be vigilant of our own limitations and our own differences.

Foucault's deconstructive methodology provides an immanent critique of such a search for *the* authentic female voice or *the* sexuality, a warning against the commitment to any confessional mode as necessarily liberating, and a challenge to the notion that simply speaking or writing frees us in any simple way from patriarchy or phallocentrism. His analysis of the confessional mode in Western culture exposes the misconceptions in our definitions of truth: "The obligation to confess is now relayed through so many different points, is so deeply ingrained in us, that we no longer perceive it as the effect of a power that constrains us; on the contrary, it seems to us that truth, lodged in our most secret nature, 'demands' only to surface; that if it fails to do so, this is because a constraint holds it in place, the violence of a power weighs it down, and it can finally be articulated only at the price of a kind of liberation. Confession frees, but power reduces one to silence; truth does not belong to the order of power, but shares an original affinity with freedom: traditional themes in philosophy, which a 'political history of truth' would have to overturn by showing that truth is not by nature free—nor error servile—but that its production is thoroughly imbued with relations of power. The confession is an example of this."[21]

It is imperative that we understand and not abuse the need and/or the desire to speak and be heard, and that we question the structure of the communicative relation that is operating.

The insistence on analyzing power in terms of its local, discursive, and specific formations implies a critique of a polemics of patriarchy that conceives of exclusive and exhaustive divisions between oppressor and oppressed, between a dominant or false and a subversive or true discourse. What is useful for us is the suggestion to be read out of Foucault's work that we analyze the historically and discursively specific ways in which woman has figured as a constitutive absence. To totalize or universalize Otherness as an answer to the question of woman is to leave ourselves with no possibility for understanding or intervening in the processes through which meaning is produced, distributed, and transformed in relation to the shifting articulation of power in our world.

On the other hand, it is imperative that we not dismiss the importance of the concepts patriarchy and oppression as they have been developed by radical feminist thinkers. The radical feminist articulation of the universality and totality of the oppression of women constitutes the condition of possibility for feminist deconstructive work. The assertion even of a fiction of the unity of woman and the globality of patriarchy has created a space for us from which to interpret as well as to speak. Our task is to deconstruct, to undo our own meanings and categories, the identities and the positions from which we intervene at any given point so as not to close the question of woman and discourse around new certainties and absolutes. We cannot afford to refuse to take a political stance "which pins us to our sex" for the sake of an abstract theoretical correctness, but we can refuse to be content with fixed identities or to universalize ourselves as revolutionary subjects. Our deconstructions are neither identical nor synchronous with those of the male avant-garde in spite of the very significant points of convergence in our interests.

In her introduction to Monique Plaza's critique of Foucault's position on rape in the British feminist journal *m/f*, Leslie Stern argues quite convincingly that "Foucault's approach to questions of sex and power is useful for those of us who see the need to disengage from a polemic of oppression and to concentrate on identifying and analyzing sites of struggle, but there is a danger in too virulent a critique of the notion of oppression. If it is conceptualized out of existence, rendered immaterial, this is to have serious repercussions upon material intervention."[22] And Plaza goes on to demonstrate in a polemical attack on Foucault's approach to rape law in France that his strategy of removing sexuality from control by the law (punishing rape, then, as assault but not as a sexual crime) evidences a denial of the power differences that characterize relations between the sexes in society. She maintains that "these arguments, far from furnishing a theoretico-political support for our struggle, denote, on the contrary, a closure, a major containment, which is all the more pernicious given that they are in other respects, and in part, abstractly (idealistically) correct. Foucault's is an ideology which is undoubtedly more refined than the traditional one, but threatens to lock us into a 'double bind' of the most politically dangerous kind."[23] To speak from a position of abstract correctness, rather than grounding oneself within the limitations of one's own material and ideological reality, is a privilege that can only reproduce the androcentric and fundamentally humanist universalizing "I," this time in the apparent form of the "Not-I."

The struggle for control over representational and social practices through which and across which sex has been defined and organized has been a heterosexist struggle between and among men in which woman has figured as the object of knowledge and the metaphor for truths. Having achieved a position from which to enter the struggle over definition, we are confronted with the avant-garde's observations that sexual difference, sexual identity, sexuality itself are fictions, and that the perpetuation of those categories can only further enhance the workings of power. Men will no longer speak for mankind. Should women, by implication, no longer (i.e., never) speak as women? The question of woman, like all questions of meaning, must be particularized, localized, specified, and robbed of the mystical and ontological. However, if we fail now to assert the category woman from our own shifting and open-ended points of view, our oppression may easily be lost among the pluralities of new theories of ideology and power. There is the danger that Foucault's challenges to traditional categories, if taken to a "logical" conclusion, if made into imperatives rather than left as hypotheses and/or methodological provocations, could make the question of women's oppression obsolete.

It seems clear that the intersection of poststructuralist, antihumanist strategies with feminist analyses provides the possibility for a materialist critical practice and political struggle. In terms of cultural criticism, the convergences between the feminist and poststructuralist projects of Foucault make it possible for us to divest ourselves of the bourgeois heritage that has taught us to consider texts as the expressions of fixed meanings intended by an author, transparent to the educated critic, and approached quite passively by most other readers. As feminists we have based our critical practice on authorial intentionality and classical notions of language for too long. We have been engaged on the one hand in exposing sexism in male texts on the level of manifest content, condemning what we document to be a history of sexist images and preserving those images of women that seem to conform in isolation to a pre-given conception of a positive portrayal; and on the other hand, we have worked on creating a canon of women writers and developing an analysis of their writing that might unify woman as artist. Certainly, both projects have been crucial to the development of a feminist cultural criticism and alternative cultural sphere; however, they are limited by an approach to language and culture that interprets images as the more or less authentic reflection of a preconceived reality or truth, and assumes that women, by virtue of our powerlessness, can create new meanings without simultaneously engaging in a careful analysis of the processes through which meanings are negotiated across various discursive practices at any given historical moment.

A materialist cultural interpretive practice insists that we read not only individual texts but literary histories and critical discourse as well, not as reflections of a truth or lie with respect to a pre-given real, but as instruments for the exercise of power, as paradigmatic enactments of those struggles over meaning. For feminists, the task is to elaborate the ways in which sexual difference, the meaning of woman, figures in these processes by creating alternative points from which to approach traditionally accepted meanings. Feminism does, in fact, provide a context out of which we can pluralize meaning by opening apparently fixed constructs onto their social, economic, and political determinacies.

Notes

1. Michel Foucault, *Power/Knowledge: Selected Interviews and Other Writings*, ed. Colin Gordon (New York: Pantheon, 1980), p. 80.
2. Ibid.
3. Michel Foucault, *The History of Sexuality, Volume I: An Introduction*, trans. Robert Hurley (New York: Vintage Books, 1980).
4. Fran Bennett, Beatrix Campbell, Rosalind Coward, Anne S. Sassoon, Carole Snee, "Women's Editorial," *Politics and Power Three* (London: Routledge and Kegan Paul, 1982), p. 5.

5. "Men's Editorial," written by the male members of the editorial staff, *Politics and Power Three*, p. 12.
6. Ibid., p. 17.
7. Heidi Hartmann, "Summary and Response: Continuing the Discussion," in *Women and Revolution*, ed. Lydia Sargent (Boston: South End Press, 1981), p. 364.
8. Ibid., p. 371.
9. Quoted in Alan Sheridan, *Michel Foucault: The Will to Truth* (New York: Tavistock Publications, 1980), p. 217.
10. Ibid., p. 218.
11. Ibid., p. 219.
12. Ibid., p. 217.
13. Foucault, *History of Sexuality*, p. 139.
14. Ibid., p. 5.
15. Ibid., p. 7.
16. Sheridan, *Michel Foucault*, p. 191.
17. Foucault, *History of Sexuality*, p. 23.
18. Ibid., p. 121.
19. Adrienne Rich, "Compulsory Heterosexuality and Lesbian Existence," *Signs* 5 (Summer 1980): 631–60.
20. Foucault, *Power/Knowledge*, pp. 219–20.
21. Foucault, *History of Sexuality*, p. 60.
22. Leslie Stern, "Introduction to Plaza," *m/f* 4 (1980): 23.
23. Monique Plaza, "Our Costs and Their Benefits," *m/f* 4 (1980): 28.

Meaghan Morris

The Pirate's Fiancée: Feminists and Philosophers, or maybe tonight it'll happen

Lacking faith in their ability to change anything, resigned to the status quo, they *have* to see beauty in turds because, so far as they can see, turds are all they'll ever have.

I would like to make a few slanted suggestions about the possible value of Foucault's work to those feminists who might be reading it. This isn't a theoretical text; though that is not because I wish to avoid being caught at commentary, or to tick down my allegiance automatically to a politics (which I do support) of the provisional and the definitely uncertain. Still less does it claim to have anything to do with a genealogical analysis; far from being patiently documentary, it's rather a matter of some impatient speculations on some affairs currently absorbing (in theory) a small section of the women's movement.

Discipline and Punish and *The History of Sexuality*, vol. 1, arrive in troubled times: their propositions have a kind of rampant inappropriateness around them. Foucault's recent work is not enamoured of psychoanalysis, being much more concerned with the possibility of its emergence. It displaces some of the traditional concerns of Marxism, and has scant respect for semiotics: "Neither the dialectic (as logic of contradiction) nor semiotics (as structure of communication) can account for the intrinsic intelligibility of confrontations. The 'dialectic' is a way of evading the always hazardous and open reality of this intelligibility, by reducing it to the hegelian skeleton; and 'semiology' is a way of evading its violent, bloody and deadly character, by reducing it to the pacified and platonic form of language and dialogue."[1]

In the English-speaking world, Marxism and psychoanalysis have been playing a positive role in many women's work for some time; and semiology, while making a major public appearance for the British in a baffling book called *Language and Materialism*, has yet to emerge fully into the limelight. And for backdrop, we have a general proliferation of references to French texts (many of them creative English fictions), which leads some people to call for the cultural vice squad to intervene.

The Foucault problem that these conditions create cannot be entirely dismissed by saying, with some malicious souls, that for a culture where the traditional duty of the intellectual is to prove forever after that he is not a swot and came top of the class without really trying, this is all too much for the mind. (In Australia, this is essentially a masculine model: the witty drinking companion. Most female intellectuals one can unearth tend to be discreet writers, but raving workaholics.)

• In many places in Australia, students and teachers can fall into fatal disfavor for introducing Marxism, psychoanalysis, semiotics (outside the relatively safe place of the modern language department, where they disappear into the innocuous category "foreign culture"). Whether these are worth fighting "for" is a non-question in this context; real struggles take place around them, and through them.

• Marxism (and specifically, Marxist political economy) has a local subversive potential unthinkable to most European intellectuals, when deployed in a culture where the most elementary affirmation of the existence of class struggles past or present is capable of triggering explosions left and right.

• Marxism and psychoanalysis have been all the more effective in opening up possibilities for political struggles, in that much Australian activism is still organized by the ritual form of the Catholic canonical Index: the "what you should not read." Marx and Freud have had less the status of master thinkers, and more the exhilarating effect of an indecent adventure (outside the universities, at least).

• For many feminists, Marxism and psychoanalytic theory (semiotics in the past only drew a few strays) have played the role of unblocking a dead end encountered after a certain period of feminist practice—that of separatism for some, "women's studies" for others. Secondly, with the passing of time, Marxist and/or Freudian feminism now functions for some women as a beginning, what used to be called "radicalization." Thirdly, given the anxiety and aggression that has surrounded the mysterious entity "theory" in the women's movement (and the complex history of that would be well worth looking at), Marxism and psychoanalysis have helped to organize the beginnings of a resistance to the appalling behaviorist and sociological bog that swallows up so much valuable feminist empirical research; at the same time, they have helped to make incursions into the institutionalized exclusion of women from certain kinds of knowledge (and a statement like that these days is no longer an empty rhetorical gesture, but a fully loaded one).

In fact, the first thing that one might want to say about Foucault's recent work (particularly the notion of the specific intellectual, and the analyses of the place of resistance in power relations) is that it is Foucault's work itself that provides a strategic thought, sparing one the absurd paralysis of wondering whether participation in the real struggles going on is corrupting to one's revolutionary essence. (Although a little political *nous* might do the same job just as well.) If there is indeed—in those few ordered little spaces where Anglo-Althusserianism calls the shots— a totalitarian reading of Foucault that rifles for References in order and interrogates his respect for Marx, there is also an authoritarian and equally abusive reading, which brandishes the texts at feminists working with Marxism and psychoanalysis, casts the anathema of co-optation, and then hopes for recantations.

This is a body of work that asks for patient and cautious appraisal. It should be obvious, however, that the last thing that the concept of "regime of truth" can lend itself to is a politics of the pointing finger (even if, in the ritual of self-criticism, one points it at oneself). Nor can "truth" be invoked every time someone (especially a "known Marxist") opens his or her mouth to make a statement: the concept retains its rigor; and if catatonia operates within the theater of thought, Foucault's work is not a prop to quell others into mutism, "Theatrum Philosophicum" is not a monologue on the final effacement of all distinctions.

With that said, however, more interesting questions can arise than the "demoralization in the current conjuncture" which some people fear might follow from reading Foucault's work. For instance, it would be nice to eye a body of work that offers itself as a toolbox and start asking what use its tools might be to us; or, more positively, what use we might make of them. But wielding a feminist "we" is tricky at the moment.

The roar of battle surrounds the pronoun: "I" spells a host of sins, from the humanist horror of talking heads to the simple vulgarity of claims to authenticity; "one" has been written into the masculine; and as for "we," that embarrassing macro-binary constraint from the days of units and solidarity, whatever is to be done with "we"? How many disparate and displacing "you's" and "I's" are being dispossessed?

We are not only choking on the utterance act. Worse, we seem to be sliding on our signifieds, and the scare quote stalks in to fence off the space of a disaster zone: "woman," "women," "Woman" are the warning signs of an increasingly unposable problem, all of a heap, wrong from the start. Yet when the watchful scare quotes are absent, the result is irresistibly comic: one article stolidly observes, "Thus women cannot be taken as an unproblematic collection of subjects, once the concept of subjects is challenged."[2] (Indeed, one would hope not . . .)

In the name of the patriarchal mode of production, Monique Plaza berates Luce Irigaray for flirting with the unseemly proposition in which it is said that woman does not exist;[3] and Mark Cousins (who asserts in a different sense that women do not exist) also cautions that, in Marxist terms at least, what cannot be said to exist is the patriarchal mode of production.[4]

While it is frustrating to read too many of these arguments (and if at times it seems as though Valerie Solanas's observation, *"the ultimate male insight is that life is absurd,"* only needs a little rephrasing in the days of the profound examination of the nonexistence of women), it is nevertheless a little too easy to make fun of them.

Feminisms both past and present have run into some very solid brick walls through trusting too lightly to "the obvious," assuming a continuous and evenly distributed, consistently significant oppression of the eternal natural object "woman" or "women" through the ages. Much of the work going on at the moment that is questioning the "existence" of women (within different or incompatible frameworks) is attempting to break this wall down and so solidify—or diversify—the grounds for an extension of women's struggles. The research that might roughly be called Marxist-Freudian-feminist (sign of a strange conglomeration) is insisting that women are "constructed" in a variety of practices, and attempting to find a way of integrating feminist and class analysis: another kind of investigation is being carried out in terms of women's language, the possibility of discovering or rediscovering a speech that articulates the diversities of women's reality.

However, I would like to use a couple of aspects of Foucault's recent work to raise some questions about the terms in which two particular skirmishes going on *within* these general areas at the moment are being carried out: one around the programme for a so-called theory of the subject (with "language" and "subjectivity" as two defining terms); the other around the celebration of a "feminine" writing ("discourse" and "femininity")—blending an old Anglo-American interest in women writers with the newer discovery of the work going on in France on "feminine specificity."

In doing so, I don't mean to suggest that these are in any sense the main or "leading" theoretical tendencies of feminism. Whatever one thinks about woman, feminism, at least, is never one; and Marxist feminism, for example, is very far from being reducible to the theory of the subject, or to any form of Freudian inclination at all. The two debates in question probably impassion remarkably few women. But they do pose fairly acutely, even if only in passing, an ever-discreditable and ridiculous political question—the (shaky and shifting) place within the women's movement, and beside it, of academics and intellectuals, or "theorists," in British-inspired terminology.

These three terms are used with a variety of connotations by different people in different situations. They cover abuse, dismissal, distrust (it's a strange thing to hear two women, each employed in tertiary teaching, describe each other contemptuously for some *other* reason as "typical academics"), self-abasement, fierce or shy self-assertion. They also hide a multitude of problems. Problems of practice, for even if one leaves aside the proposition that the real task of feminist and other revolutionary intellectuals is to use a privileged relation to truth to explain matters gently to the People, there is always the pressure to feel that "Practice" always lies *elsewhere* (on the streets, on the beaches . . .) and never there where one works, which is rarely an ivory tower of dreams called Theory, but the school, the university, the college, the hospital, the clinic, the media . . . contexts in which, if it becomes impossible to cling to the simplicities of sex war, then it also becomes impossible to escape specification as "a woman." Problems too of formulation, since behind much of the embarrassment and muddle lies a barely broached question sometimes labeled "women and philosophy," or "women and theory," which women working *in* either are the first to realize cannot be posed like that at all.

It's worth insisting that in looking at this—obliquely—through Foucault's work, the point is to use it and not to "apply" it. Even if his texts did not take their own precautions against application, I doubt whether Foucault would apply himself at all well if put directly to work for women. Foucault is a profoundly androcentric writer; it may be frivolous to say so (or worse, old-fashioned), but one only needs to flirt with the possibility of censorship in the act of translating his texts to feel "Homme . . ." resound like a mantra. "The Life of Infamous People" just would not do, it would not do at all.

In fact, the nicest thing about Foucault (in this respect, at least) is that not only do the offers of a philosopher to self-destruct appear to be positively serious on this occasion, but that any feminists drawn in to sending love letters to Foucault would be in no danger of reciprocation. Foucault's work is not the work of a ladies' man: and (confounding the received opinions of the advocates of plain speech, straight sex) some recent flirtations between feminists and other more susceptible thinkers would seem to suggest that there are far worse fates than wanking (like being thoroughly screwed).

However *The History of Sexuality,* vol. 1, contains a number of perspectives of immediate interest to feminists. Apart from the suggestive references to the hysterisation of women, the chapter "Right of Death and Power over Life," for example, casts a curious light on the question of abortion and its history, on the research that has been surfacing on eugenics and the history of feminisms, and on the "professionalisation of birth control."[5] At the same time, it seems to me that for such serious research projects, more would eventually be gained from attention to Foucault's proposals on the analysis of power, knowledge, and struggle than from simply *isolating* the more obviously "relevant" material on sexuality. For if it *is* extracted in isolation, then it becomes only too tempting to observe that much of the book's analytical force is directed against a generalised dream of "sex liberation" that the women's movement began by resisting—by resisting the invitation, floating festively above the tents of the revolution of a decade ago, calling "Free Pussy . . ."

> . . . they've seen the whole show—every bit of it—the fucking scene, the sucking scene, the dick scene, the dyke scene—they've covered the whole waterfront, been under every dock and pier—the peter pier, the pussy pier . . . you've got to go through a lot of sex to get to anti-sex, and SCUM's been through it all, and they're now ready for a new show; they want to crawl out from under the dock, move, take off, sink out. But SCUM doesn't yet prevail; SCUM's still in the gutter of our "society," which, if it's not deflected from its present course and if the Bomb doesn't drop on it, will hump itself to death.

The project of a theory of the subject and the project of a feminine writing have many incompatibilities, and at least one thing in common: the unlikely tool of Lacanian analysis. But the manipulation of the tool is itself a source of dispute. The advocates of "feminine writing" play with a Lacan who flirts with Derrida, admire ruse and dirty fighting, cultivate the tactics of the pricktease; the rigidity of solid philosophical discourse is taunted and tautened unto dissolution. In contrast, the theory of the subject aims to be nothing if not solid; in Coward and Ellis's *Language and Materialism,* or in the pages of the journal *m/f*, there is not much fooling around. The Lacan solicited there is one who could be put to bed with Marx, discomfiting the latter considerably, no doubt, but all in the cause of knowledge rather than desire, science coupled with science breeds science. The language of Lacan is scanned and straightened out; divested of its power to tease, it becomes simply "Hard." It stimulates exegesis, not exhibitionism.

Yet *Language and Materialism* crystallised a new attention to language, an attention that displaced for Marxist feminists much of the earlier work on "the subject" which had sprung up around Juliet Mitchell's *Psychoanalysis and Feminism.* The earlier work relied heavily on the notion of symptomatic reading, in which the text is a sort of medium facilitating the location and diagnosis of tainted concepts, and tried to use healthy pieces of Lacan to "fill in the gaps" in Althusser's comments on ideology. Theories of signification, and the implications of text and discourse analysis, received relatively little attention in themselves –partly because of the (continuing) unavailability of most of the material in English and partly because, despite its apparent exoticism and "structuralist" overtones, the method of symptomatic reading did not involve any attention to "language" at all. Coward and Ellis point to one immediate consequence of the absence of "a radical understanding of signification, of identity and the sign" in Mitchell's book itself:[6] the Lacanian analysis of the unconscious was ignored, and as a result the unconscious was treated as a repository of the structural relations of patriarchy. Marxist feminists then spent a great deal of time arguing whether this was an *acceptable* formulation, or not (a difficult subject, since while curiously attractive to their feminism, it was quite indigestible for their Marxism, and had some rather horrifying implications all around).

Language and Materialism offered a new set of possibilities. By restoring something of the complexity of Lacanian analysis, *and*—at the same time—by interpreting its importance through some concepts extracted from Kristeva's early work, Coward and Ellis were able not only to insist that subjects, and therefore the unconscious, are "produced" by language,[7] but also to dismantle the fairly simple, monolithic, and determined subject of the work inspired by Mitchell. Positions were cleared for plurality, diversity, multiplicity, heterogeneity, disruption, contradiction; the payoff was not only another crack at a theory of ideology, but also a reopened possibility for struggle, which might, into the bargain, allow Marxism to catch up finally on some of its opponents in the ideological domain.

The mention of this possibility prompts questions about the method of *Language and Materialism* itself. Despite its hard-core conceptual approach, there are a number of strange and paradoxical things about it. One is the blithe narrativisation of "developments" in semiology—a discipline (some would say science) whose development is virtually absent from the story except for some glancing asides on Hjelmslev and Greimas. Another is the tendency, disarming in a text written so much in praise of heterogeneity, to synthesise unrelated or conflicting discourses by looking at them through the unifying lens provided by the concept of the "subject in process," with the equally disarming prospect of a study of the "subject in crisis" in poetic language, performed in the most placid and imperturbable of philosophical styles, in which "insights" are clear or unclear, "appropriations" correct or incorrect. *Language and Materialism* is a monument to the spirit of system and, courageously enough, builds itself up with the aid of *S/Z*—one of the fiercest attacks on systemisation and on semiotics as a science ever written. The *lexie*, for example, with its nonchalant arbitrariness, is not only a tool for a new kind of analysis, it is also an inspired and lethal joke.[8]

But the terrain of the theory of the subject is not the terrain of the joker, and it really accords only a very circumscribed place to the productivity of language. Lacanian analysis and semiotics are courted only for their use value: they *account for*. If they also explode as well as explain, then the degree of disruption is carefully controlled—the explosion is limited to the site of the "subject," and not to "the theory of." The status, function, and writing of "theory" remain untouched. One can write that "Narration rather sets the subject in place as the point of intelligibility of its activity: the subject is then in a position of observation, understanding, synthesising"[9] as part of the process of constructing a text that precisely has that position of the subject—among other things—in common with the procedures of narration. There is no "contradiction" at all, in truth, since apart from the text's necessary and worthwhile pedagogical intention, a very traditional mode of distinguishing discourses is at work; the theory of the subject is science, and not literature.

> We have tried to show in this book how the problematic of language has influenced the developments of both Marxism and psychoanalysis in a way that their encounter must necessarily produce a new object of knowledge. This new object is the scientific knowledge of the subject.[10]

The critique of the instrumental theories of language is purely instrumental for the theory. There is therefore every reason why the pursuit of this new object should most rigorously not involve being lured off the path (by Barthes, Kristeva, Lacan) into the thorny territory of the disarticulation of classical rationalism. There things are sloppy, confused, indistinct, unclear; and as one enthusiast for the theory said, there are perfectly sound philosophical objections to that part of it anyway. (Indeed—and from what place might we speak if there were not?)

If the object at stake is the scientific knowledge of the subject, then the political function of knowledge is that of equipment *for* ideological struggle. "Until Marxism can produce a more adequate account of the role of ideology, subjective contradiction and the family, it will never provide a real alternative to such operations of bourgeois ideology."[11] Knowledge guides struggle, somehow but surely; theoretical competence improves political performance.

If one steps outside this framework—which is not reducible to *Language and Materialism* itself, nor coextensive with it —then innocent and discreditable questions arise again; although it seems to me that to pose them it is neither necessary to adopt the facilities of "feminine writing," and claim that this is all too cocky for words, nor sufficient to harangue it self-righteously in general terms for complicity with Truth (nor for pretensions to such complicity; the argument has rather the imprint of utopian desires and all discussion of it needs to take account of its marginality). Instead one can ask in a more limited way what the local implications of these developments might be for women's struggles. What is happening there where women work so hard on distinguishing the penis and the phallus? What is going on when the privileged areas of a Marxist theory become "the subject" on one hand and "language" on the other?

In one sense, it is easy to see the immediate value of this, since constructing a theory of the subject involves trying to work on two legendary disaster-and-devastation zones: one being the outcome of a pugnaciously practical feminism actively hostile to any reflection, confiding itself trustfully to the tender care of sociology, ignoring the claims of economy, and proceeding from the attempt to pit all women against all men at all times to the discovery that the main enemy, when not in The Head, was other women; the other being the failures of an economistic Marxism that not only failed to account for subjective contradictions and the appeals of bourgeois ideology but could not even begin to account for its own remarkable failure to appeal.

Yet the way in which the repair project has been undertaken has some awkward consequences, related at least in part to the Althusserian inheritance at work in the plan's scientific design. Since it is of the first importance to distinguish science from ideology, it therefore becomes extremely important for "theory" to take up a position of combating the enemy *within*. Bourgeois ideology, idealism, humanism . . . if the procedure by which the theory of the subject constructs its *object* is one of forging an identity from (and between) a series of discourses flourishing outside Marxism, then it establishes its own *necessity* by demonstrating that idealism and humanism have infiltrated Marxism itself (and that feminism is fairly seething with both). This is not really a manoeuvre of dogmatism, but of defence, since error leads to practical ineffectiveness.

The first consequence is that it becomes, strictly speaking, unthinkable to question the tools of the necessity-demonstration in any fundamental way, although their refinement, correction, and adjustment are allowed to be not only possible but necessary. For example, when psychoanalytic theory is accepted both for its explanation value *and* for its use in combating humanism in Marxism and feminism, then not only do critiques of the social function of psychoanalysis become irrelevant, or at best a carefully defined "separate" question; but no problems can arise within the space of the theory about the *history* of the relations between (for example) psychoanalysis on the one hand and humanism on the other.[12]

As long as a "science" of the subject can be distinguished from an "ideology" of the subject, the former accounting for the wanderings and limitations of the latter, then there is nothing disturbing about the peculiar convergence of their concerns. Only the naive humanist feminist thinks she can change something by changing her consciousness; the rigorous feminist plumbs the hidden depths of subjectivity, studies its construction in language, follows the diffusing implications of Benveniste's empty instance through to its fulfillments elsewhere, winds through the labyrinth to find not a monster but a new position of the subject. . .

Robert Castel has argued in *Le psychanalysme* that the famous decentering of the subject (and today one needs to add detotalising, deglobalising, and deunifying) serves precisely to displace the subject's functions by carrying them elsewhere and further: but one has trouble arguing effectively in this way with a science. For Castel's observation rests on a series of assumptions, guiding his own research as well as that of Michel Foucault: it depends on assuming that it be *significant* that there is a relation between analytic knowledge and practice, and sociopolitical power relations; that this analytic knowledge and power inscribes itself in a certain socioeconomic form (the contractualisation of subjectivity); and it further depends on insisting that this knowledge cannot be unravelled intact from the networks of power in which it is actively enmeshed, networks whose proliferation can be mapped by *historical* research.

Few proponents of a theory of the subject would deny that these assumptions point to real questions; what is at stake, however, is their importance and the time of their asking. A theory of the subject cannot incorporate them if a theory of the subject is to be possible in the first place. (It might be unkind to suggest that this can be an example of a moment of tactical option, in which false unities dissolve indeed; as when, within the space of Marxist epistemology, an observation of similarities between Althusser and Popper leads some Marxists to take a good hard look again at Althusser, and others to warm to Popper once more.) So one awkward consequence of the Freudo-Marxist marriage presided over by language is to open up an inviting space for Marxist and feminist labours that can only be defined by the systematic evacuation of certain questions—political, economic, and above all historical questions. Unfortunately, this strange form of materialism has its nonintentional relays in practice as well: leaving aside the transfer of some theorists from armchair to couch, the work on constructing a theory of the subject has had some success in partially neutralising the crude and direct assault on psychoanalytics that was once a major tactic for the struggles of women and homosexuals. Long before *Language and Materialism* this was shown to be mistaken, not because it wasn't having effects (which it was, though not all of them brilliant), but because in erroneously assuming that a wide variety of theories, institutions, and practices could be called "psychoanalysis" its aggressively operational ignorance was obscuring the possibility of something much better for the long run—an adequate "analysis."

Other problems appear when the task of assuring internal security takes top priority, if not for its own sake, then at least for the welfare and further development of the struggles under investigation. It then becomes a *point of departure* for "theory" to insist on the presence of humanism, etc. in feminist discourses and practices (a fairly easy job, in fact). The immediate disadvantage of this is not that it can lead to a delirious enumeration of theoretical errors and dangers, though these do diversify delightfully in the site of the hapless subject: apart from the old favourites idealism, humanism, and empiricism, there can be essentialism, moralism, unification, centralisation, necessitation, globalisation, and totalisation. Nor is it that this is the speech of policemen or judges: the "theorist" on these occasions is, rather, in the speaking position of the impotent and ex-centered chieftains of South American tribes, pouring out words (in times of peace) while others go about their business.

The immediate disadvantage is that *"the"* subject looms up even more hugely as problem and as formulation, though this is often a subject that is indeed an effect of language, emerging from a convenient shorthand term for a multiplicity of problems and enlarging itself to assume the status of a reading grid. *"The"* subject as a concept in some British works has assumed a massiveness that is probably equaled only in the concepts of French new philosophy. The construction of "the" subject as problem in the discourse and practice of others means not only that one is forced into the constraints of that form of analysis which consists in demonstrating that women willy-nilly reproduce or reintroduce exactly what they thought they were fighting, but that

1. there is no escape from "the" subject as an effective concept in the analysis of political struggles, and
2. in the process, analysis is largely deprived of any operative means of distinguishing between strategies of power and tactics of resistance, between statements in common (Right to Life, Right to Choose, for example) on the one hand, and antagonistic discourses on the other.

The most one can do is acknowledge difference in vague and general

terms, in an admissive mode: "It may be necessary at this time . . .";
since the foundation of the whole procedure is not to use research itself
to diversify the possibility of struggles, but to establish identity, equivalence, significant similarity. Theory as watchdog is a poor creature: not
because it is nasty or destructive, but because for attacking the analysis
of confrontations it simply has no teeth.

One of the great beauties of Foucault's recent work is the way that
his displacement of the problematics of science and ideology, in favour
of an analysis of the fundamental *implications* of power-knowledge and
their historical transformations, permits the beginnings of an analysis of
that favourite rhetorical flourish, "struggle": and in so doing, displaces
the problematics of humanism—and thus of "anti-humanism"—altogether (a displacement marked by the wickedness of "soul" in *Discipline
and Punish*).

It is this displacement, for example, that allows Foucault to continue
his detailed analyses of the technologies of subjection and subjugation,
and at the same time to speak of "the insurrection of subjugated knowledges" in history, of the revolts of disqualified knowledges, and of their
insistent emergence in the political struggles in recent years.[13] It is this
that permits a rigorous distinction, for example, between "prison reform"
projects initiated through officials, commissioners, and functionaries, and
the demands made by prisoners themselves and those who work for them
on their terms. It is this that could permit a more productive approach
to the articulation—and extension—of the struggles of those resistant
objects of knowledge, "women." For in a perspective in which bodies
and souls are seen as not simply constituted but also invested and *traversed*
by relations of power-knowledge (and that unevenly and inequitably—
it is not a question of a uniform distribution or a stable "effect"), then
what becomes possible in relation to "women," special category in the
catalogues of the human sciences, is something more than a history of
a "construction": it is, rather, the possibility of a history of a strategic
specification—a real one, productive perhaps not only of "specificity" but
also of its status as "intrinsic" in fiction and in truth—and at the same
time, a history of that in women which *defies* specification, which escapes
its hold: the positively *not specific*, the unwomanly in history.

> Men who are rational, however, won't kick or struggle or
> raise a distressing fuss, but will just sit back, relax, enjoy
> the show and ride the waves to their demise.[14]

Passing from the realm of the theory of the subject to the shifty spaces of feminine writing is like emerging from a horror movie to a costume ball. The world of "theorization" is a grim one, haunted by mad scientists breeding monsters through hybridization, the hunted ghosts of a hundred isms, and the massive shadow of the subject surging up at every turn. Feminine writing lures with an invitation to license, gaiety, laughter, desire, and dissolution, a fluid exchange of partners of indefinite identity. All that custom requires is infinite variety, infinite disguise. Only overalls are distinctly out of place; this is the world of "style." Women are not welcome here garbed in the durable gear of men; men, instead, get up in drag. Lacan reigns here not as lawgiver, but as queen.

Each performance has its code, however, and the naive feminist blunders in at her peril. The audiences gather to watch her slip on a central shibboleth, the language of psychoanalysis. In Frankenstein's castle, the penalty for careless definition is swift but clean dismemberment: in the shimmering world of feminine impersonation, a worse fate awaits the woman with the wrong style of argument—she is exposed for the straight that she is, stripped bare to reveal (to her shame and surprise) that she is only equipped with a phallus. In either case, however, there is no forgiveness for not knowing what you do when you speak.

But when it comes to a competition between these two rather risqué forms of entertainment for feminists, the gothic stories of science seem to lose out well and truly. Feminine writing is never One, by definition cannot be defined, asserts itself as irreducible difference, as always other and elsewhere, and, when confronted by an "incisive argument," just laughingly melts away. And with certain eminent philosophers laying bets on the lady, all that wheezing science can do is demonstrate, laboriously, its own limitations.

Traditional political criticism in France has indeed had great difficulties with feminine writing when the latter assumes, chameleon-style, an explicitly political or philosophical colour. Christine Delphy has most success in transfixing Annie Leclerc;[15] but then Annie Leclerc's writing is drivel rather than flow. Yet even here, in the midst of a fine dissection of Leclerc's personal "I" of unquestionable authenticity, Delphy is irritated into matching the mawkishness of her opponent by a melodramatic gesture in the direction of another (if impersonal) mode of authentication—". . . psychologism, biologism, and idealism are the three udders of ideology."[16] One cannot win this argument like that; one can only call for approving cheers from those who are always already on side.

Monique Plaza tries a similar tactic at times in her heroic assault on

Luce Irigaray, " 'Phallomorphic power' and the psychology of 'woman.' "[17] Plaza's theme is naturalism. However, it is impossible to pin down the formidable Irigaray in this way—her ploys are much more lethal than the simperings of Annie Leclerc and have practically nothing in common with them. On the shifting, treacherous ground of femininitude, there is nothing more dangerous than appeals to underlying similarity and resemblance, or to kinship. Annie Leclerc, for example, does believe in a "natural" woman, socially devalorised; Luce Irigaray is very far from confusing the anatomical and the social, but she works with a deadly deliberation *on* the point (the site and the purpose) of the confusion of anatomical and *cultural*.

If a systematic analysis born of concepts like mode of production and reproduction is certainly absent from *Speculum*, then in a sense the power of that form of analysis is actively deflated in the text (although its questions are fleetingly re-raised); but to reinstate its potency, Plaza is forced into merely ignoring the problematics of discourse and the unconscious assaulted in Irigaray's work, and thus in trying to make the charge of naturalism stick she is obliged to read it largely in terms of Freud rather than the terms of Lacan. Plaza's sense of nature, culture, and society is oddly prelinguistic—baby talk. While it is immensely cheering to read an analysis in which it is Lacan rather than women reduced to effective nonexistence, this is achieved at the cost of triumphantly confronting a text with an argument that is already only one of its own antecedents. So too does Plaza find it sufficient to reveal the ambiguity of Irigaray's project and number its contradictions—when ambiguity and contradiction are openly flaunted as its most tormenting methods in the first place.

Irigaray's text itself infuriatingly resists definition as feminine; for her the feminine is conditional or future tense, an interrogative mood. These pervade her writing, with possibility, it is true, but the speculum is a masculine instrument; the feminine is suspended and explored, and the circular form with the fitting contours for the job is one beloved of classical ("masculine") intelligibility fondling its own limits—the paradox. Irigaray remains the recalcitrant outsider at the festival of feminine specificity— she lounges ironically at the door. For what goes on inside, celebrated in the joyful present tense of Hélène Cixous or Marguerite Duras, is nothing more powerful than literature.

And where political criticism and philosophy flounder before a menace of some kind, literary criticism runs up joyfully to embrace feminine writing. Men in literature departments love it (the "display" of power)— relieved of the tedium of exposition, they too can flaunt and fling and giggle with the girls. For in practice, the feminine writing that has "come" has very little to do with biological sex and unspeakable desire, and everything to do with gender and gesture. The language of the feminine body, woman's desire, is a deliriously cultural ploy, entirely organised by the binary logic which Luce Irigaray alone attempts (and wittingly refuses) to dismantle.

It is here, however, that Plaza does point to a way of sneaking up on specificity and stabbing it in the back. "Woman," she says, "exists too much as signifier. Woman exists too much as subjected, exploited individual." It is the absolute irrelevance of women to feminine writing that is the giveaway; and Plaza shows this up best not when she herself hurls socialism head-on against biologism, but when she points to a possible undermining of the binary problematization of difference itself, and to the desirability of the study of its destruction. (A major exploit for which some marauding philosophers do deserve our admiration is their effort to think difference in terms of more than two.)

Women are irrelevant to feminine writing when what is at stake is a binary stirring, a revolution (turning over) *in the name of* "Woman." In "Long Hair, Short Ideas," Michèle Le Doeuff suggested that Hegel's listing of Pythagorean oppositions was not out of date: limit and infinity / unity and multiplicity / masculine and feminine / light and darkness / good and evil.[18] Feminine writing—and much of the proudly obscure literature of "disruptive" multiplicity—would seem to suggest that this list is indeed not out of date, and that the terms of the final couple are changing places. In the feminine "beyond," we are only invited to dance in the next same old two-step.

"Woman" not only exists too much as signifier; she has existed too long as such for too much triumphant celebration of the "coming" of woman in writing to be undertaken without some protective paranoia, least of all when the context is a cult of the signifier itself. The problem "women and literature," for example, has a history, although that is also a history of the diversity of its formulation: but it is difficult to claim any significance for this once the tantalizing suggestion that woman does not exist is converted—as it has often been in the debates on feminine writing in France—to a flat dismissal of the possibility of anything of interest to the present having been said or done by or about women in the past. What a systematic study of the history of specificity as problem could expose I do not know. But even the most cursory glance at the underground of the recent debates in France alone—if a girl takes her eyes off Lacan and Derrida long enough to look—shows up the outline of a couple of regular features.

For one thing, those texts that pose their problem in the name of the *specificity* of women, in some sense, are rarely specifically about women. To take just four examples: there is the complex debate (analysed by Georges May in *Le dilemme du roman au dix-huitième siècle*) that raged around the status of the novel from the late seventeenth to the middle of the eighteenth century, with "ècole des dames," the school for women, as one of its key terms—the problem of women reading, women writing, what they read and wrote and how, became the symbolic battleground of a whole series of social, political, and moral conflicts, and transformations. At the end of the eighteenth century, one finds the hilariously inciting text of Mme de Genlis, *De l'influence des femmes sur la littérature comme protectrices des arts et des auteurs;* here the greatest pedagogue of the age argues in terms of "influence," and the most monstrously prolific of scandalous women writers speaks coyly and decently of "protectors"; but what is elaborated here—*through* a conception (and prescription) of woman's nature and ideal function—is an outline of the woman-function as "model" for social conduct, social control. Closer to home is Theodore Joran, *Les féministes avant le féminisme*, in 1910; this is the age of significant biography, and Joran's second volume uses a series of wonderfully vicious attacks on the manners, morals, abilities, and reputations of a parade of women writers through the ages in order to oppose the notion of women having a "right" to vote—and across that, the concept of "rights" in itself. Finally, in Jean Larnac's gallant defense of women in 1929, *Histoire de la littérature féminine en France*, "feminine literature" becomes the fascinating and dramatic site of a pressing problem of knowledge: can the structure of a brain inhibited and weakened by thousands of years of patriarchal oppression be modified by sudden and rapid social change?

Whatever conclusions could be drawn from this, something more is at stake than a general observation that talking about women involves talking about everything and nothing. When feminine specificity is taken as a point of departure, or as defining the contours of a problem, then we are on the verge of a "something else"; a reorganisation, major or minuscule, in the articulation of power and knowledge. This can be, and has been, exploited by real women (who are never "only" women). But it can also suggest that women wishing to examine the underside of their present specificity as women might come closer to succeeding by taking their own point of departure somewhere else entirely.

While the practice of Writing and experiments in the artifice of dissemination may seem light-years away from the naive evolutionism of Larnac, "woman" as signifier seems to show a remarkable stability: as *site* of change and changeability, innovation, rebirth, renewal, experiment and experimentation, the place for the planting of otherwise discredited questions. The speaking body of feminine writing is perhaps (like the silent muse) only the condition of possibility for the birth of something other. Whether this use, this time, can be of benefit or solace to women is impossible to say; but since, on this occasion, it is a raid on philosophy that feminine writing is not only being summoned to accompany, but being urged to put its body in the forefront of and incited to say its piece, it can do no harm to go humming, "Promises, promises . . ."

For another feature that seems to recur in the histories of feminine writing, which might make us wary of incitements to speak a feminine truth, and to burst across the threshold of "discourse" to the thunder of public applause, is that this theme of shocking visibility ("Let the priests tremble, we're going to show them our sexts")[19] is involved in a reaffirmation of a Literature blending disruption and revelation. If Foucault is right in suggesting that literature has occupied a special place in the systems of constraint bringing the "everyday" into discourse—a special place defined by transgression, the task of saying the most unsayable—then it becomes noticeable that this literature has itself accorded a special place to the discourse of women.[20] Here again, it is Georges May who has made the most extensive study of feminism and realism in the early eighteenth century; whatever the vicissitudes of the relationship would turn out to be, there is surely something in the belief that the novel is the ultimate "feminine" genre, and something more in the belief that the feminine novel is a patriarchal plot.

May plays with the traditional idea that in the period of transition from romance to novel men left the field temporarily free for women because of the debased status of the indistinct and undistinguished new form. Foucault (without reference to women) suggests that we are living through the death of the great writer as model intellectual: "All the fevered theorisation of writing which we witnessed during the sixties was no doubt only a swan song: the writer was desperately struggling for the maintenance of his political privilege."[21] To make any extrapolations from that to speculate on the appearance of the great "feminine" writer aureoled with political import would be both abusive and too paranoid for words.

Besides, in our own culture, political privilege has not weighed upon the writer-intellectual for some time; it is, rather, invested in the writer as journalist. (Had the New Philosophers been Americans, they would certainly have written for *Rolling Stone*—though had they been Australians, they would probably have emigrated to Paris.) Yet there is, in each place, a highly prized and profitable form of feminine writing (very carefully delimited as such, and never disrupted by shrillness or imperative mood). In the cult(ure) of the signifier and the irruption of the repressed, it is that of the speaking sext: in the culture of the solid signified, the hard facts, the true story, and Amazing Scenes, it's the literature of "what it's *really* like for women"—*Fear of Flying, Kinflicks, The Women's Room, Memoirs of an Ex–Prom Queen*.

Foucault gives a passing pat of approval, if not quite to the sext show, then at least to chatter boxing, in an interview called "Non au sexe roi":[22] tactical reversal and resistance, women are turning their sex saturation back on the sexuality apparatus (sex you have said we are, sex we will be . . .) and in so doing, women begin to outflank it. Perhaps. But if it becomes hard not to sense just a wee tinge of vacuity in this, it certainly also becomes futile to think the phenomenon of feminine writing in terms of co-optation, since nothing follows from that formulation but fear, paralysis, the injunction to secrecy, silence, and surveillance—or, less melodramatically, the form of "feminist criticism" that consists in showing that women who have succeeded in reaching some large audience are prostitutes (selling out) or pimps (selling out women), while those who do not or will not are hopeless autoerotics (wanking). The position of women desiring both, or neither, would certainly be unspeakable.

It is not a question of co-optation *in general*, but of the efficacy of different methods of attack in different situations, of the possibility of multiplying rather than restricting (for "safety's sake") the points from which women's struggle can develop, and of refusing to think in terms of all or nothing—conserving one's virginity for the ultimate event. Take two films, for example, which define two poles of a debate on women and experiment in the cinema: we do not have to adjudicate between Marguerite Duras's *India Song* and Nelly Kaplan's *La fiancée du pirate*, either on the grounds that the former has been heralded as a work of genius, an avant-garde "classic," and the latter has subversively escaped that fate; or on the grounds that the former deconstructs traditional narrative, while the latter is a "bourgeois" simple tale about a witch.

But to refuse the logic of all or nothing is not to assert equivalence, or to propose a bland avoidance of conflict at all. The seductions of Duras's "profoundly absent" Anne-Marie Stretter, and the well-orchestrated irruptions of the unintelligible language of her mad and colonised double in *India Song*, those of Irigaray's woman thinking of everything and nothing, and of the coming of Cixous's woman giving birth to herself: in all these ladylike textual exhibitions, *a* language is whispering uncommonly loud of desire, the same language which in another dialect and in a harsher register promises knowledge through fidelity to a theory of the subject. That this language can be the language of women—or of their present political struggle—sounds extremely unlikely.

At any rate, the seductive sound and the fury have been drowning out another kind of women's speech; feminism already has its store of forgotten and ignoble texts—aggressive fairy tales, mostly, like Kaplan's dream of the serving girl who didn't hang round waiting for any black freighters to cruise in and pick her up; sentimental celebrations of a women's language that was never unconscious, and a desire that was most unrepressed, like Monique Wittig's *The Guérillères;* or fanatical attempts to make the metaphorical war a real one, like the crazy Tactical-Strategy Charts of Ti-Grace Atkinson's *Amazon Odyssey*. Savagely ingenuous texts: not solid science, but then most unsusceptible to the teasing of pricks. Genuinely disastrous texts, too, in many ways: with (in differing degrees) their simplistic view of class and sex, their binary vision of power, their imperative utopianism. Texts disgraced and disqualified: it seems impossible to mention them at the moment without incurring suspicion of nostalgia, saccharine celebration, necrophilia, romantic anarchism, belief in the timeless subversive integrity of texts irreducibly outside truth. . . Besides, if in France one philosopher can accuse another of being the last dinosaur of the Classical age, the most dreadful condemnation stray feminists have to fear here is dismissal with the last dinosaurs of the late sixties; apart from reassuringly familiar brays about co-optation from other dinosaurs.

However, these museum pieces of *women's* writing do have both a potent charm and a power: which is not to lure back, but to point elsewhere, further, and beyond. As Valerie Solanas (a woman who wrote most certainly in order to become something else than a great writer) reminds us from a place far beyond the construction sites of "theory" or the dressings-up of analytical practice, stretching binary schemes to their limits, defining male sex in terms of "feminine" soul and its undoing, bringing a speech of "refuse" into being—not to dig deep in the truth of every day, but to wheel round for an extraordinary future—there are lots of other things to do:

> Life in this society being, at best, an utter bore and no aspect of society being at all relevant to women, there remains to civic-minded, responsible, thrillseeking females only to overthrow the government, eliminate the money system, institute complete automation, and destroy the male sex.

Notes

1. Michel Foucault, "Truth and Power" (Sydney: Feral, 1979).
2. P. Adams and J. Minson, "The 'Subject' of Feminism," *m/f* 2 (1978): 44.
3. Monique Plaza, " 'Phallomorphic power' and the psychology of 'woman,' " *Ideology and Consciousness* 4 (1978): 4–36. This text is a critique of Luce Irigaray, *Speculum de l'autre femme* (Paris: Minuit, 1974), and *Ce sexe qui n'en est pas un* (Paris: Minuit, 1977); cf. also "Women's exile: interview with Luce Irigaray," *Ideology and Consciousness* 1 (1977): 62–67; and "That sex which is not one," in P. Foss and Meaghan Morris, *Language, Sexuality and Subversion* (Sydney: Feral, 1978), pp. 161–72.
4. Mark Cousins, "Material Arguments and Feminism," *m/f* 2 (1978): 62–70.
5. Cf. Linda Gordon, *Woman's Body, Woman's Right* (London: Penguin, 1977).
6. Rosalind Coward and John Ellis, *Language and Materialism: Developments in Semiology and the Theory of the Subject* (London: Routledge and Kegan Paul, 1977), p. 155.
7. "It is this concentration on language—language producing the subject and therefore the unconscious—which points a way to avoiding incorrect appropriations of psychoanalysis to Marxist thought. These are characterised by seeing the concerns of psychoanalysis as pre-existing the social operations analysed by historical materialism." Ibid.
8. It is a fundamental principle of the scientific semiotics of A. J. Greimas, for example, that the methods of analysis be such that an analysis *is repeatable* with a multiplicity of texts: while *S/Z* might just conceivably give rise to imitations, by means of the *lexie* it aspires to absolute unrepeatability.
9. Coward and Ellis, *Language and Materialism*, p. 50.
10. Ibid., p. 156.
11. Ibid., p. 154.
12. A guide to other unposable questions is contained in Luce Irigaray's account of an expulsion, "Questions," in *Ce sexe qui n'en est pas un*, pp. 117–64.
13. Lecture at the Collège de France, 7/1/1976. Throughout this section I am alluding in part to the method of argument adopted in Adams and Minson, "The 'Subject' of Feminism." This is a text with which one could initiate a lengthy argument of interpretation in relation to Foucault's work: for example, on the status of "discourse" in *The Archaeology of Knowledge* and *Birth of the Clinic*, or whether Foucault ever appeals to "the body" in general in the sense that Adams and Minson suggest. A text with a very different interpretation of these questions (pointing out, for example, that for Foucault the "pre-discursive referent" is *not a natural object*), is P. Veyne, "Foucault révolutionne l'histoire," in *Commen on écrit l'histoire*, 2d ed. (Paris, 1978), pp. 347–85.
14. I would like to thank André Frankovits for his relaxed assistance in the ordering of this article.
15. Christine Delphy, "Proto-féminisme et anti-féminisme," *Les Temps Modernes* 346 (1975): 1469–1500 (translation in *The Main Enemy*, London, WRRC, 1977). Works by Annie Leclerc are *Parole de femme* (Paris: Grasset, 1974); *Epousailles* (Paris: Grasset, 1976); "La lettre d'amour," in Hélène Cixous, M. Gagnon, Annie Leclerc, *La venue à l'écriture* (Paris: U.G.E., 1977); and, with M. Cardinal, *Autrement Dit* (Paris: Grasset, 1977). An introduction to the work discussed in this section is Elaine Marks, "Women and Literature in France," and C. Greenstein Burke, "Report from Paris: Women's Writing and the Women's Movement," both in *Signs* 3, no. 4: 843–55.

16. Delphy, "Proto-féminisme et anti-féminisme," p. 1475.
17. Plaza, " 'Phallomorphic power.' "
18. Le Doeuff, "Women and Philosophy," *Radical Philosophy* 17 (1977): 6.
19. Hélène Cixous, "The Laugh of the Medusa," quoted as epigraph to Marks, "Women and Literature in France."
20. Foucault, "The Life of Infamous Men," in Morris and Patten, *Foucault.*
21. Foucault, "Truth and Power," in Morris and Patten, *Foucault.*
22. Foucault, "Non au sexe roi," *Le Nouvel Observateur* 644 (1977).

Erotica

L'Arc 58, *Jacques Lacan* (1974).
Derrida, Jacques. "The Question of Style." In *The New Nietzsche*, ed. David B. Allison. New York: Delta, 1977.
———. "Becoming Woman." *Semiotext(e): Nietzsche's Return* 3, no. 1 (1978).
———. "The Purveyor of Truth." *Yale French Studies* 52 (1975).
Gallop, Jane. "The Ladies' Man." *Diacritics* (Winter 1976).
Lacan, Jacques. *Le Séminaire Livre XX: Encore*. Paris: Seuil, 1975.
Lyotard, Jean-François. "One of the Things at Stake in Women's Struggles." *SubStance* 20 (1978).

Frances Bartkowski

Epistemic Drift in Foucault

There are two distinct parts of this essay that resonate with the history of publication and the biological fact of Foucault's death as a punctuation, terminal, albeit not final, of his own project—the silencing of a magisterial voice that puts the possibility of its own production everywhere into question and on display. I imagine an encounter of Foucault with others who are also interrogating aspects of subjectivity in the everyday life of institutions to be already going on. Among those others are the ones who have been posing questions about the speaking female subject and her place in language, a realm whose borders follow the traces of authority.

Michel Foucault's first volume of the *History of Sexuality* did not situate itself within the ongoing feminist discussions of sexuality; yet because it appeared when and where it did I wished to read it against itself as a part of such discussions.[1] To wish a dialogue where there may be none expected was a goal; but such a wish raises several questions. These have to do with the means of production of this discourse on sexuality. Whose desire is being brought into the discourse? Who is listening? How are these discourses recirculated and redistributed by the apparatus of power-knowledge-pleasure? By what means is the discourse appropriated by the will to know? Given the will to know and the demands of power and pleasure, how do silence and secrecy function? How does confession work to produce "truth"? If sex functions as unique signifier and universal signified (p. 204), how then is the hermeneutic function of the listener (p. 89) validated? Foucault's text itself posed some of these questions, but could not answer them.

The tripartite axis of power-knowledge-pleasure is missing a fourth term, which is everywhere present in the text but rarely directly discussed: resistance. In focusing more closely on the relation between power and *resistance* we may discover aspects of this history that tend to privilege the triadic power-knowledge-pleasure relationship, never giving us as committed a look at resistance as we most certainly get at power, even though Foucault acknowledges quite clearly that "you can't have one without the other." In *Beginnings* Edward Said notes Foucault's predilection for three- and four-part structures. Perhaps a look at the fourth term will more fully disclose the workings of *this* history of sexuality, for resistance is a term of the same order as power. How can a discourse on the history of sexuality and the will to know neglect to come to terms with that which motivates the ever-insistent discourse on power? Foucault's view of the history of the power-knowledge-pleasure axis was itself presented from the seat of power. While Foucault's gaze and ear are "on the side" of the marginal, his words emanate that very power so eloquently placed into question. There is also the pleasure Foucault takes in his own discourse of knowledge and power; he knows of what he speaks. Yet it is only in *The Order of Discourse* that Foucault sincerely, albeit ritually, addresses his own power-knowledge-pleasure maneuvers, noting the bonds between discourse, desire, and power.[2] In *The Birth of the Clinic* Foucault marked the gaze as the source of determining and determined power. In *The Order of Things* it is resemblance. In the *History of Sexuality* it is the receptive ear that structures and sifts what will enter the domain of the axis of power-knowledge-pleasure. But the ear is an organ dependent on the presence of an other's mouth to do its work.

The receptive locus of power once again speaks of and for itself about that which is given no voice—resistance. By overlooking the mouth (who has spoken?) that produces the "truth" of confession, we get yet another patriarchal history of sexuality, which may know itself as such but gives no voice to its "other half."

History, like philosophy, has long been one of the preserves of patriarchal discourse, and we should not, perhaps, be surprised that Foucault's history speaks so comfortably from and of the realm of power. In *Oublier Foucault* Baudrillard speaks admiringly *and* critically of the way in which Foucault's discourse is the "mirror of the powers he describes."[3] The confession of which Foucault speaks at length is an attempt to give voice to the resistance: yet what we (readers/confessors) hear are not the voices of women, children, homosexuals, perverts, but the voice of power as it institutionalizes, rationalizes, domesticates, and suppresses those very discourses by which it shores itself up.

The thesis of volume 1 has been widely affirmed and made use of: that the discourse of sex was not repressed but has long been spoken from the confessional to the couch. But that is just the point: if the place of sexual discourse is so specifically localized, sex cannot be spoken of except in certain kinds of ways. The church and psychoanalysis have had the monopoly on controlling and recirculating the discourse they have each so comfortably assumed were rightfully their domain. In this text, as in all of Foucault's works, there are no actors in the theater of representation; these archives are not the dramatic texts of history, and this may indeed teach us another way to read from them. But to write a history in which only those listening are heard is to ignore totally the means and relations of the production of that discourse. Those who listen have the power; they regulate, with both approval and disapproval, the behavior described in the confessional and on the couch. And the subject, we are again reminded, is not only the one who speaks, but also the one subjected.

In the deployment of sexuality the space of power is extremely privatized, even closeted. Both sex and sexuality are codified behind closed doors. The entire scene of confession/transference is one of hushed tones and genteel remonstrances. It is perhaps this kind of representation that does support the more traditional view, which Foucault has turned on its head, that the history of sexuality is one of repression. This is another history of discipline and punishment; we are all prisoners of sex.

Baudrillard in his critique is seduced by Foucault's discourse at the same time that he wishes to expose the power play of the text. He seems to foresee both an end to power as we come to know it in *this* text, *and* an end to sex as it has been domesticated by the bourgeoisie. One of the most significant gestures toward closure that Foucault offers is the irony he locates in movements of liberation, which, even as they operate, are constrained by the power-knowledge-pleasure apparatus of the dominant order. Yet while Baudrillard remains entirely too apocalyptic in his edenic reversal, Foucault gives, perhaps, too little place to the power of resistance. We have long listened to power explaining and justifying itself in economic, biological, and sociological terms; what has been spoken in recent years is the history of the resistance that confronts power everywhere. Liberation is not a vision of the end of power or sex; it is an attempt to renegotiate the terms of power-knowledge-pleasure, as in the discourse of contemporary feminism. Foucault's text seems politically informed by the analyses of power-knowledge-pleasure that have come from outside, from resistance. Yet this work, if it was in any sense a last gasp (as Baudrillard would have it), may function as such because it is dissecting an apparatus of sexuality that may already be obsolescent. It is precisely the *scientia sexualis* that has come under attack from many of the voices of resistance. Men and women, gay and straight, have long realized the limitations of codified adult genital sexuality. It would appear that Deleuze and Guattari have attempted a new *ars erotica* in *Anti-Oedipus*, though it is couched in rather aptly technological terms. Where Foucault would speak of pleasure, Deleuze and Guattari make desire their focus. As we saw in this first volume, Foucault mentioned desire only rarely, and even pleasure is the least operative term in the dialectic power-knowledge-pleasure.

Just as the confession is confined to a closed space, the intimacy of the confessional, so the analyst's couch is mirrored in the space of sex itself: that silent closed bedroom of the heterosexual reproductive couple. The appropriation is complete: both the body and the words of women become the property of the discourse of power and sexuality, sanctioning the activity, both sex and confession, which is always privatized. Knowledge is in the possession of the listeners; it is produced through voyeurism and sanctioned eavesdropping. The listening men then recirculate the desire(s) of women into the economy of power and knowledge. The voices of resistance are retranslated into witchcraft and, later, into hysteria as medical institutions take over the functions of the church.

In *La Jeune Née* Catherine Clément cites Freud, who finds in the *Malleus Maleficarum* descriptions uncannily like the symptoms he classified as hysteria in *The Birth of Psychoanalysis*.[4] Those women "possessed by the devil" are heard only in order to be dispossessed and repossessed by those whose will to know *will* be satisfied. Indeed, it is the resistance of the hysteric in her will to know that must be and is managed and manipulated, as it is in the *Studies on Hysteria*. While Freud and his predecessors, the exorcists, recognized and "cured" male hysterics and male witches, that knowledge was and is peripheral to the predominant symbolism of these related "diseases" as the province of the minds/bodies of women.

What Foucault has done is to reproduce and produce as history the patriarchal history of sexuality. As Cixous and Clément point out in *La Jeune Née*, at those times when women have acceded to knowledge it has always been from without, as excluded from and other than the realm of power (and, to be sure, pleasure); for there is the pleasure in the exercise of power, and it is this with which Foucault's text seduces us if we stop here.

What Irigaray, Cixous, Clément, and others are re-creating and inventing are some of the histories of resistance, but again marginalized, ghettoized by publishers, critics, and the like. If we accept Foucault's framework of seventeenth- and eighteenth-century domination by the church and nineteenth-century domination by the practitioners of medicine, we ask again who is listening to whom for whom? Foucault's three centuries of *scientia sexualis* pick up where the witch burnings of western and central Europe left off. Clément's contribution to *La Jeune Née*, "*Sorcière-Hystérique*," fills in the patriarchal lacunae that recall Freud's classification of hysteria as resembling the symptoms of medieval possession—the word is apt. These are among the confessions that we did not hear in Foucault's first volume. But Foucault knows this history; he recalls that confession has always been closely associated with torture. Yet somehow in Foucault's text the words of those who confess are more camouflaged than the covert operations of power that proceed from the satisfied will to know that extorts the confession.

Foucault works as the archaeologist of power and knowledge as it shows itself in operation in areas that bourgeois history has often deemed marginal: prisons, madness, clinics, and sexuality. His history is not one of dates, but one of ruptures—the struggles of the history of resistance are not marked so clearly. As Foucault points out, history does not operate as a force, but remains dispersed, split, random. This book not only should be, but (wittingly or not) is very much a part of the ongoing feminist discovery of the "nature" of sexuality as it has been codified for/of/by the voices, eyes, and ears of those in the seat of power, hidden in the confessional and behind the analyst's couch—*"encore un chuchotement profitable sur un lit"* (p. 11).

Why this turning over/*bouleversement* of the repression hypothesis? Is it a mere methodological reversal that opens the archive to the resistance, which has not been mute in spite of the "triple interdiction"? Foucault rejects the notion of repression as the mode of power-knowledge-pleasure because it is too easy: the naive belief that we liberate *ourselves*, that one who speaks (of) repression is therefore outside its force, that we transgress and therefore subvert. For if, in fact, listening were taking place, power could not so comfortably retain its hierarchical structure and status.

In *Social Text #1*, working from Frantz Fanon's notion of an oppositional language and Volosinov's idea of the materiality of the sign as ideology, Bruce Boone discusses gay language as an antagonistic political praxis. Boone's article places itself among ongoing discussions of "women's language." In France such discussions have often turned to what has been named *écriture féminine*. While such critical practices take the risk of positing notions of essential femininity, they may also try to varying degrees to retain a historical specificity that would always assert that such language practice is ideological. Its status as oppositional and antagonistic speaks simultaneously of the desire(s) and need for a practice denied by the dominant modes of discourse (where that discourse is identified as patriarchal). To recognize resistance as the motor of the discursive productions of power-knowledge-pleasure would be to include the oppositional practice of women, gays, even children in the history of sexuality. This is what Clément and Cixous do when they attempt to read, necessarily through Freud, the language of Dora, *"la perle des hystériques."* Their reading makes for an understanding of the repression at work in making of Dora's speech a case study. What is at work in the discourse of Freud is the re-covering, the covering over/again, of a discourse that must remain unheard, mute, invisible except as it is appropriated by the magisterial narrative. Here the work of Fanon, Boone, and feminists comes together to examine how that which is strange and other is turned against itself by those who listen only to reinforce the dominant and dominating structures of knowledge. The desire of the other (the hysteric who "wants it all") is translated into the patriarchal discourse of desire that, according to Foucault's scheme, manifests itself in (1) the control of population (read: reproduction, the bodies of women as the agents of this control); (2) the specification of homosexuality; (3) the segregation of and attention to infantile, child, and adolescent sexuality; and (4) the fixing of perversions through the necessity to speak of them. These operations of power leading to a proliferation of sexualities and a concurrent "sensualization of power" (p. 61) demonstrate the finally interlocking and interwoven apparatus of power and pleasure. And it is here that the intermediary term of knowledge begins to slide once we can see it as confined by and centered between pleasure and power; Foucault is quite clear about those who listen and look but refuse to hear and see what must remain inadmissible as evidence. Through what he terms an "obstinate will not to know" (p. 74), the discourse of sexuality begins to assign truth and falsehood as criteria, developing the morbid and solemn *scientia sexualis*. This "scientific" sexuality will derive its truth from the ritual of confession and its other side, torture.

And yet what must be spoken must also remain secret. Isn't this contradiction one that arises out of the above-mentioned clos(et)ed space of the confessional discourse? It must not be spoken everywhere, but is privileged by the coupled place of the inquisitor-victim, confessor-confessant, analyst-analysand, master-slave. Isn't it this reversal of recent years that now makes sexual discourse marketable and, perhaps in everyday life, liberating? That is, while the speaking of sexuality may still be under the yoke of power and its technicians, the adversary position it achieves by speaking "everywhere" redefines the contemporary relations of the production of this discourse. Isn't this a part of the basic "faith" (and it may also be ironic, as Foucault's final statement would insist) that sexuality is no longer privatized by the forms of patriarchy, as in the bedroom, confessional, and psychiatrist's office? Isn't it this transformation that can see the oppositional function of gay or women's language and that can question, use, and question again what its place is and how it might permit us the possibility of another reading of the history of sexuality in which resistance and power might indeed hear each other? Isn't this how the translation of the two discourses for and by each other might serve to illuminate that always-problematic area of claims toward both equality and difference? Couldn't such a dialogue remain complex and self-critical so that the power of discourse would not necessarily entail the "subordination of the feminine," as an essay by Irigaray suggests it always does?[5] Aren't the confessions of today made as much, if not more, for those in the position of the dominated than for those in the position of the dominating?

These questions return us to those opening, resistant questions, imitating a circularity apparent in many sections of the *History of Sexuality*. Leo Bersani discusses this lack of closure and linearity in the text, a device that is a cornerstone of Foucault's archaeology of knowledge. It is this very omission that may allow us to see and hear as Bersani does that "Foucault's own discourse conforms to the cultural imperatives he denounces" even as "every resistance to power is an exciting counter-exercise of power."[6] This reminder may help us to keep in view that though resistance is not as hypostatized by this text as are power-knowledge-pleasure, the impetus for the work and its production of the discourse of knowledge is what Bersani terms the "rejoicing strength" of the counter-exercise, or resistance to power. It is in the claims made for and in favor of difference that we can distinguish forms of resistance that engender other forms of power less totalizing and normative than those Foucault analyzed. It is not the end of power or sex, as Baudrillard seems to both hope and fear, but in political terms it is a transformation of the relations of power-knowledge-pleasure-resistance. We read Foucault for the view he gives us of the desire that motivates (t)his will to know as it finds pleasure in its own power and resistance to the knowledge *(savoir)* it discloses. This renders circular and complex the discourse that produces its own object—power, always there and always resistant. To read the history of power within the history of sexuality we have to be willing to accept Foucault's reversal of the repressive hypothesis. But to begin to balance this history and admit the vis-à-vis of power and resistance, we must continue to listen to the voices that find strength in the counter-exercise of the history of repression, oppression, suppression. We know from Foucault that the reversal is not so simple or visible. We must listen to *and* hear the languages of opposition even as they test the syntax of the dominating discourses. Foucault's own reversal is an example of an intellectual performance that both mocks and imitates its object of knowledge.

While it may be an effort of grafting, I still want to read Foucault's project in *The History of Sexuality* as singular yet broken. Epistemic break and rupture have become a form of methodological drift. Where volume 1 may be easily aligned with the studies of madness, the clinic, prisons, and forms of representation, volumes 2 and 3 are more reminiscent of the ways Foucault worked in the *Archaeology of Knowledge* and *The Order of Discourse*. The continuity is present even in the change in the continued concern with questions of marginality. What is unexpected is Foucault's turn to an epoch where heterosexuality has yet to become central or compulsory in his genealogy of the man of desire. Drift is not only method but also object of these studies—the glance is microscopic and the time-table of this hermeneutics of the self is evolutionary. The theoretical splash and broad strokes of volume 1 have given way to the naturalist's eye for fine distinctions. A search for an ethics of practice will displace the installation of norms and taboos through the workings of power and knowledge.

In thinking about Foucault's archaeological and geological metaphors, an image that came to me was of Foucault as Camus's Sisyphus. The key turn that Camus takes with that myth is to say "we must imagine Sisyphus as happy in his task." And I think that we must imagine Foucault as happy in his task in volumes 2 and 3.

Soon after the publication of volume 1, Foucault announced that his direction in this project had changed. So the question was, in what way would that change become apparent? I would suggest that there is an intermediate text here—the memoirs of Herculine Barbin; there you have Foucault working in a place of resistance, going to some specific archival materials to do so.[7]

With this image of Foucault as the happy Sisyphus, I see him in volumes 2 and 3 not at the top of the mountain in an act of rejoicing strength, which is how Leo Bersani described the mode of volume 1, but at a bend in the course and heading back uphill and knowing that this will be another slow progress. One of the things Foucault said in a late interview about the nature of his work in volumes 2 and 3 is that he is taking care of himself, and there you have a form of *Le Souci de Soi*— the whole project of how to care for the self, how to construct the self, what sort of self was constructed in ancient Greece, in early Rome. This taking care of the self, this moving back up the hill slowly, gives us Foucault in a heroic, and desiring, posture. Heroic act, heroic gesture, and a manly one at that.

The world of volumes 2 and 3 is a world of men, and since one of my interests is to keep the questions of gender and feminism in view, it is noteworthy that Foucault is one of the male thinkers, intellectuals, writers, to whom feminists have turned much more frequently and much more readily than to other French writers and thinkers. Eve Sedgwick, in *Between Men*, says that the projects of feminism and anti-homophobia are allied in ways that must be made clear. I think that is one of the reasons why feminists do find a way to turn to Foucault more than, say, to Derrida, or even Barthes. Now, for feminists to say that there is a reason to enter this world of men is something that I would like to put forth, since there are aspects of Foucault's work in volumes 2 and 3 that allow us to see a very clear consciousness of gender in a way that volume 1 did not offer us.

One of the landmark texts for beginning readers in French feminism is Hélène Cixous's *Laugh of the Medusa*. In that essay she says, "men still have everything to tell us about their sexuality."[8] Let me suggest that Foucault is one of the men who is responding to that call, implicitly or explicitly. And in volumes 2 and 3 there is a kind of unabashed search for origins, of looking toward the birth of ethics and the ways of self-examination and generation as they come through the body in discourse.

At the end of volume 1 Foucault speaks of "the austere monarchy of sex," and about the fact that we have been asked to bring to that our attention and our care *(notre souci)*. He would focus on bodies and their pleasures rather than on desire. In those closing moments, there is a bridge to volumes 2 and 3 and to the kind of work he does here.[9] The use of pleasure, the uses of pleasures, the proper use of pleasure is about measure, it is about quantity and management. Excess and passivity are the two forms of immorality for the (male) subject of desire, and the admitted subject of desire in volumes 2 and 3 is *l'homme du désir*, the man of desire. This is going to be a model where hierarchy always counts and where constancy in power relations must be fixed. Foucault works with the ways in which the body and sexual practices have always been problematized in Western culture. But his gaze has shifted toward the stylization of pleasures rather than the justification of taboos.

Volume 2 begins with the themes of austerity—in relationships among men, particularly older and younger men, in marriage, and in the political economy. The economy of the body, the domestic economy, the political economy are worked over by analogy; that is, from the proper use of pleasure will arise the proper management of the household and thereby the proper management of the city-state. Austerity is required in the gaining of wisdom, and the method for the gaining of wisdom is through measure and quantity as they concern the appetites: food, drink, and sex. Those are the areas that are regimented. One of the chapters in volume 2 is about diet, diet as regime, as regiment, as one of the first instances of how the body must deal with what it encounters—food, drink, and other bodies. It is not just *L'Usage des Plaisirs* but *le bon usage*—and this is kind of a grammar of pleasures that Foucault is studying. There is another triple strategy to this proper use of pleasure: it is about need, timing, and the status of those involved in the taking of pleasure. One must/does turn to food, drink, and sex when there is need, not excessively, and at the proper time. So that clean and proper sexual objects are said to be at times women, slaves, boys, but women and slaves inhabit separate categories; this man of desire is a free man. What is gained through this proper use of pleasure, this proper management of the pleasures is mastery over the self. This mastery of the self will produce a man of temperance and, curiously, a man of virtue. What is important here is that the ethical negativity is in being passive in regard to pleasures. One should not let oneself go. One must master oneself.

Volume 2 ends on a chapter called "True Love," discussing how true love becomes possible between men and boys or men and younger men, who are boys. This is problematic, of course, because these boys become men. So, how are they properly to stylize their pleasures when they become men after having been the passive objects of the desire of older men? There must be a reversal; it becomes necessary to find ways of establishing notions of reciprocity. Volume 2 and volume 3 both end by conceptualizing notions of reciprocity in relationships between older and younger men. That comes about at both points, in classical Greek texts and in early Roman texts, through a negation of sexuality—sexual activity between these men. It is the body that needs; it is the soul that desires. It is the control of the body and its demands that leads to this mastery of the self that offers the possibility for reciprocity between older and younger men.

In volume 3 Foucault begins to examine inflections, not ruptures— the slow evolutions in this study of the morality of the body. What volume 3 is moving toward is the way that the late Roman period lays the groundwork for the early Christian period. The meditative ego makes a "continuing exercise" *(exercice permanente)* of existence, and darkness and silence become necessary for the proper examination of the self.

The text that Foucault is working with at the beginning of volume 3 is Artemidorus's *Interpretation of Dreams*, in which dreams are part of the practices of daily life that have to do with proper management of the self. Dreams are divided into categories. The dream book deals with sexual acts that are represented in dreams and how they are to be interpreted. Some acts are within the law, some are against the law, and some are against nature. What is important is not whether acts represented in dreams are against the law or conform to the law, but rather whether the figures represented in dreams retain their proper hierarchical status — so that the free man is in the position of the free man, in the active position, and not in the position of one who is passive or a slave. If dreams represent or dramatize a kind of reversal of hierarchical positions, then they augur ill for daily life. An ideal of the man of desire is to find a form of *jouissance* that is without desire and without disquiet *(sans désir, sans trouble)*. In this new relation to the self, certain words begin to appear, certain terms begin to shift. Notions of evil and notions of the law begin to take their place in line with questions of self, strength, and technique, so that some of the tensions that will become more apparent in the Christian pastoral ethic are already being anticipated here by Foucault.

I think the volumes following volume 1 will eventually bring us back to it as the overarching theoretical structure. The closing of volume 3 is important as a reading of the direction that the work on the self will take. The story told at the end of *Le Souci de Soi* is from a text by Lucian. Two friends meet, and one presents his dilemma to the other. He finds that he loves equally women and young men. The question he poses to his friend is, which is the proper object of his desire? The friend in responding offers him a narrative—frames within narrative frames—of a Greek text about such a dialogue between two adversaries, one the lover of men, one the lover of women. The dialogue tells the story of a young man who has unlawfully spent the night in a temple of Aphrodite. Foucault's French text (and the Greek text) says that this young man soiled the statue and treated her as one would a man. So the question to be decided between the two adversaries is whether the young man has properly loved the statue of Aphrodite. Is this a tribute to the love of women, or is this a defilement of the statue of Aphrodite? Is it about love of men? The two adversaries conclude that love of women takes one into a world of what Foucault terms "gracious reciprocity," while love of men takes one into a world of "virtuous community." Again, we can see that the notion of virtue is part of what constitutes masculinity in the Greek world, and in the Roman world.

It has become a commonplace for us to think of virtue, certainly since the eighteenth century, as an attribute of femininity. At the end of volume 3 Foucault talks about some of the Alexandrian romances, early pastoral forms. This may be a transitional moment, where virtue begins to slip and becomes (or is on its way to becoming) an attribute attached to the world of women. What has happened to the codes of masculinity may be a question of the last volume. Ending on this model of reciprocity in both volume 2 and volume 3 is a very provocative move for Foucault in a study of love among men. If the struggle is one in which passivity is to be denied, where are we to go in shifting the model? Where Foucault seems to want to go at the end of both volumes is toward a notion of reciprocity. That ideal begins to draw women into the world of men for a political and sexual economy that becomes recognizable as one that shapes the early modern world.

Another word that appears at the end of volume 3, in a very brief discussion, is virginity. Once talk of virginity enters this discourse then it is no longer a question of the use of pleasure, since to valorize virginity is to be talking not about use but rather about a state of rest, about forms of preservation and accumulation, in preparation for reproduction. Foucault points out that to valorize virginity is a step away from the valorization of friendship toward its replacement with "spiritual marriage"— a choice whereby the hero abstains and resists: double virginity, symmetry of austerity.

Contemporary feminist theory, until the last several years, has tried to deal with questions of power in ways that have avoided the complexities and contradictions in that realm. (If we think about early feminist texts, we can see this to be particularly true.) In the last few years the question of power has been taken up in ways that are much more subtle.[10] The early models of consensus and reciprocity have also been put into question. But are there models that present us with the notions of conflict and resolution of conflict, hierarchy and questions of status within worlds of women? Joanna Russ's 1975 novel *The Female Man* may be read as an "aphrodisia" for women and girls.[11] It resembles a futuristic version of classical texts in its treatment of the proper uses of pleasure and the proper relations among women of different generations, women of different cultures, women who do different kinds of work, and women of different histories. Russ presents conflict and hierarchical struggle through literary conventions appropriate to science fiction. Her protagonists are four women from different times and places whose ethics and norms are in collision. Russ's text is marked both by the rhetoric of United States feminism circa 1975 and that of an imagined post-gender world (her future is located on the planet Whileaway). It is this ability to speak clearly from a very specific historical moment and also to imagine it spatially and temporally subsumed that gives Russ's text a privileged place. This place is acknowledged in a recent essay by Donna Haraway, "A Manifesto for Cyborgs," which also takes up issues of power and forms of resistance and cites a host of other feminist science-fiction and feminist utopian novels.[12] Haraway suggests that the female self that feminists must code exists in a post-gender world, a postmodern world, a world that is beyond Foucault, in which affinity restructures identity through difference. She offers the phrase the "informatics of domination" as a more accurate description of the current regime, and says in one of her footnotes that "it is time to write the death of the clinic." She talks about how power is no longer subjected merely to the clinical gaze of public hygiene but is dealt with in terms of "stress management." Her text is full of the kind of language to which we have all become not only accustomed, but probably immune. Yet she uses that language to evoke for us the world in which we live, and to point out that we are already cyborgs, that we all consist only of partial identities. The self encoded in Western culture that Foucault traces is already part fossil for its tracks to be so clearly marked and legible. The cyborg is part animal, part human, part machine. Haraway's points of reference range from corporate technology to current scientific research to early feminist work as she tries to imagine what socialist feminism might have to gain by accepting a notion of this partial self that is constructed through forms of domination and forms of resistance to them—more effective theories of experience, how not to be *man*, and regeneration, not rebirth.

The reciprocity Foucault seeks arises not only in terms of the model of heterosexuality and marriage; it also comes up as a possibility, a necessary possibility, among men. I think that this is really what interests Foucault, because so much in the texts that he examines deals with the proper place of the subjects participating in taking pleasure and maintaining their proper place. The adversary in the Greek dialogue that Foucault cites who advocates love among men says that reciprocity is possible here too. There are situations where the young man, grown older, is the lover and the older man has become the beloved, which is not where they began; it is circular. There has been a dialectical reversal and displacement. Reciprocity in marriage has to do with its long-term status; this becomes true here, too. So there is still groundwork that comes out of the heterosexual model, but I think that for Foucault it is important that he locate moments when what is valorized is the love possible between men, which is about his commitment to searching out and finding reciprocity there. The last chapter in volume 3 is called "A New Erotic"; its subject is the erotics of reciprocity, as opposed to an erotics based on a differential in power. In this "new" model what matters is the long-term nature of the bond and its ties to fidelity; older men do not abandon younger men once their beards grow. It is possible to anticipate how these forms of pleasure will be deployed within the Christian pastoral ethic and its concomitant privileging of heterosexuality.

At the end of volume 2 Foucault observes that philosophy arises in culture when certain basic needs have been seen to, have been taken care of. A surplus economy supports philosophy and pederasty: men can take time away from the domestic scene to love other men because the reproduction of the family and the state is assured. To leave the domestic scene is to take up philosophy. In a text like Russ's *The Female Man* there is also a surplus economy, love among women, and philosophy.

And it is certainly the case that as feminism thrives in moments of psycho-social and sexuo-economic surplus, so do the possibilities for feminist theory to expand the borders of women's ideas and the experiences of their bodies and their pleasures.

Notes

The work on volume 1 of *The History of Sexuality* in this essay is a revision of a paper presented to the Midwest Modern Language Association in November 1979 in Indianapolis; the work on volumes 2 and 3 was first presented at a lecture at Brown University in November 1985. Among the critical readers, I want to acknowledge my appreciation for the words/thoughts of Steve Ungar, Peggy Kamuf, Elizabeth Weed, and Linda Singer.

1. Michel Foucault, *Histoire de la sexualité, 1, La Volonte de savoir* (Paris: Gallimard, 1976); *The History of Sexuality, Vol. I: An Introduction*, trans. Robert Hurley (New York: Random House, 1980). All page numbers cited in this essay refer to the original; translations are mine.
2. Michel Foucault, *L'Ordre du discours* (Paris: Gallimard, 1971), p. 12.
3. Jean Baudrillard, *Oublier Foucault* (Paris: Galilée, 1977), p. 11.
4. Hélène Cixous and Catherine Clément, *La Jeune Née* (Paris: 10/18, 1975); *The Newly Born Woman*, trans. Betsy Wing (Minneapolis: University of Minnesota Press, 1986).
5. Luce Irigaray, *Ce Sexe qui n'en est pas un* (Paris: Minuit, 1977); *This Sex Which Is Not One*, trans. Catherine Porter with Carolyn Burke (Ithaca, N.Y.: Cornell University Press, 1985), in the essay of the same name.
6. Leo Bersani, "The Subject of Power," *Diacritics* (Fall 1977): 5–6.
7. *Herculine Barbin dite Alexina B.*, presente par Michel Foucault (Paris: Gallimard, 1978), *Herculine Barbin· Being the Recently Discovered Memoirs of a Nineteenth Century French Hermaphrodite*, trans. Richard McDougall (New York: Pantheon, 1980).
8. Hélène Cixous, "Le Rire de la Méduse," *L'Arc* (1975): 39–54; "The Laugh of the Medusa," trans. Keith Cohen and Paula Cohen, *Signs* 1, no. 4 (Summer 1976): 875–93; also reprinted in *New French Feminisms*, ed. Elaine Marks and Isabelle de Courtivron (Amherst: University of Massachusetts Press, 1980), 245–64.
9. Michel Foucault, *Histoire de la sexualité, L'Usage des plaisirs, 3, Le Souci de soi* (Paris: Gallimard, 1984); *The Use of Pleasure*, trans. Robert Hurley (New York: Pantheon, 1985).
10. I am interested in marking at least three phases in the feminist study of the workings and conceptualization of power (sexual politics); the first might best be represented by essays collected in the early movement anthologies such as *Sisterhood is Powerful*, ed. Robin Morgan (New York: Random House, 1970), and *Voices from Women's Liberation*, ed. Leslie B. Tanner (New York: New American Library, 1970).

    A distinct shift occurs in the direction of more ideologically textured notions of power with the publication of *Capitalist Patriarchy and the Case for Socialist Feminism*, ed. Zillah Eisenstein (New York: Monthly Review Press, 1979), and Nancy Chodorow, *The Reproduction of Motherhood: Psychoanalysis and the Sociology of Gender* (Berkeley: University of California Press, 1978), or even earlier, though somewhat less widely read at the time, I suspect, Juliet Mitchell, *Psychoanalysis and Feminism* (New York: Random House, 1974).

I read a third moment in the appearance of two anthologies that deal with sexual politics as reinvigorated by attacks on feminism from the U.S. New Right and through a return to the again effaced discourse on sexuality, *Powers of Desire*, ed. Ann Snitow, Christine Stansell, and Sharon Thompson (New York: Monthly Review Press, 1983), and *Pleasure and Danger*, ed. Carole S. Vance (Boston: Routledge and Kegan Paul, 1984).

11. Joanna Russ, *The Female Man* (New York: Bantam, 1975).
12. Donna Haraway, "A Manifesto for Cyborgs: Science, Technology, and Socialist Feminism in the 1980s," *Socialist Review*, no. 80 (March–April 1985): 65–107.

Discipline and the Female Subject

II

Sandra Lee Bartky

Foucault, Femininity, and the Modernization of Patriarchal Power

I

In a striking critique of modern society, Michel Foucault has argued that the rise of parliamentary institutions and of new conceptions of political liberty was accompanied by a darker counter-movement, by the emergence of a new and unprecedented discipline directed against the body. More is required of the body now than mere political allegiance or the appropriation of the products of its labor: the new discipline invades the body and seeks to regulate its very forces and operations, the economy and efficiency of its movements.

The disciplinary practices Foucault describes are tied to peculiarly modern forms of the army, the school, the hospital, the prison, and the manufactory; the aim of these disciplines is to increase the utility of the body, to augment its forces:

> What was then being formed was a policy of coercions that act upon the body, a calculated manipulation of its elements, its gestures, its behaviour. The human body was entering a machinery of power that explores it, breaks it down and re-arranges it. A "political anatomy", which was also a "mechanics of power", was being born; it defined how one may have a hold over others' bodies, not only so that they may do what one wishes, but so that they may operate as one wishes, with the techniques, the speed and the efficiency that one determines. Thus, dis-cipline produces subjected and practiced bodies, "docile" bodies.[1]

The production of "docile bodies" requires that an uninterrupted coercion be directed to the very processes of bodily activity, not just their result; this "micro-physics of power" fragments and partitions the body's time, its space, and its movements.[2]

The student, then, is enclosed within a classroom and assigned to a desk he cannot leave; his ranking in the class can be read off the position of his desk in the serially ordered and segmented space of the classroom itself. Foucault tells us that "Jean-Baptiste de la Salle dreamt of a class-room in which the spatial distribution might provide a whole series of distinctions at once, according to the pupil's progress, worth, character, application, cleanliness and parents' fortune."[3] The student must sit up-right, feet upon the floor, head erect; he may not slouch or fidget; his animate body is brought into a fixed correlation with the inanimate desk.

The minute breakdown of gestures and movements required of soldiers at drill is far more relentless:

> Bring the weapon forward. In three stages. Raise the rifle with the right hand, bringing it close to the body so as to hold it perpendicular with the right knee, the end of the barrel at eye level, grasping it by striking it with the right hand, the arm held close to the body at waist height. At the second stage, bring the rifle in front of you with the left hand, the barrel in the middle between the two eyes, vertical, the right hand grasping it at the small of the butt, the arm outstretched, the triggerguard resting on the first finger, the left hand at the height of the notch, the thumb lying along the barrel against the moulding. At the third stage . . .[4]

These "body-object articulations" of the soldier and his weapon, the student and his desk effect a "coercive link with the apparatus of pro-duction." We are far indeed from older forms of control that "demanded of the body only signs or products, forms of expression or the result of labour."[5]

The body's time, in these regimes of power, is as rigidly controlled as its space: the factory whistle and the school bell mark a division of time into discrete and segmented units that regulate the various activities of the day. The following timetable, similar in spirit to the ordering of my grammar school classroom, is suggested for French "écoles mutuelles" of the early nineteenth century:

> 8:45 entrance of the monitor, 8:52 the monitor's summons, 8:56 entrance of the children and prayer, 9:00 the children go to their benches, 9:04 first slate, 9:08 end of dictation, 9:12 second slate, etc.[6]

Control this rigid and precise cannot be maintained without a minute and relentless surveillance.

Jeremy Bentham's design for the Panopticon, a model prison, captures for Foucault the essence of the disciplinary society. At the periphery of the Panopticon, a circular structure; at the center, a tower with wide windows that opens onto the inner side of the ring. The structure on the periphery is divided into cells, each with two windows, one facing the windows of the tower, the other facing the outside, allowing an effect of backlighting to make any figure visible within the cell. "All that is needed, then, is to place a supervisor in a central tower and to shut up in each cell a madman, a patient, a condemned man, a worker or a schoolboy."[7] Each inmate is alone, shut off from effective communication with his fellows, but constantly visible from the tower. The effect of this is "to induce in the inmate a state of conscious and permanent visibility that assures the automatic functioning of power"; each becomes to himself his own jailer.[8] This "state of conscious and permanent visibility" is a sign that the tight, disciplinary control of the body has gotten a hold on the mind as well. In the perpetual self-surveillance of the inmate lies the genesis of the celebrated "individualism" and heightened self-consciousness that are hallmarks of modern times. For Foucault, the structure and effects of the Panopticon resonate throughout society: Is it surprising that "prisons resemble factories, schools, barracks, hospitals, which all resemble prisons"?[9]

Foucault's account in *Discipline and Punish* of the disciplinary practices that produce the "docile bodies" of modernity is a genuine *tour de force*, incorporating a rich theoretical account of the ways in which instrumental reason takes hold of the body with a mass of historical detail. But Foucault treats the body throughout as if it were one, as if the bodily experiences of men and women did not differ and as if men and women bore the same relationship to the characteristic institutions of modern life. Where is the account of the disciplinary practices that engender the "docile bodies" of women, bodies more docile than the bodies of men? Women, like men, are subject to many of the same disciplinary practices Foucault describes. But he is blind to those disciplines that produce a modality of embodiment that is peculiarly feminine. To overlook the forms of subjection that engender the feminine body is to perpetuate the silence and powerlessness of those upon whom these disciplines have been imposed. Hence, even though a liberatory note is sounded in Foucault's critique of power, his analysis as a whole reproduces that sexism which is endemic throughout Western political theory.

We are born male or female, but not masculine or feminine. Femininity is an artifice, an achievement, "a mode of enacting and reenacting received gender norms which surface as so many styles of the flesh."[10] In what follows, I shall examine those disciplinary practices that produce a body which in gesture and appearance is recognizably feminine. I consider three categories of such practices: those that aim to produce a body of a certain size and general configuration; those that bring forth from this body a specific repertoire of gestures, postures, and movements; and those that are directed toward the display of this body as an ornamented surface. I shall examine the nature of these disciplines, how they are imposed and by whom. I shall probe the effects of the imposition of such discipline on female identity and subjectivity. In the final section I shall argue that these disciplinary practices must be understood in the light of the modernization of patriarchal domination, a modernization that unfolds historically according to the general pattern described by Foucault.

II

Styles of the female figure vary over time and across cultures: they reflect cultural obsessions and preoccupations in ways that are still poorly understood. Today, massiveness, power, or abundance in a woman's body is met with distaste. The current body of fashion is taut, small-breasted, narrow-hipped, and of a slimness bordering on emaciation; it is a silhouette that seems more appropriate to an adolescent boy or a newly pubescent girl than to an adult woman. Since ordinary women have normally quite different dimensions, they must of course diet.

Mass-circulation women's magazines run articles on dieting in virtually every issue. The *Ladies' Home Journal* of February 1986 carries a "Fat Burning Exercise Guide," while *Mademoiselle* offers to "Help Stamp Out

Cellulite" with "Six Sleek-Down Strategies." After the diet-busting Christmas holidays and, later, before summer bikini season, the titles of these features become shriller and more arresting. The reader is now addressed in the imperative mode: Jump into shape for summer! Shed ugly winter fat with the all-new Grapefruit Diet! More women than men visit diet doctors, while women greatly outnumber men in such self-help groups as Weight Watchers and Overeaters Anonymous—in the case of the latter, by well over 90 percent.[11]

Dieting disciplines the body's hungers: appetite must be monitored at all times and governed by an iron will. Since the innocent need of the organism for food will not be denied, the body becomes one's enemy, an alien being bent on thwarting the disciplinary project. Anorexia nervosa, which has now assumed epidemic proportions, is to women of the late twentieth century what hysteria was to women of an earlier day: the crystallization in a pathological mode of a widespread cultural obsession.[12] A survey taken recently at UCLA is astounding: of 260 students interviewed, 27.3 percent of women but only 5.8 percent of men said they were "terrified" of getting fat; 28.7 percent of women but only 7.5 percent of men said they were obsessed or "totally preoccupied" with food. The body images of women and men are strikingly different as well: 35 percent of women but only 12.5 percent of men said they felt fat though other people told them they were thin. Women in the survey wanted to weigh ten pounds less than their average weight; men felt they were within a pound of their ideal weight. A total of 5.9 percent of women and no men met the psychiatric criteria for anorexia or bulimia.[13]

Dieting is one discipline imposed upon a body subject to the "tyranny of slenderness"; exercise is another.[14] Since men as well as women exercise, it is not always easy in the case of women to distinguish what is done for the sake of physical fitness from what is done in obedience to the requirements of femininity. Men as well as women lift weights and do yoga, calisthenics, and aerobics, though "jazzercise" is a largely female pursuit. Men and women alike engage themselves with a variety of machines, each designed to call forth from the body a different exertion: there are Nautilus machines, rowing machines, ordinary and motorized exercycles, portable hip and leg cycles, belt massagers, trampolines, treadmills, and arm and leg pulleys. However, given the widespread female obsession with weight, one suspects that many women are working out with these apparatuses in the health club or at the gym with an aim in mind and in a spirit quite different from men's.

But there are classes of exercises meant for women alone, these designed not to firm or to reduce the body's size overall, but to resculpture its various parts on the current model. M. J. Saffon, "international beauty expert," assures us that his twelve basic facial exercises can erase frown lines, smooth the forehead, raise hollow cheeks, banish crow's feet, and tighten the muscles under the chin.[15] There are exercises to build the breasts and exercises to banish "cellulite," said by "figure consultants" to be a special type of female fat. There is "spot-reducing," an umbrella term that covers dozens of punishing exercises designed to reduce "problem areas" like thick ankles or "saddlebag" thighs. The very idea of "spot-reducing" is both scientifically unsound and cruel, for it raises expectations in women that can never be realized—the pattern in which fat is deposited or removed is known to be genetically determined.

It is not only her natural appetite or unreconstructed contours that pose a danger to woman: the very expressions of her face can subvert the disciplinary project of bodily perfection. An expressive face lines and creases more readily than an inexpressive one. Hence, if women are unable to suppress strong emotions, they can at least learn to inhibit the tendency of the face to register them. Sophia Loren recommends a unique solution to this problem: a piece of tape applied to the forehead or between the brows will tug at the skin when one frowns and act as a reminder to relax the face.[16] The tape is to be worn whenever a woman is home alone.

III

There are significant gender differences in gesture, posture, movement, and general bodily comportment: women are far more restricted than men in their manner of movement and in their spatiality. In her classic paper on the subject, Iris Young observes that a space seems to surround women in imagination that they are hesitant to move beyond: this manifests itself both in a reluctance to reach, stretch, and extend the body to meet resistances of matter in motion—as in sport or in the performance of physical tasks—and in a typically constricted posture and general style of movement. Woman's space is not a field in which her bodily intentionality can be freely realized but an enclosure in which she feels herself positioned and by which she is confined.[17] The "loose woman" violates these norms: her looseness is manifest not only in her morals, but in her manner of speech and quite literally in the free and easy way she moves.

In an extraordinary series of over two thousand photographs, many candid shots taken in the street, the German photographer Marianne Wex has documented differences in typical masculine and feminine body posture. Women sit waiting for trains with arms close to the body, hands folded together in their laps, toes pointing straight ahead or turned inward, and legs pressed together.[18] The women in these photographs make themselves small and narrow, harmless; they seem tense; they take up little space. Men, on the other hand, expand into the available space; they sit with legs far apart and arms flung out at some distance from the body. Most common in these sitting male figures is what Wex calls the "proffering position": the men sit with legs thrown wide apart, crotch visible, feet pointing outward, often with an arm and a casually dangling hand resting comfortably on an open, spread thigh.

In proportion to total body size, a man's stride is longer than a woman's. The man has more spring and rhythm to his step; he walks with toes pointed outward, holds his arms at a greater distance from his body and swings them farther; he tends to point the whole hand in the direction he is moving. The woman holds her arms closer to her body, palms against her sides; her walk is circumspect. If she has subjected herself to the additional constraint of high-heeled shoes, her body is thrown forward and off balance: the struggle to walk under these conditions shortens her stride still more.[19]

But women's movement is subjected to a still finer discipline. Feminine faces, as well as bodies, are trained to the expression of deference. Under male scrutiny, women will avert their eyes or cast them downward; the female gaze is trained to abandon its claim to the sovereign status of seer. The "nice" girl learns to avoid the bold and unfettered staring of the "loose" woman who looks at whatever and whomever she pleases. Women are trained to smile more than men, too. In the economy of smiles, as elsewhere, there is evidence that women are exploited, for they give more than they receive in return; in a smile elicitation study, one researcher found that the rate of smile return by women was 93 percent, by men only 67 percent.[20] In many typical women's jobs, graciousness, deference, and the readiness to serve are part of the work; this requires the worker to fix a smile on her face for a good part of the working day, whatever her inner state.[21] The economy of touching is out of balance, too: men touch women more often and on more parts of the body than women touch men: female secretaries, factory workers, and waitresses report that such liberties are taken routinely with their bodies.[22]

Feminine movement, gesture, and posture must exhibit not only constriction, but grace and a certain eroticism restrained by modesty: all three. Here is field for the operation for a whole new training: a woman must stand with stomach pulled in, shoulders thrown slightly back and chest out, this to display her bosom to maximum advantage. While she must walk in the confined fashion appropriate to women, her movements must, at the same time, be combined with a subtle but provocative hip-roll. But too much display is taboo: women in short, low-cut dresses are told to avoid bending over at all, but if they must, great care must be taken to avoid an unseemly display of breast or rump. From time to time, fashion magazines offer quite precise instructions on the proper way of getting in and out of cars. These instructions combine all three imperatives of women's movement: a woman must not allow her arms and legs to flail about in all directions; she must try to manage her movements with the appearance of grace—no small accomplishment when one is climbing out of the back seat of a Fiat—and she is well-advised to use the opportunity for a certain display of leg.

All the movements we have described so far are self-movements; they arise from within the woman's own body. But in a way that normally goes unnoticed, males in couples may literally steer a woman everywhere she goes: down the street, around corners, into elevators, through doorways, into her chair at the dinner table, around the dance floor. The man's movement "is not necessarily heavy and pushy or physical in an ugly way; it is light and gentle but firm in the way of the most confident equestrians with the best trained horses."[23]

IV

We have examined some of the disciplinary practices a woman must master in pursuit of a body of the right size and shape that also displays the proper styles of feminine motility. But woman's body is an ornamented surface too, and there is much discipline involved in this production as well. Here, especially in the application of makeup and the selection of clothes, art and discipline converge, though, as I shall argue, there is less art involved than one might suppose.

A woman's skin must be soft, supple, hairless, and smooth; ideally, it should betray no sign of wear, experience, age, or deep thought. Hair must be removed not only from the face but from large surfaces of the body as well, from legs and thighs, an operation accomplished by shaving, buffing with fine sandpaper, or applying foul-smelling depilatories. With the new high-leg bathing suits and leotards, a substantial amount of pubic hair must be removed too.[24] The removal of facial hair can be more specialized. Eyebrows are plucked out by the roots with a tweezer. Hot wax is sometimes poured onto the mustache and cheeks and then ripped away when it cools. The woman who wants a more permanent result may try electrolysis: this involves the killing of a hair root by the passage of an electric current down a needle that has been inserted into its base. The procedure is painful and expensive.

The development of what one "beauty expert" calls "good skincare habits" requires not only attention to health, the avoidance of strong facial expressions, and the performance of facial exercises, but the regular use of skincare preparations, many to be applied more often than once a day: cleansing lotions (ordinary soap and water "upsets the skin's acid and alkaline balance"), wash-off cleansers (milder than cleansing lotions), astringents, toners, makeup removers, night creams, nourishing creams, eye creams, moisturizers, skin balancers, body lotions, hand creams, lip pomades, suntan lotions, sunscreens, and facial masks. Provision of the proper facial mask is complex: there are sulfur masks for pimples; oil or hot masks for dry areas; if these fail, then tightening masks; conditioning masks; peeling masks; cleansing masks made of herbs, cornmeal, or almonds; and mudpacks. Black women may wish to use "fade creams" to "even skin tone." Skincare preparations are never just sloshed onto the skin, but applied according to precise rules: eye cream is dabbed on gently in movements toward, never away from, the nose; cleansing cream is applied in outward directions only, straight across the forehead, the upper lip, and the chin, never up but straight down the nose and up and out on the cheeks.[25]

The normalizing discourse of modern medicine is enlisted by the cosmetics industry to gain credibility for its claims. Dr. Christiaan Barnard lends his enormous prestige to the Glycel line of "cellular treatment activators"; these contain "glycosphingolipids" that can "make older skin behave and look like younger skin." The Clinique computer at any Clinique counter will select a combination of preparations just right for you. Ultima II contains "procollagen" in its anti-aging eye cream that "provides hydration" to "demoralizing lines." "Biotherm" eye cream dramatically improves the "biomechanical properties of the skin."[26] The Park Avenue clinic of Dr. Zizmor, "chief of dermatology at one of New York's leading hospitals," offers not only such medical treatment as derma-brasion and chemical peeling, but "total deep skin cleansing" as well.[27]

Really good skincare habits require the use of a variety of aids and devices: facial steamers, faucet filters to collect impurities in the water, borax to soften it, a humidifier for the bedroom, electric massagers, backbrushes, complexion brushes, loofahs, pumice stones, and blackhead removers. I will not detail the implements or techniques involved in the manicure or pedicure.

The ordinary circumstances of life as well as a wide variety of activities cause a crisis in skincare and require a stepping-up of the regimen as well as an additional laying-on of preparations. Skincare discipline requires a specialized knowledge: a woman must know what to do if she has been skiing, taking medication, doing vigorous exercise, boating, or swimming in chlorinated pools; or if she has been exposed to pollution, heated rooms, cold, sun, harsh weather, the pressurized cabins on airplanes, saunas or steam rooms, fatigue, or stress. Like the schoolchild or prisoner, the woman mastering good skincare habits is put on a timetable: Georgette Klinger requires that a shorter or longer period of attention be paid to the complexion at least four times a day.[28] Haircare, like skincare, requires a similar investment of time, the use of a wide variety of preparations, the mastery of a set of techniques, and, again, the acquisition of a specialized knowledge.

The crown and pinnacle of good haircare and skincare is, of course, the arrangement of the hair and the application of cosmetics. Here the regimen of haircare, skincare, manicure, and pedicure is recapitulated in another mode. A woman must learn the proper manipulation of a large number of devices—the blow dryer, styling brush, curling iron, hot curlers, wire curlers, eye-liner, lipliner, lipstick brush, eyelash curler, and mascara brush. And she must learn to apply a wide variety of products—foundation, toner, covering stick, mascara, eyeshadow, eyegloss, blusher, lipstick, rouge, lip gloss, hair dye, hair rinse, hair lightener, hair "relaxer," and so on.

In the language of fashion magazines and cosmetic ads, making-up is typically portrayed as an aesthetic activity in which a woman can express her individuality. In reality, while cosmetic styles change every decade or so, and while some variation in makeup is permitted depending on the occasion, making-up the face is, in fact, a highly stylized activity that gives little rein to self-expression. Painting the face is not like painting a picture; at best, it might be described as painting the same picture over and over again with minor variations. Little latitude is permitted in what is considered appropriate makeup for the office and for most social occasions; indeed, the woman who uses cosmetics in a genuinely novel and imaginative way is liable to be seen not as an artist but as an eccentric. Furthermore, since a properly made-up face is, if not a card of entree, at least a badge of acceptability in most social and professional contexts, the woman who chooses not to wear cosmetics at all faces sanctions of a sort that will never be applied to someone who chooses not to paint a watercolor.

V

Are we dealing in all this merely with sexual *difference?* Scarcely. The disciplinary practices I have described are part of the process by which the ideal body of femininity—and hence the feminine body-subject—is constructed; in doing this, they produce a "practiced and subjected" body, that is, a body on which an inferior status has been inscribed. A woman's face must be made-up, that is to say, made-over, and so must her body: she is ten pounds overweight; her lips must be made more kissable, her complexion dewier, her eyes more mysterious. The "art" of makeup is the art of disguise, but this presupposes that a woman's face, unpainted, is defective. Soap and water, a shave, and routine attention to hygiene may be enough for *him;* for *her* they are not. The strategy of much beauty-related advertising is to suggest to women that their bodies are deficient; but even without such more or less explicit teaching, the media images of perfect female beauty that bombard us daily leave no doubt in the minds of most women that they fail to measure up. The technologies of femininity are taken up and practiced by women against the background of a pervasive sense of bodily deficiency: this accounts for what is often their compulsive or even ritualistic character.

The disciplinary project of femininity is a "setup": it requires such radical and extensive measures of bodily transformation that virtually every woman who gives herself to it is destined in some degree to fail. Thus, a measure of shame is added to a woman's sense that the body she inhabits is deficient: she ought to take better care of herself; she might after all have jogged that last mile. Many women are without the time or resources to provide themselves with even the minimum of what such a regimen requires, for example, a decent diet. Here is an additional source of shame for poor women, who must bear what our society regards as the more general shame of poverty. The burdens poor women bear in this regard are not merely psychological, since conformity to the prevailing standards of bodily acceptability is a known factor in economic mobility.

The larger disciplines that construct a "feminine" body out of a female one are by no means race- or class-specific. There is little evidence that women of color or working-class women are in general less committed to the incarnation of an ideal femininity than their more privileged sisters: this is not to deny the many ways in which factors of race, class, locality, ethnicity, or personal taste can be expressed within the kinds of practices I have described. The rising young corporate executive may buy her cosmetics at Bergdorf-Goodman, while the counter-server at McDonald's gets hers at the K-Mart; the one may join an expensive "upscale" health club, while the other may have to make do with the $9.49 GFX Body-Flex II Home-Gym advertised in the *National Enquirer:* both are aiming at the same general result.[29]

In the regime of institutionalized heterosexuality, woman must make herself "object and prey" for the man: it is for him that these eyes are limpid pools, this cheek baby-smooth.[30] In contemporary patriarchal culture, a panoptical male connoisseur resides within the consciousness of most women: they stand perpetually before his gaze and under his judgment. Woman lives her body as seen by another, by an anonymous patriarchal Other. We are often told that "women dress for other women." There is some truth in this: who but someone engaged in a project similar to my own can appreciate the panache with which I bring it off? But women know for whom this game is played: they know that a pretty young woman is likelier to become a flight attendant than a plain one, and that a well-preserved older woman has a better chance of holding onto her husband than one who has "let herself go."

Here it might be objected that performance for another in no way signals the inferiority of the performer to the one for whom the performance is intended: the actor, for example, depends on his audience but is in no way inferior to it; he is not demeaned by his dependency. While femininity is surely something enacted, the analogy to theater breaks down in a number of ways. First, as I argued earlier, the self-determination we think of as requisite to an artistic career is lacking here: femininity as spectacle is something in which virtually every woman is required to participate. Second, the precise nature of the criteria by which women are judged, not only the inescapability of judgment itself, reflects gross imbalances in the social power of the sexes that do not mark the relationship of artists and their audiences. An aesthetic of femininity, for example, that mandates fragility and a lack of muscular strength produces female bodies that can offer little resistance to physical abuse, and the physical abuse of women by men, as we know, is widespread. It is true that the current fitness movement has permitted women to develop more muscular strength and endurance than was heretofore allowed; indeed, images of women have begun to appear in the mass media that seem to eroticize this new muscularity. But a woman may by no means develop more muscular strength than her partner; the bride who would tenderly carry her groom across the threshold is a figure of comedy, not romance.[31]

Under the current "tyranny of slenderness" women are forbidden to become large or massive; they must take up as little space as possible. The very contours a woman's body takes on as she matures—the fuller breasts and rounded hips—have become distasteful. The body by which a woman feels herself judged and which by rigorous discipline she must try to assume is the body of early adolescence, slight and unformed, a body lacking flesh or substance, a body in whose very contours the image of immaturity has been inscribed. The requirement that a woman maintain a smooth and hairless skin carries further the theme of inexperience, for an infantilized face must accompany her infantilized body, a face that never ages or furrows its brow in thought. The face of the ideally feminine woman must never display the marks of character, wisdom, and experience that we so admire in men.

To succeed in the provision of a beautiful or sexy body gains a woman attention and some admiration but little real respect and rarely any social power. A woman's effort to master feminine body discipline will lack importance just because she does it: her activity partakes of the general depreciation of everything female. In spite of unrelenting pressure to "make the most of what she has," women are ridiculed and dismissed for their interest in such "trivial" things as clothes and makeup. Further, the narrow identification of woman with sexuality and the body in a society that has for centuries displayed profound suspicion toward both does little to raise her status. Even the most adored female bodies complain routinely of their situation in ways that reveal an implicit understanding that there is something demeaning in the kind of attention they receive. Marilyn Monroe, Elizabeth Taylor, and Farrah Fawcett have all wanted passionately to become actresses-artists—and not just "sex objects."

But it is perhaps in their more restricted motility and comportment that the inferiorization of women's bodies is most evident: women's typical body-language, a language of relative tension and constriction, is understood to be a language of subordination when it is enacted by men in male status hierarchies. In groups of men, those with higher status typically assume looser and more relaxed postures: the boss lounges comfortably behind the desk, while the applicant sits tense and rigid on the edge of his seat. Higher status individuals may touch their subordinates more than they themselves get touched; they initiate more eye contact and are smiled at by their inferiors more than they are observed to smile in return.[32] What is announced in the comportment of superiors is confidence and ease, especially ease of access to the Other. Female constraint in posture and movement is no doubt overdetermined: the fact that women tend to sit and stand with legs, feet, and knees close or touching may well be a coded declaration of sexual circumspection in a society that still maintains a double standard, or an effort, albeit unconscious, to guard the genital area. In the latter case, a woman's tight and constricted posture must be seen as the expression of her need to ward off real or symbolic sexual attack. Whatever proportions must be assigned in the final display to fear or deference, one thing is clear: woman's body language speaks eloquently, though silently, of her subordinate status in a hierarchy of gender.

VI

If what we have described is a genuine discipline—a system of "micro-power" that is "essentially non-egalitarian and asymmetrical"—who then are the disciplinarians?[33] Who is the top sergeant in the disciplinary regime of femininity? Historically, the law has had some responsibility for enforcement: in times gone by, for example, individuals who appeared in public in the clothes of the other sex could be arrested. While cross-dressers are still liable to some harassment, the kind of discipline we are considering is not the business of the police or the courts. Parents and teachers, of course, have extensive influence, admonishing girls to be demure and ladylike, to "smile pretty," to sit with their legs together. The influence of the media is pervasive, too, constructing as it does an image of the female body as spectacle, nor can we ignore the role played by "beauty experts" or by emblematic public personages such as Jane Fonda and Lynn Redgrave.

But none of these individuals—the skincare consultant, the parent, the policeman—does in fact wield the kind of authority that is typically invested in those who manage more straightforward disciplinary institutions. The disciplinary power that inscribes femininity in the female body is everywhere and it is nowhere; the disciplinarian is everyone and yet no one in particular. Women regarded as overweight, for example, report that they are regularly admonished to diet, sometimes by people they scarcely know. These intrusions are often softened by reference to the natural prettiness just waiting to emerge: "People have always said that I had a beautiful face and 'if you'd only lose weight you'd be really beautiful.' "[34] Here, "people"—friends and casual acquaintances alike—act to enforce prevailing standards of body size.

Foucault tends to identify the imposition of discipline upon the body with the operation of specific institutions, for example, the school, the factory, the prison. To do this, however, is to overlook the extent to which discipline can be institutionally *unbound* as well as institutionally bound.[35] The anonymity of disciplinary power and its wide dispersion have consequences that are crucial to a proper understanding of the subordination of women. The absence of a formal institutional structure and of authorities invested with the power to carry out institutional directives creates the impression that the production of femininity is either entirely voluntary or natural. The several senses of "discipline" are instructive here. On the one hand, discipline is something imposed on subjects of an "essentially non-egalitarian and asymmetrical" system of authority. Schoolchildren, convicts, and draftees are subject to discipline in this sense. But discipline can be sought voluntarily as well—for example, when an individual seeks initiation into the spiritual discipline of Zen Buddhism. Discipline can, of course, be both at once: the volunteer may seek the physical and occupational training offered by the army without the army's ceasing in any way to be the instrument by which he and other members of his class are kept in disciplined subjection. Feminine bodily discipline has this dual character: on the one hand, no one is marched off for electrolysis at gunpoint, nor can we fail to appreciate the initiative and ingenuity displayed by countless women in an attempt to master the rituals of beauty. Nevertheless, insofar as the disciplinary practices of femininity produce a "subjected and practiced," an inferiorized, body, they must be understood as aspects of a far larger discipline, an oppressive and inegalitarian system of sexual subordination. This system aims at turning women into the docile and compliant companions of men just as surely as the army aims to turn its raw recruits into soldiers.

Now the transformation of oneself into a properly feminine body may be any or all of the following: a rite of passage into adulthood, the adoption and celebration of a particular aesthetic, a way of announcing one's economic level and social status, a way to triumph over other women in the competition for men or jobs, or an opportunity for massive narcissistic indulgence.[36] The social construction of the feminine body is all these things, but at its base it is discipline, too, and discipline of the inegalitarian sort. The absence of formally identifiable disciplinarians and of a public schedule of sanctions only disguises the extent to which the imperative to be "feminine" serves the interest of domination. This is a lie in which all concur: making-up is merely artful play; one's first pair of high-heeled shoes is an innocent part of growing up, not the modern equivalent of foot-binding.

Why aren't all women feminists? In modern industrial societies, women are not kept in line by fear of retaliatory male violence; their victimization is not that of the South African black. Nor will it suffice to say that a false consciousness engendered in women by patriarchal ideology is at the basis of female subordination. This is not to deny that women are often subject to gross male violence or that women and men alike are ideologically mystified by the dominant gender arrangements. What I wish to suggest instead is that an adequate understanding of women's oppression will require an appreciation of the extent to which not only women's lives but their very subjectivities are structured within an ensemble of systematically duplicitous practices. The feminine discipline of the body is a case in point: the practices that construct this body have an overt aim and character far removed, indeed, radically distinct, from their covert function. In this regard, the system of gender subordination, like the wage-bargain under capitalism, illustrates in its own way the ancient tension between what-is and what-appears: the phenomenal forms in which it is manifested are often quite different from the real relations that form its deeper structure.

VII

The lack of formal public sanctions does not mean that a woman who is unable or unwilling to submit herself to the appropriate body discipline will face no sanctions at all. On the contrary, she faces a very severe sanction indeed in a world dominated by men: the refusal of male patronage. For the heterosexual woman, this may mean the loss of a badly needed intimacy; for both heterosexual women and lesbians, it may well mean the refusal of a decent livelihood.

As noted earlier, women punish themselves too for the failure to conform. The growing literature on women's body size is filled with wrenching confessions of shame from the overweight:

> I felt clumsy and huge. I felt that I would knock over furniture, bump into things, tip over chairs, not fit into VW's, especially when people were trying to crowd

into the back seat. I felt like I was taking over the whole room. . . . I felt disgusting and like a slob. In the summer I felt hot and sweaty and I knew people saw my sweat as evidence that I was too fat.

I feel so terrible about the way I look that I cut off connection with my body. I operate from the neck up. I do not look in mirrors. I do not want to spend time buying clothes. I do not want to spend time with make-up because it's painful for me to look at myself.[37]

I can no longer bear to look at myself. . . . Whenever I have to stand in front of a mirror to comb my hair I tie a large towel around my neck. Even at night I slip my nightgown on before I take off my blouse and pants. But all this has only made it worse and worse. It's been so long since I've really looked at my body.[38]

The depth of these women's shame is a measure of the extent to which all women have internalized patriarchal standards of bodily acceptability. A fuller examination of what is meant here by "internalization" may shed light on a question posed earlier: Why isn't every woman a feminist?

Something is "internalized" when it gets incorporated into the structure of the self. By "structure of the self" I refer to those modes of perception and of self-perception that allow a self to distinguish itself both from other selves and from things that are not selves. I have described elsewhere how a generalized male witness comes to structure woman's consciousness of herself as a bodily being.[39] This, then, is one meaning of "internalization." The sense of oneself as a distinct and valuable individual is tied not only to the sense of how one is perceived, but also to what one knows, especially to what one knows how to do; this is a second sense of "internalization." Whatever its ultimate effect, discipline can provide the individual upon whom it is imposed with a sense of mastery as well as a secure sense of identity. There is a certain contradiction here: while its imposition may promote a larger disempowerment, discipline may bring with it a certain development of a person's powers. Women, then, like other skilled individuals, have a stake in the perpetuation of their skills, whatever it may have cost to acquire them and quite apart from the question whether, as a gender, they would have been better off had they never had to acquire them in the first place. Hence, feminism, especially a genuinely radical feminism that questions the patriarchal construction of the female body, threatens women with a certain de-skilling, something people normally resist; beyond this, it calls into question that aspect of personal identity that is tied to the development of a sense of competence.

Resistance from this source may be joined by a reluctance to part with the rewards of compliance; further, many women will resist the abandonment of an aesthetic that defines what they take to be beautiful. But there is still another source of resistance, one more subtle, perhaps, but tied once again to questions of identity and internalization. To have a body felt to be "feminine"—a body socially constructed through the appropriate practices—is in most cases crucial to a woman's sense of herself as female and, since persons currently can *be* only as male or female, to her sense of herself as an existing individual. To possess such a body may also be essential to her sense of herself as a sexually desiring and desirable subject. Hence, any political project that aims to dismantle the machinery that turns a female body into a feminine one may well be apprehended by a woman as something that threatens her with de-sexualization, if not outright annihilation.

The categories of masculinity and femininity do more than assist in the construction of personal identities; they are critical elements in our informal social ontology. This may account to some degree for the otherwise puzzling phenomenon of homophobia and for the revulsion felt by many at the sight of female bodybuilders; neither the homosexual nor the muscular woman can be assimilated easily into the categories that structure everyday life. The radical feminist critique of femininity, then, may pose a threat not only to a woman's sense of her own identity and desirability but to the very structure of her social universe.

Of course, many women *are* feminists, favoring a program of political and economic reform in the struggle to gain equality with men.[40] But many "reform," or liberal, feminists (indeed, many orthodox Marxists) are committed to the idea that the preservation of a woman's femininity is quite compatible with her struggle for liberation.[41] These thinkers have rejected a normative femininity based upon the notion of "separate spheres" and the traditional sexual division of labor, while accepting at the same time conventional standards of feminine body display. If my analysis is correct, such a feminism is incoherent. Foucault has argued that modern bourgeois democracy is deeply flawed in that it seeks political rights for individuals constituted as unfree by a variety of disciplinary micropowers that lie beyond the realm of what is ordinarily defined as the "political." "The man described for us whom we are invited to free," he says, "is already in himself the effect of a subjection much more profound than himself."[42] If, as I have argued, female subjectivity is constituted in any significant measure in and through the disciplinary practices that construct the feminine body, what Foucault says here of "man" is perhaps even truer of "woman." Marxists have maintained from the first the inadequacy of a purely liberal feminism: we have reached the same conclusion through a different route, casting doubt at the same time on the adequacy of traditional Marxist prescriptions for women's liberation as well. Liberals call for equal rights for women, traditional Marxists for the entry of women into production on an equal footing with men, the socialization of housework, and proletarian revolution; neither calls for the deconstruction of the categories of masculinity and femininity.[43] Femininity as a certain "style of the flesh" will have to be surpassed in the direction of something quite different—not masculinity, which is in many ways only its mirror opposite, but a radical and as yet unimagined transformation of the female body.

VIII

Foucault has argued that the transition from traditional to modern societies has been characterized by a profound transformation in the exercise of power, by what he calls "a reversal of the political axis of individualization."[44] In older authoritarian systems, power was embodied in the person of the monarch and exercised upon a largely anonymous body of subjects; violation of the law was seen as an insult to the royal individual. While the methods employed to enforce compliance in the past were often quite brutal, involving gross assaults against the body, power in such a system operated in a haphazard and discontinuous fashion; much in the social totality lay beyond its reach.

By contrast, modern society has seen the emergence of increasingly invasive apparatuses of power: these exercise a far more restrictive social and psychological control than was heretofore possible. In modern societies, effects of power "circulate through progressively finer channels, gaining access to individuals themselves, to their bodies, their gestures and all their daily actions."[45] Power now seeks to transform the minds of those individuals who might be tempted to resist it, not merely to punish or imprison their bodies. This requires two things: a finer control of the body's time and of its movements—a control that cannot be achieved without ceaseless surveillance and a better understanding of the specific person, of the genesis and nature of his "case." The power these new apparatuses seek to exercise requires a new knowledge of the individual: modern psychology and sociology are born. Whether the new modes of control have charge of correction, production, education, or the provision of welfare, they resemble one another; they exercise power in a bureaucratic mode—faceless, centralized, and pervasive. A reversal has occurred: power has now become anonymous, while the project of control has brought into being a new individuality. In fact, Foucault believes that the operation of power constitutes the very subjectivity of the subject. Here, the image of the Panopticon returns: knowing that he may be observed from the tower at any time, the inmate takes over the job of policing himself. The gaze that is inscribed in the very structure of the disciplinary institution is internalized by the inmate: modern technologies of behavior are thus oriented toward the production of isolated and self-policing subjects.[46]

Women have their own experience of the modernization of power, one that begins later but follows in many respects the course outlined by Foucault. In important ways, a woman's behavior is less regulated now than it was in the past. She has more mobility and is less confined to domestic space. She enjoys what to previous generations would have been an unimaginable sexual liberty. Divorce, access to paid work outside the home, and the increasing secularization of modern life have loosened the hold over her of the traditional family and, in spite of the current fundamentalist revival, of the church. Power in these institutions was wielded by individuals known to her. Husbands and fathers enforced patriarchal authority in the family. As in the ancien régime, a woman's body was subject to sanctions if she disobeyed. Not Foucault's royal individual but the Divine Individual decreed that her desire be always "unto her husband," while the person of the priest made known to her God's more specific intentions concerning her place and duties. In the days when civil and ecclesiastical authority were still conjoined, individuals formally invested with power were charged with the correction of recalcitrant women whom the family had somehow failed to constrain.

By contrast, the disciplinary power that is increasingly charged with the production of a properly embodied femininity is dispersed and anonymous; there are no individuals formally empowered to wield it; it is, as we have seen, invested in everyone and in no one in particular. This disciplinary power is peculiarly modern: it does not rely upon violent or public sanctions, nor does it seek to restrain the freedom of the female body to move from place to place. For all that, its invasion of the body is well-nigh total: the female body enters "a machinery of power that explores it, breaks it down and rearranges it."[47] The disciplinary techniques through which the "docile bodies" of women are constructed aim at a regulation that is perpetual and exhaustive—a regulation of the body's size and contours, its appetite, posture, gestures and general comportment in space, and the appearance of each of its visible parts.

As modern industrial societies change and as women themselves offer resistance to patriarchy, older forms of domination are eroded. But new forms arise, spread, and become consolidated. Women are no longer required to be chaste or modest, to restrict their sphere of activity to the home, or even to realize their properly feminine destiny in maternity: normative femininity is coming more and more to be centered on woman's body—not its duties and obligations or even its capacity to bear children, but its sexuality, more precisely, its presumed heterosexuality and its appearance. There is, of course, nothing new in women's preoccupation with youth and beauty. What is new is the growing power of the image in a society increasingly oriented toward the visual media. Images of normative femininity, it might be ventured, have replaced the religiously oriented tracts of the past. New too is the spread of this discipline to all classes of women and its deployment throughout the life cycle. What was formerly the specialty of the aristocrat or courtesan is now the routine obligation of every woman, be she a grandmother or a barely pubescent girl.

To subject oneself to the new disciplinary power is to be up-to-date, to be "with-it"; as I have argued, it is presented to us in ways that are regularly disguised. It is fully compatible with the current need for women's wage labor, the cult of youth and fitness, and the need of advanced capitalism to maintain high levels of consumption. Further, it represents a saving in the economy of enforcement, since it is women themselves who practice this discipline on and against their own bodies, men get off scot-free.

The woman who checks her makeup half a dozen times a day to see if her foundation has caked or her mascara has run, who worries that the wind or the rain may spoil her hairdo, who looks frequently to see if her stockings have bagged at the ankle or who, feeling fat, monitors everything she eats, has become, just as surely as the inmate of the Panopticon, a self-policing subject, a self committed to a relentless self-surveillance. This self-surveillance is a form of obedience to patriarchy. It is also the reflection in woman's consciousness of the fact that *she* is under surveillance in ways that *he* is not, that whatever else she may become, she is importantly a body designed to please or to excite. There has been induced in many women, then, in Foucault's words, "a state of conscious and permanent visibility that assures the automatic functioning of power."[48] Since the standards of female bodily acceptability are impossible fully to realize, requiring as they do a virtual transcendence of nature, a woman may live much of her life with a pervasive feeling of bodily deficiency. Hence a tighter control of the body has gained a new kind of hold over the mind.

Foucault often writes as if power constitutes the very individuals upon whom it operates:

> The individual is not to be conceived as a sort of elementary nucleus, a primitive atom, a multiple and inert material on which power comes to fasten or against which it happens to strike. . . . In fact, it is already one of the prime effects of power that certain bodies, certain gestures, certain discourses, certain desires, come to be identified and constituted as individuals.[49]

Nevertheless, if individuals were wholly constituted by the power-knowledge regime Foucault describes, it would make no sense to speak of resistance to discipline at all. Foucault seems sometimes on the verge of depriving us of a vocabulary in which to conceptualize the nature and meaning of those periodic refusals of control that, just as much as the imposition of control, mark the course of human history.

Peter Dews accuses Foucault of lacking a theory of the "libidinal body," that is, the body upon which discipline is imposed and whose bedrock impulse toward spontaneity and pleasure might perhaps become the locus of resistance.[50] Do women's "libidinal" bodies, then, not rebel against the pain, constriction, tedium, semistarvation, and constant self-surveillance to which they are currently condemned? Certainly they do, but the rebellion is put down every time a woman picks up her eyebrow tweezers or embarks upon a new diet. The harshness of a regimen alone does not guarantee its rejection, for hardships can be endured if they are thought to be necessary or inevitable.

While "nature," in the form of a "libidinal" body, may not be the origin of a revolt against "culture," domination (and the discipline it requires) are never imposed without some cost. Historically, the forms and occasions of resistance are manifold. Sometimes, instances of resistance appear to spring from the introduction of new and conflicting factors into the lives of the dominated: the juxtaposition of old and new and the resulting incoherence or "contradiction" may make submission to the old ways seem increasingly unnecessary. In the present instance, what may be a major factor in the relentless and escalating objectification of women's bodies—namely, women's growing independence—produces in many women a sense of incoherence that calls into question the meaning and necessity of the current discipline. As women (albeit a small minority of women) begin to realize an unprecedented political, economic, and sexual self-determination, they fall ever more completely under the dominating gaze of patriarchy. It is this paradox, not the "libidinal body," that produces, here and there, pockets of resistance.

In the current political climate, there is no reason to anticipate either widespread resistance to currently fashionable modes of feminine embodiment or joyous experimentation with new "styles of the flesh"; moreover, such novelties would face profound opposition from material and psychological sources identified earlier in this essay (see section VII). In spite of this, a number of oppositional discourses and practices have appeared in recent years. An increasing number of women are "pumping iron," a few with little concern for the limits of body development imposed by current canons of femininity. Women in radical lesbian communities have also rejected hegemonic images of femininity and are struggling to develop a new female aesthetic. A striking feature of such communities is the extent to which they have overcome the oppressive identification of female beauty and desirability with youth: here, the physical features of aging—"character" lines and graying hair—not only do not diminish a woman's attractiveness, they may even enhance it. A popular literature of resistance is growing, some of it analytical and reflective, like Kim Chernin's *The Obsession*, some oriented toward practical self-help, like Marcia Hutchinson's recent *Transforming Body Image, Learning to Love the Body You Have*.[51] This literature reflects a mood akin in some ways to that other and earlier mood of quiet desperation to which Betty Friedan gave voice in *The Feminine Mystique*. Nor should we forget that a mass-based women's movement is in place in this country that has begun a critical questioning of the meaning of femininity, if not yet in the corporeal presentation of self, then in other domains of life. We women cannot begin the re-vision of our own bodies until we learn to read the cultural messages we inscribe upon them daily and until we come to see that even when the mastery of the disciplines of femininity produces a triumphant result, we are still only women.[52]

Notes

1. Michel Foucault, *Discipline and Punish: The Birth of the Prison*, trans. Alan Sheridan (New York: Vintage Books, 1979), p. 138.
2. Ibid., p. 28.
3. Ibid., p. 147.
4. Ibid., p. 153. Foucault is citing an eighteenth-century military manual, "Ordonnance du Ier janvier 1766 . . ., titre XI, article 2."
5. Ibid., p. 153.

6. Ibid., p. 150.
7. Ibid., p. 200.
8. Ibid., p. 201.
9. Ibid., p. 228.
10. Judith Butler, "Embodied Identity in de Beauvoir's *The Second Sex*" (unpublished manuscript presented to American Philosophical Association, Pacific Division, March 22, 1985), p. 11.
11. Marcia Millman, *Such a Pretty Face: Being Fat in America* (New York: W. W. Norton, 1980), p. 46.
12. Susan Bordo, "Anorexia Nervosa: Psychopathology as the Crystallization of Culture," *Philosophical Forum* 17, no. 2 (Winter 1985–86): 73–104 (reprinted in this volume).
13. *USA Today* (Thursday, May 30, 1985).
14. Phrase taken from the title of Kim Chernin, *The Obsession: Reflections on the Tyranny of Slenderness* (New York: Harper and Row, 1981), an examination from a feminist perspective of women's eating disorders and of the current female preoccupation with body size.
15. M. J. Saffon, *The 15-Minute-A-Day Natural Face Lift* (New York: Warner Books, 1981).
16. Sophia Loren, *Women and Beauty* (New York: William Morrow, 1984), p. 57.
17. Iris Young, "Throwing Like a Girl: A Phenomenology of Feminine Body Comportment, Motility and Spatiality," *Human Studies* 3 (1980): 137–56.
18. Marianne Wex, *Let's Take Back Our Space: "Female" and "Male" Body Language as a Result of Patriarchal Structures* (Berlin: Frauenliteraturverlag Hermine Fees, 1979). Wex claims (p. 23) that Japanese women are still taught to position their feet so that the toes point inward, a traditional sign of submissiveness.
19. In heels, the "female foot and leg are turned into ornamental objects and the impractical shoe, which offers little protection against dust, rain and snow, induces helplessness and dependence. . . . The extra wiggle in the hips, exaggerating a slight natural tendency, is seen as sexually flirtatious while the smaller steps and tentative, insecure tread suggest daintiness, modesty and refinement. Finally, the overall hobbling effect with its sadomasochistic tinge is suggestive of the restraining leg irons and ankle chains endured by captive animals, prisoners and slaves who were also festooned with decorative symbols of their bondage." Susan Brownmiller, *Femininity* (New York: Simon and Schuster, 1984), p. 184.
20. Nancy Henley, *Body Politics* (Englewood Cliffs, N.J.: Prentice-Hall, 1977), p. 176.
21. For an account of the sometimes devastating effects on workers, like flight attendants, whose conditions of employment require the display of a perpetual friendliness, see Arlie Hochschild, *The Managed Heart: The Commercialization of Human Feeling* (Berkeley: University of California Press, 1983).
22. Henley, *Body Politics*, p. 108.
23. Ibid., p. 149.
24. Clairol has just introduced a small electric shaver, the "Bikini," apparently intended for just such use.
25. Georgette Klinger and Barbara Rowes, *Georgette Klinger's Skincare* (New York: William Morrow, 1978), pp. 102, 105, 151, 188, and passim.
26. *Chicago Magazine* (March 1986), pp. 43, 10, 18, and 62.
27. *Essence* (April 1986), p. 25. I am indebted to Laurie Shrage for calling this to my attention and for providing most of these examples.
28. Klinger, *Skincare*, pp. 137–40.

29. In light of this, one is surprised to see a 2-ounce jar of "Skin Regeneration Formula," a "Proteolytic Enzyme Cream with Bromelain and Papain," selling for $23.95 in the tabloid *Globe* (April 8, 1986, p. 29) and an unidentified amount of Tova Borgnine's "amazing new formula Beverly Hills" (otherwise unnamed) going for $41.75 in the *National Enquirer* (April 8, 1986, p. 15).

30. ". . . it is required of woman that in order to realize her femininity she must make herself object and prey, which is to say that she must renounce her claims as sovereign subject." Simone de Beauvoir, *The Second Sex* (New York: Bantam Books, 1968), p. 642.

31. The film *Pumping Iron II* portrays very clearly the tension for female bodybuilders (a tension that enters into formal judging in the sport) between muscular development and a properly feminine appearance.

32. Henley, *Body Politics*, pp. 101, 153, and passim.

33. Foucault, *Discipline and Punish*, p. 222: "The general, juridical form that guaranteed a system of rights that were egalitarian in principle was supported by these tiny, everyday, physical mechanisms, by all those systems of micro-power that are essentially non-egalitarian and asymmetrical that we call disciplines."

34. Millman, *Such a Pretty Face*, p. 80. Such remarks are made so commonly to heavy women that sociologist Millman takes the most clichéd as title of her study of the lives of the overweight.

35. I am indebted to Nancy Fraser for the formulation of this point.

36. See my paper "Narcissism, Femininity and Alienation," in *Social Theory and Practice* 8, no. 2 (Summer 1982): 127–43.

37. Millman, *Such a Pretty Face*, pp. 80, 195.

38. Chernin, *The Obsession*, p. 53.

39. Bartky, "Narcissism, Femininity and Alienation."

40. For a claim that the project of liberal or "mainstream" feminism is covertly racist, see Bell Hooks, *Ain't I Woman: Black Women and Feminism* (Boston: South End Press, 1981), chap. 4. For an authoritative general critique of liberal feminism, see Alison Jaggar, *Feminist Politics and Human Nature* (Totowa, N.J.: Rowman and Allanheld, 1983), chaps. 3 and 7.

41. See, for example, Mihailo Markovic, "Women's Liberation and Human Emancipation," in *Women and Philosophy*, ed. Carol C. Gould and Marx W. Wartofsky (New York: G. P. Putnam's Sons, 1976), pp. 165–66.

42. Foucault, *Discipline and Punish*, p. 30.

43. Some radical feminists have called for just such a deconstruction. See especially Monique Wittig, *The Lesbian Body* (New York: Avon Books, 1976).

44. Foucault, *Discipline and Punish*, p. 44.

45. Michel Foucault, *Power/Knowledge: Selected Interviews and Other Writings, 1972–1977*, ed. Colin Gordon (Brighton, U.K.: 1980), p. 151. Quoted in Peter Dews, "Power and Subjectivity in Foucault," *New Left Review*, no. 144 (March–April 1984): 17.

46. Dews, "Power and Subjectivity in Foucault," p. 77.

47. Foucault, *Discipline and Punish*, p. 138.

48. Ibid., p. 201.

49. Foucault, *Power/Knowledge*, p. 98. In fact, Foucault is not entirely consistent on this point. For an excellent discussion of contending Foucault interpretations and for the difficulty of deriving a consistent set of claims from Foucault's work generally, see Nancy Fraser, "Michel Foucault: A 'Young Conservative'?" *Ethics* 96 (October 1985): 165–84.

50. Dews, "Power and Subjectivity in Foucault," p. 92.

51. See Marcia Hutchinson, *Transforming Body Image: Learning to Love the Body You Have* (Trumansburg, N.Y.: Crossing Press, 1985). See also Bordo, "Anorexia Nervosa."

52. An earlier version of this paper was read to the Southwestern Philosophical Society, November 1985. Subsequent versions were read to the Society for Women in Philosophy, March 1986, and to the American Philosophical Association, May 1986. Many people in discussion at those meetings offered incisive comments and criticisms. I would like to thank in particular the following persons for their critiques of earlier drafts of this paper: Nancy Fraser; Alison Jaggar; Jeffner Allen; Laurie Shrage; Robert Yanal; Martha Gimenez; Joyce Trebilcot, Rob Crawford, and Iris Young.

Susan Bordo

Anorexia Nervosa: Psychopathology as the Crystallization of Culture

Historians long ago began to write the history of the body.
They have studied the body in the field of historical de-
mography or pathology; they have considered it as the seat
of needs and appetites, as the locus of physiological processes and metabolisms, as a target for the attacks of
germs or viruses; they have shown to what extent historical
processes were involved in what might seem to be the
purely biological base of existence; and what place should
be given in the history of society to biological "events" such
as the circulation of bacilli, or the extension of the lifespan.
But the body is also directly involved in a political field;
power relations have an immediate hold upon it; they invest

it, mark it, train it, torture it, force it to carry out tasks, to
perform ceremonies, to emit signs.

—*Michel Foucault, Discipline and Punish*

I believe in being the best I can be,
I believe in watching every calorie . . .

—*"Crystal Light" commercial*

Psychopathology, as Jules Henry has said, "is the
final outcome of all that is wrong with a culture."[1] In no case is this
more strikingly true than in the case of anorexia nervosa and bulimia,
barely known a century ago, yet reaching epidemic proportions today.
Far from being the result of a superficial fashion phenomenon, these
disorders reflect and call our attention to some of the central ills of our
culture—from our historical heritage of disdain for the body, to our
modern fear of loss of control over our futures, to the disquieting meaning
of contemporary beauty ideals in an era of female presence and power.

Changes in the incidence of anorexia[2] have been dramatic:[3] In 1945,
when Ludwig Binswanger chronicled the now famous case of Ellen West,
he was able to say that "from a psychiatric point of view we are dealing
here with something new, with a new symptom." In 1973, Hilde Bruch,
one of the pioneers in understanding and treating eating disorders, could
still say that anorexia was "rare indeed."[4] In 1984, it was estimated that
as many as one in every 200–250 women between the ages of thirteen
and twenty-two suffers from anorexia (*TO*, p.1), and that anywhere from
12 to 33 percent of college women control their weight through vomiting,
diuretics, and laxatives.[5] The New York Center for the Study of Anorexia
and Bulimia reports that in the first five months of 1984 it received 252
requests for treatment, compared to 30 requests received in all of 1980.[6]
Even allowing for increased social awareness of eating disorders and a
greater willingness to report the illness, these statistics are startling and
provocative. So, too, is the fact that 90 percent of all anorexics are women,
and that of the 5,000 people each year who have their intestines removed
to lose weight 80 percent are women.[7]

Anorexia nervosa is clearly, as Paul Garfinkel and David Garner call
it, a "multidetermined disorder,"[8] with familial, psychological and possibly biological factors[9] interacting in varying combinations in different
individuals to produce a "final common pathway."[10] Over the last several
years, with growing evidence, not only of an overall increase in frequency
of the disease, but of its higher incidence in certain populations,[11] attention

has begun to turn, too, to cultural factors as significant in the pathogenesis of eating disorders. Until very recently, however, the most that one could expect in the way of cultural or social analysis, with very few exceptions,[12] was the (unavoidable) recognition that anorexia is related to the increasing emphasis that fashion has placed on slenderness over the last fifteen years. This, unfortunately, is only to replace one mystery with another, more profound mystery than the first.

What we need to ask is *why* our culture is so obsessed with keeping our bodies slim, tight, and young that when 500 people were asked, in a recent poll, what they feared most in the world, 190 replied "getting fat."[13] So, too, do we need to explore the fact that it is women who are most oppressed by what Kim Chernin calls "the tyranny of slenderness,"[14] and that this particular oppression is a post-1960s, post-feminist phenomenon. In the 1950s, by contrast, with women once again out of the factories and safely immured in the home, the dominant ideal of female beauty was exemplified by Marilyn Monroe—hardly your androgynous, athletic, adolescent body type. At the peak of her popularity, Monroe was often described as "femininity incarnate," "femaleness embodied"; last term, a student of mine described her as "a cow." Is this merely a change in what size hips, breasts, and waist are considered attractive, or has the very idea of incarnate femaleness come to have a different meaning, different associations, the capacity to stir up different fantasies and images, for the culture of the 1980s? These are the sorts of questions that need to be addressed if we are to achieve a deep understanding of the current epidemic of eating disorders.

The central point of intellectual orientation for this paper is expressed in its subtitle. I take the psychopathologies that develop within a culture, far from being anomalies or aberrations, as characteristic expressions of that culture, as the crystallization, indeed, of much that is wrong with it. For that reason they are important to examine, as keys to cultural self-diagnosis and self-scrutiny. "Every age," says Christopher Lasch, "develops its own peculiar forms of pathology, which express in exaggerated form its underlying character structure."[15] The only thing with which I would disagree in this formulation, with respect to anorexia, is the idea of the expression of an underlying, unitary cultural character structure. Anorexia appears less as the extreme expression of a character structure than as a remarkably overdetermined *symptom* of some of the multifaceted and heterogeneous distresses of our age. Just as it functions in a variety of ways in the psychic economy of the anorexic individual, so a variety of cultural currents or streams converge in anorexia, find their perfect, precise expression in it.

I will call those streams or currents "axes of continuity": *axes* because they meet or converge in the anorexic syndrome; *continuity* refers to the fact that when we place or locate anorexia on these axes, its family resemblances and connections with other phenomena emerge. Some of these axes represent anorexia's *synchronicity* with other contemporary cultural practices and forms—bodybuilding and jogging, for example. Other axes will bring to light *historical* connections: for example, between anorexia and earlier examples of extreme manipulation of the female body, such as corseting, or between anorexia and long-standing traditions and ideologies in Western culture, such as our Greco-Christian traditions of dualism. The three axes that I will discuss in this paper (although they by no means exhaust the possibilities for cultural understanding of anorexia) are *the dualist axis, the control axis, and the gender/power axis*.[16]

Throughout my discussion, it will be assumed that the body, far from being some fundamentally stable, acultural constant to which we must *contrast* all culturally relative and institutional forms, is constantly "in the grip," as Foucault puts it, of cultural practices. Not that this is a matter of cultural *repression* of the instinctual or natural body. Rather, there *is* no "natural" body. Cultural practices, far from exerting their power *against* spontaneous needs, "basic" pleasures or instincts, or "fundamental" structures of body experience, are already and always inscribed, as Foucault has emphasized, "on our bodies and their materiality, their forces, energies, sensations, and pleasures."[17] Our bodies, no less than anything else that is human, are constituted by culture.

The malleability of the body is often but not exclusively a matter of the body-as-experienced (the "lived body," as the phenomenologists put it) rather than the physical body. For example, Foucault points to the medicalization of sexuality in the nineteenth century, which recast sex from a family matter into a private, dark, bodily secret that was appropriately investigated by doctors, psychiatrists, school educators, etc. The constant probing and interrogation, Foucault argues, ferreted out, eroticized, and solidified all sorts of sexual types and perversions, which people then experienced (although they hadn't originally) as defining their bodily possibilities and pleasures. The practice of the medical confessional, in other words, in its constant foraging for sexual secrets and hidden stories, actually *created* new sexual secrets—and eroticized the acts of interrogation and confession, too.[18] Here, social practice changed people's *experience* of their bodies and their possibilities. Similarly, as we shall see, the practice of dieting—of saying "no" to hunger—contributes to the anorexic's increasing sense of hunger as a dangerous eruption, which comes from some alien part of the self, and to a growing intoxication with controlling that eruption.

Although the malleability of the body is frequently a matter of the body-as-experienced, the *physical* body can also be an instrument and medium of power. Foucault gives the classic example of public torture during the ancien régime, through which "the sovereign's power was literally and publicly inscribed on the criminal's body in a manner as controlled, scenic and well-attended as possible."[19] Similarly, the nineteenth-century corset appears, in addition to the actual physical incapacitation it caused the wearer, as a virtual emblem of the power of culture to impose its designs on the female body.

Indeed, women's bodies in general have historically been more vulnerable to extremes in both forms of cultural manipulation of the body. When we later turn to consider some aspects of the history of medicine and fashion, the social manipulation of the female body emerges as an absolutely central strategy in the maintenance of power relations between the sexes over the last hundred years. This historical understanding must deeply affect our understanding of anorexia, and of our contemporary preoccupation with slenderness.

This is *not* to say that I take what I am doing here to be the unearthing of a long-standing male conspiracy against women, or the fixing of blame on *any* particular participants in the play of social forces. In this, I once again follow Foucault, who reminds us that although a perfectly clear logic may characterize historical power relations, with perfectly decipherable aims and objectives, it is nonetheless "often the case that no one was there to have invented" these aims and strategies, either through choice of individuals or through the rational game plan of some presiding "headquarters."[20] This does not mean that individuals do not *consciously* pursue goals that advance their own positions, and advance certain power positions in the process. But it does deny that in doing so, they are directing the overall movement of relations, or engineering their shape. They may not even know what that shape is. Nor does the fact that power relations involve the domination of particular groups—say, prisoners by guards, females by males, amateurs by experts—entail that the dominators are in control of the situation, or that the dominated do not sometimes advance and extend the situation themselves.[21] Nowhere, as we shall see, is this more clear than in the case of anorexia.

The Dualist Axis

I will begin with the most general and attenuated axis of continuity—
the one that begins with Plato, winds its way to its most lurid expression
in Augustine, and finally becomes metaphysically solidified and "scientized" by Descartes. I am referring, of course, to our dualistic heritage:
the view that human existence is bifurcated into two realms or sub-
stances—the bodily or material on the one hand, and the mental or spiritual on the other. Despite some fascinating historical variations, which
I will not go into here, the basic imagery of dualism has remained fairly
constant. Let me briefly describe its central features; they will turn out,
as we will see, to constitute the basic body imagery of the anorexic.

First, the body is experienced as alien, as the not-self, the not-me. *It*
is "fastened and glued" to me, "nailed" and "riveted" to me, as Plato
describes it in the *Phaedo*.[22] For Descartes, it is the brute material en-
velope for the inner and essential self, the thinking thing—ontologically
distinct from it, as mechanical in its operations as a machine, comparable
to animal existence.

Second, the body is experienced as *confinement* and *limitation:* a "prison," a "swamp," a "cage," a "fog"—all images that occur in Plato,
Descartes, and Augustine—from which the soul, will, or mind struggles
to escape. "The enemy ['the madness of lust'] held my will in his power
and from it he made a chain and shackled me," says Augustine.[23] In all
three, images of the soul being "dragged" by the body are prominent.
The body is "heavy, ponderous," as Plato describes it;[24] it exerts a
downward pull.

Third, the body is the *enemy*, as Augustine explicitly describes it time
and again, and as Plato and Descartes strongly suggest in their diatribes
against the body as the source of obscurity and confusion in our thinking.
"A source of countless distractions by reason of the mere requirement
of food," says Plato, "liable also to diseases which overtake and impede
us in the pursuit of truth: it fills us full of loves, and lusts, and fears,
and fancies of all kinds, and endless foolery, and in very truth, as men
say, takes away from us the power of thinking at all. Whence come wars,
and fightings, and factions? Whence but from the body and the lusts of
the body."[25]

Finally, whether as an impediment to reason or as the home of the
"slimy desires of the flesh" (as Augustine calls them), the body is the
locus of all that threatens our attempts at *control*. It overtakes, it over-
whelms, it erupts and disrupts. This situation, for the dualist, becomes

an incitement to battle the unruly forces of the body, to show it who is boss; for as Plato says, "Nature orders the soul to rule and govern and the body to obey and serve."[26] All three, Plato, Augustine, and, most explicitly, Descartes provide instructions, rules, or models of how to gain control over the body,[27] with the ultimate aim of learning to live without it. That is: to achieve intellectual independence from the lure of its illusions, to become impervious to its distractions, and most importantly, to kill off its desires and hungers. Once control has become the central issue for the soul, these are the only possible terms of victory, as Alan Watts makes clear:

> Willed control brings about a sense of duality in the organism, of consciousness in conflict with appetite. . . . But this mode of control is a peculiar example of the proverb that nothing fails like success. For the more consciousness is individualized by the success of the will, the more everything outside the individual seems to be a threat—including . . . the uncontrolled spontaneity of one's own body. . . . Every success in control therefore demands a further success, so that the process cannot stop short of omnipotence.[28]

Dualism here appears as the offspring, the by-product, of the identification of the self with control, an identification that Watts sees as lying at the center of Christianity's ethic of antisexuality. The attempt to subdue the spontaneities of the body in the interests of control only succeeds in constituting them as more alien, and more powerful, and thus more needful of control. The only way to win this no-win game is to go beyond control, is to kill off the body's spontaneities entirely. That is: to cease to *experience* our hungers and desires.

This is what many anorexics describe as their ultimate goal. "[I want] to reach the point," as one put it, "when I don't need to eat at all." (*ED*, p. 84). Kim Chernin recalls her surprise when, after fasting, her hunger returned: "I realized [then] that my secret goal in dieting must have been the intention to kill off my appetite completely" (*TS*, p. 8).

It is not usually noted, in the popular literature on the subject, that anorexic women are as obsessed with *hunger* as they are with being slim. Far from losing her appetite, the typical anorexic is haunted by her appetite (in much the same way as Augustine describes being haunted by sexual desire) and is in constant dread of being overwhelmed by it. Many describe the dread of hunger—"of not having control, of giving in to biological urge," to "the craving, never satisfied thing"[29] as the "original fear" (as one puts it—*GC*, p. 4), or, as Ellen West describes it, "the real obsession." "I don't think the dread of becoming fat is the real . . . neurosis," she writes, "but the constant desire for food. . . . [H]unger, or the dread of hunger, pursues me all morning. . . . Even when I am full, I am afraid of the coming hour in which hunger will start again." Dread of becoming fat, she interprets, rather than being originary, served as a "brake" to her horror of her own unregulatable, runaway desire for food ("EW'," p. 253). Bruch reports that her patients are often terrified by the prospect of taking just one bite of food, lest they never be able to stop (*ED*, p. 253). (Bulimic anorexics, who binge on enormous quantities of food—sometimes consuming up to 15,000 calories a day [*TO*, p. 6] indeed *cannot* stop.)

For these women, hunger is experienced as an alien invader, marching to the tune of its own seemingly arbitrary whims, disconnected from any normal self-regulating mechanisms. How could it be so connected? (For it is experienced as coming from an area *outside* the self.) One patient of Bruch's says she ate breakfast because "my stomach wanted it" (*ED*, p. 270), expressing here the same sense of alienation from her hungers (and her physical self) that Augustine expresses when he speaks of his "captor," "the law of sin that was in my member."[30] Bruch notes that this "basic delusion," as she calls it, "of not owning the body and its sensations" is a typical symptom of all eating disorders. "These patients act," she says, "as if for them the regulation of food intake was outside [the self]" (*ED*, p. 50). This experience of bodily sensation as foreign, strikingly, is not limited to the experience of hunger. Patients with eating disorders have similar problems in identifying cold, heat, emotions, and anxiety as originating in the self (*ED*, p. 254).

While the body is experienced as alien and outside, the soul or will is described as being trapped or confined in an alien "jail," as one woman puts it.[31] A typical fantasy, as it is for Plato, is of total liberation from the bodily prison: "I wish I could get out of my body entirely and fly!"[32] "Please dear God, help me. . . . I want to get out of my body, I want to get out!"[33] Ellen West, astute as always, sees a central meaning of her self-starvation in this "ideal of being too thin, of being *without a body*" ("EW," p. 251; emphasis added).

Anorexia is not a philosophical attitude; it is a debilitating affliction. Yet quite often a highly conscious and articulate scheme of images and associations—one could go so far as to call it a metaphysics—is presented by these women. The scheme is strikingly Augustinian, with evocations of Plato. This is not to say, of course, that anorexics are followers of Plato or Augustine, but that in the anorexic's "metaphysics" elements are made explicit, historically grounded in Plato and Augustine, that run deep in our culture.[34] As Augustine often speaks of the "two wills" within him, "one the servant of the flesh, the other of the spirit," who "between them tore my soul apart,"[35] so the anorexic describes a "spiritual struggle," a "contest between good and evil" (*Solitaire*, p. 109), often conceived explicitly as a battle between mind or will and appetite or body. "I feel myself, quite passively," says West, "the stage on which two hostile forces are mangling each other" ("EW," p. 343). Sometimes there is a more aggressive alliance with mind against body: "When I fail to exercise as often as I prefer, I become guilty that I have let my body 'win' another day from my mind. I can't wait 'til this semester is over. . . . My body is going to pay the price for the lack of work it is currently getting. I can't wait!"[36]

In this battle, thinness represents a triumph of the will over the body, and the thin body (that is, the nonbody) is associated with "absolute purity, hyperintellectuality and transcendence of the flesh. My soul seemed to grow as my body waned; I felt like one of those early Christian saints who starved themselves in the desert sun. I felt invulnerable, clean and hard as the bones etched into my silhouette."[37] Fat (i.e., becoming *all* body) is associated with the "taint" of matter and flesh, "wantonness" (*Solitaire*, p. 109), mental stupor and mental decay.[38] One woman describes how after eating sugar she felt "polluted, disgusting, sticky through the arms, as if something bad had gotten inside."[39] Very often, sexuality is brought into this scheme of associations, and hunger and sexuality are psychically connected. Cherry Boone O'Neill describes a late-night binge, eating scraps of leftovers from the dog's dish:

> I started slowly, relishing the flavor and texture of each marvelous bite. Soon I was ripping the meager remains from the bones, stuffing the meat into my mouth as fast as I could detach it.
>
> [Her boyfriend surprises her, with a look of "total disgust" on his face.]
>
> I had been caught red-handed . . . in an animalistic orgy on the floor, in the dark, alone. Here was the horrid truth for Dan to see. I felt so evil, tainted, pagan. . . . In Dan's mind that day, I had been whoring after food.[40]

A hundred pages earlier, she had described her first romantic involvement in much the same terms: "I felt secretive, deceptive, and . . . tainted by the ongoing relationship" (which never went beyond kisses).[41] Sexuality, similarly, is "an abominable business" to Aimée Liu; for her, staying reed-thin is seen as a way of avoiding sexuality, by becoming "androgynous," as she puts it (*Solitaire*, p. 101). In the same way, Sarah, a patient of Levenkron's, connects her dread of gaining weight with "not wanting to be a 'temptation' to men" (*TO*, p. 122). In Aimée Liu's case, and in Sarah's, the desire to appear unattractive to men is connected to anxiety and guilt over earlier sexual abuse. Whether or not such episodes are common to many cases of anorexia,[42] "the avoidance of any sexual encounter, a shrinking from all bodily contact," according to Bruch, is characteristic.[43]

The Control Axis

Having pointed to the axis of continuity from Plato to anorexia, we should feel cautioned against the impulse to regard anorexia as expressing entirely modern attitudes and fears. Disdain for the body, the conception of it as an alien force and impediment to the soul, is very old in our Greco-Christian traditions (although it has usually been expressed most forcefully by male philosophers and theologians rather than adolescent women!). But although dualism is as old as Plato, in many ways contemporary culture appears *more* obsessed than previous eras with the control of the unruly body. Looking now at contemporary American life, a second axis of continuity emerges on which to locate anorexia. I will call it the *control axis*.

The anorexic, typically, experiences her life as well as her hungers as being out of control. She is torn by conflicting and contradictory expectations and demands, wanting to shine in all areas of student life, confused about where to place most of her energies, what to focus on, as she develops into an adult. Characteristically, her parents expect a great deal of her in the way of individual achievement (as well as physical appearance, particularly her father), yet have made most important decisions for her (*GC*, p. 33). Usually, the anorexic syndrome emerges, *not* as a conscious decision to get as thin as possible, but as the result of her having begun a diet fairly casually, often at the suggestion of a parent, having succeeded splendidly in taking off five or ten pounds, and then having gotten *hooked* on the intoxicating feeling of accomplishment and control.

Recalling her anorexic days, Aimée Liu recreates her feelings:

> The sense of accomplishment exhilarates me, spurs me to continue on and on. It provides a sense of purpose and shapes my life with distractions from insecurity. . . . I shall become an expert [at losing weight]. . . . The constant downward trend [of the scale] somehow comforts me, gives me visible proof that I can exert control. [*Solitaire*, p. 36]

The diet, she realizes, "is the one sector of my life over which I and I alone wield total control."[44]

The frustrations of starvation, the rigors of the constant exercise and physical activity in which anorexics engage, and the pain of the numerous physical complications of anorexia do not trouble the anorexic; indeed, her ability to ignore them is further proof to her of her mastery of her body. "Energy, discipline, my own power will keep me going," says Liu. "Psychic fuel. I need nothing and no one else, and I will prove it. . . . Dropping to the floor, I roll. My tailbone crunches on the hard floor. . . . I feel no pain. I will be master of my own body, if nothing else, I vow" (*Solitaire*, p. 123). And from one of Bruch's patients: *"You make of your own body your very own kingdom where you are the tyrant, the absolute dictator"* (*GC*, p. 65).

Surely we must recognize in this last honest and explicit statement a central modus operandi for the control of contemporary bourgeois anxiety. Consider compulsive jogging and marathon running, often despite shin-splints and other painful injuries, with intense agitation over missed days or not meeting goals for particular runs. Consider the increasing pop-ularity of triathlon events like the "Iron Man," which appear to have no other purpose than to allow people to find out how far they can push their bodies before collapsing. Consider lawyer Mike Frankfurt, who runs ten miles every morning: ". . *To run with pain is the essence of life*."[45] Or the following excerpts from student journals:

> . . . [T]he best times I like to run are under the most unbearable conditions. I love to run in the hottest, most humid and steepest terrain I can find. . . . For me running and the pain associated with it aren't enough to make me stop. I am always trying to overcome it and the biggest failure I can make is to stop running because of pain. Once I ran five of a ten-mile run with a severe leg cramp but wouldn't stop—it would have meant failure.[46]

> When I run I am free. . . . The pleasure is closing off my body—as if the incessant pounding of my legs is so total that the pain ceases to exist. There is no grace, no beauty in the running—there is the jarring reality of sneaker and pavement. Bright pain that shivers and splinters sending its white hot arrows into my stomach, my lung, but it cannot pierce my mind. I am on automatic pilot—there is no re-membrance of pain, there is freedom—I am losing myself, peeling out of this heavy flesh. . . Power surges through me.[47]

None of this is to dispute that the contemporary concern with fitness has nonpathological, nondualist dimensions as well. Particularly for women, who have historically suffered from the ubiquity of rape and abuse, from the culturally instilled conviction of our own helplessness, and from lack of access to facilities and programs for rigorous physical training, the cultivation of strength, agility, and confidence has a clearly positive dimension. Nor are the objective benefits of daily exercise and concern for nutrition in question here. My focus, rather, is on a subjective stance, increasingly more prominent over the last five years, which, although preoccupied with the body and deriving narcissistic enjoyment from its appearance, takes little pleasure in the *experience* of embodiment. Rather, the fundamental identification is with mind (or will), ideals of spiritual perfection, fantasies of absolute control.

Not everyone, of course, for whom physical training is a part of daily routine exhibits such a stance. Here, an examination of the language of female bodybuilders is illustrative. Bodybuilding is particularly interesting because on the surface it appears to have the very opposite structure from anorexia: The bodybuilder is, after all, building the body *up*, not whittling it down. Bodybuilding develops strength. We imagine the bodybuilder as someone who is proud, confident, and, perhaps most of all, conscious of and accepting of her physicality. This is, indeed, how some female bodybuilders experience themselves:

> I feel . . . tranquil and stronger [says Lydia Cheng]. Working out creates a high everywhere in my body. I feel the heat. I feel the muscles rise, I see them blow out, flushed with lots of blood. . . . My whole body is sweating, and there's few things I love more than working up a good sweat. That's when I really feel like a woman.[48]

Yet a sense of joy in the body as active and alive is *not* the most prominent theme among the women interviewed by Trix Rosen in *Strong and Sexy*. Many of them, rather, talk about their bodies in ways that are disquietingly resonant with typical anorexic themes.

There is the same emphasis on will, purity, and perfection: "I've learned to be a stronger person with a more powerful will . . . pure concentration, energy and spirit." "I want to be as physically perfect as possible." "Body-building suits the perfectionist in me." "My goal is to have muscular perfection."[49] Compulsive exercisers—who Dinitia Smith, in an article for *New York*, calls "The New Puritans"—speak in similar terms: Kathy Krauch, a New York art director who bikes twelve miles a day and swims two and a half, says she is engaged in "a quest for perfection." Such people, Smith emphasizes, care little about their health: "They pursue self-denial as an end in itself, out of an almost mystical belief in the purity it confers."[50]

Among bodybuilders, as for anorexics, there are the same unnerving conceptualizations of the body as alien, the not-self:

I'm constantly amazed by my muscles. The first thing I do when I wake up in the morning is look down at my "abs" and flex my legs to see if the "cuts" are there. . . . My legs have always been my most stubborn part, and I want them to develop so badly. Every day I can see things happening to them. . . . I don't flaunt my muscles as much as I thought I would. I feel differently about them; they are my product and I protect them by wearing sweaters to keep them warm.[51]

Most strikingly, there is the same emphasis on *control*, on feeling one's life to be fundamentally out of control, and on the feeling of accomplishment derived from total mastery of the body. That sense of mastery, like the anorexic's, appears derived from two sources. First, there is the reassurance that one can overcome all physical obstacles, push oneself to any extremes in pursuit of one's goals (which, as we have seen, is a characteristic motivation of compulsive runners, as well). Second, and most dramatic (it is spoken of time and again by female bodybuilders), is the thrill of being in total charge of the shape of one's body. "Create a masterpiece," says *Fit.* "Sculpt your body contours into a work of art." As for the anorexic—who literally cannot *see* her body as other than her inner reality dictates and who is relentlessly driven by an ideal image of ascetic slenderness—so too a purely mental conception comes to have dominance over the bodybuilder's life: "You visualize what you want to look like . . . and then create the form." "The challenge presents itself; to rearrange things."[52] "It's up to you to do the chiseling; you become the master sculptress." "What a fantasy, for your body to be chang ing! . . . I keep a picture in my mind as I work out of what I want to look like and what's happened to me already."[53] The technology of dictating to nature one's own chosen design for the body is at the center of the bodybuilder's mania, as it is for the anorexic.

The sense of security derived from the attainment of this goal appears, first of all, as the pleasure of control and independence. "Nowadays," says Michael Sacks, associate professor of psychiatry at Cornell Medical College, "people no longer feel they can control events outside themselves—how well they do in their jobs or in their personal relationships, for example—but they can control the food they eat and how far they can run. Abstinence, tests of endurance, are ways of proving their self-sufficiency."[54] In a culture, moreover, in which our continued survival is often at the mercy of "specialists," machines, and sophisticated technology, the body takes on a special sort of vulnerability and dependency. We may live longer than ever before, but the circumstances surrounding illness and death may often be perceived as more alien, inscrutable, and arbitrary than ever before.

Our contemporary body fetishism, however, expresses more than a fantasy of self-mastery in an increasingly unmanageable culture. It also reflects our alliance *with* culture against all reminders of the inevitable decay and death of the body. "Everybody wants to live forever" is the refrain from the theme song of *Pumping Iron*. The most youth-worshipping of popular television shows, *Fame*, opens with a song that begins, "I want to live forever." And it is striking that although the anorexic may come very close to death (and 15% do indeed die), the dominant experience throughout the illness is of *invulnerability*.

The dream of immortality is, of course, nothing new. But what is unique to modernity is that the defeat of death has become a scientific fantasy rather than a philosophical or religious mythology. We no longer dream of eternal union with the gods; we build devices that can keep us alive indefinitely, and we work on keeping our bodies as smooth and muscular and elastic at forty as they were at eighteen. We even entertain dreams of halting the aging process completely: "Old age," according to Durk Pearson and Sandy Shaw, authors of the popular *Life Extension*, "is an unpleasant and unattractive affliction."[55] The megavitamin regime they prescribe is able, they claim, to prevent and even to *reverse* the mechanisms of aging.

Finally, it may be that in cultures characterized by gross excesses in consumption, the "will to conquer and subdue the body" (as Chernin calls it—*TS*, p. 47) expresses an aesthetic or moral rebellion. Anorexics initially came from affluent families, and the current craze for long-distance running and fasting is largely a phenomenon of young, upwardly mobile professionals (Dinitia Smith calls it "Deprivation Chic"). To those who are starving *against* their wills, of course, starvation cannot function as an expression of the power of the will. At the same time, we should caution against viewing anorexia as a trendy illness of the elite. Rather, powerlessness is its most outstanding feature.

The Gender/Power Axis

Ninety percent of all anorexics are women. We do not need, of course, to know that particular statistic to realize that the contemporary "tyranny of slenderness" is far from gender neutral. Women are more obsessed with their bodies than men, less satisfied with them,[56] and permitted less latitude with them by themselves, by men, and by the culture. In a recent *Glamour* poll of 33,000 women, 75% said that they thought they were "too fat." Yet by Metropolitan Life Insurance tables—themselves notoriously affected by cultural standards—only 25% of these women were heavier than the specified standards, and a full 30% were *below*.[57] The anorexic's distorted image of her body—her inability to see it as anything but "too fat"—while more extreme, is not radically discontinuous from fairly common female misperceptions.

Consider, too, actors like Nick Nolte and William Hurt, who are permitted a certain amount of softening, of thickening about the waist, while still retaining romantic lead status. Individual style, wit, the projection of intelligence, experience, and effectiveness still go a long way for men, even in our fitness-obsessed culture. But no female can achieve the status of romantic or sexual ideal without the appropriate *body*. That body, if we use television commercials as a gauge, has gotten steadily leaner over the past ten years.[58] What used to be acknowledged as extremes required of high-fashion models is now the dominant image that beckons to high school and college women. Over and over, extremely slender women students complain of hating their thighs or their stomachs (the anorexic's most dreaded danger spot); often, they express concern and anger over frequent teasing by their boyfriends: Janey, a former student, is 5'10" and weighs 132 pounds. Yet her boyfriend calls her "Fatso" and "Big Butt" and insists she should be 110 pounds because "that's what Brooke Shields weighs." He calls this "constructive criticism," and seems to experience extreme anxiety over the possibility of her gaining any weight: "I can tell it bothers her yet I still continue to badger her about it. I guess that I think that if I continue to remind her things will change faster. . . ."[59] This sort of relationship—within which the woman's weight has become a focal issue—is not at all atypical, as I've discovered from student journals and papers.

Hilde Bruch reports that many anorexics talk of having a "ghost" inside them or surrounding them, "a dictator who dominates me," as one woman describes it; "a little man who objects when I eat" is the description given by another (*GC*, p. 58). The little ghost, the dictator, the "other self" (as he is often described) is always male, reports Bruch. The anorexic's *other* self—the self of the uncontrollable appetites, the impurities and taints, the flabby will and tendency to mental torpor—is the body, as we have seen. But it is also (and here the anorexic's associations are surely in the mainstream of Western culture) the *female* self. These two selves are perceived as at constant war. But it is clear that it is the male side—with its associated values of greater spirituality, higher intellectuality, strength of will—is being expressed and developed in the anorexic syndrome.[60]

What is the meaning of these gender associations in the anorexic? I propose that there are two levels of meaning. One has to do with fear and disdain for traditional female *roles* and social limitations. The other has to do, more profoundly, with a deep fear of "The Female," with all its more nightmarish archetypal associations: voracious hungers and sexual insatiability. Let us examine each of these levels in turn.

Adolescent anorexics express characteristic fears about growing up to be mature, sexually developed, potentially reproductive women. "I have a deep fear," says one, "of having a womanly body, round and fully developed. I want to be tight and muscular and thin."[61] If only she could stay thin, says another, "I would never have to deal with having a woman's body; like Peter Pan I could stay a child forever."[62] The choice of Peter Pan is telling here—what she means is, stay a *boy* forever. And indeed, as Bruch reports, many anorexics, when children, dreamt and fantasized about growing up to be boys.[63] Some are quite conscious of playing out this fantasy through their anorexia: Adrienne, one of Levenkron's patients, was extremely proud of the growth of facial and body hair that often accompanies anorexia, and especially proud of her "skinny, hairy arms" (*TO*, p. 82). Many patients report, too, that their fathers had wanted a boy, were disappointed to get "less than" that,[64] or had emotionally rebuffed their daughters when they began to develop sexually (*TO*, pp. 103, 45).

In a characteristic scenario, anorexia will develop just at the beginning of puberty. Normal body changes are experienced by the anorexic, not surprisingly, as the takeover of the body by disgusting, womanish fat. "I grab my breasts," says Aimée Liu, "pinching them until they hurt. If only I could eliminate them, cut them off if need be, to become as flat-chested as a child again" (*Solitaire*, p. 79). She is exultant when her periods stop (as they do in *all* cases of anorexia) (*GC*, p. 65). The disgust with menstruation is typical: "I saw a picture at a feminist art gallery," says another woman; "there was a woman with long red yarn coming out of her, like she was menstruating. . . . I got that *feeling*—in that part of my body that I have trouble with . . . my stomach, my thighs, my pelvis. That revolted feeling."[65]

Many anorexics appear to experience anxiety over falling into the lifestyle they associate with their mothers. It is a prominent theme in Aimée Liu's *Solitaire*. One woman describes her feeling that she is "full of my mother . . . she is in me even if she isn't there" in nearly the same breath as she complains of her continuous fear of being "not human . . . of ceasing to exist" (*GC*, p. 12). And Ellen West, nearly a century earlier, had quite explicitly equated becoming fat with the inevitable (for a woman of her time) confinements of domestic life and the domestic stupor she associates with it:

> Dread is driving me mad . . . the consciousness that ultimately I will lose everything; all courage, all rebelliousness, all drive for doing; that it—my little world—will make me flabby, flabby and fainthearted and beggarly. . . . ["EW," p. 243]

Several of my students with eating disorders reported that their anorexia had developed after their families had dissuaded or forbidden them from embarking on a traditionally male career.

Here anorexia finds a true sister-phenomenon in the epidemic of female invalidism and "hysteria" that swept through the middle and upper middle classes in the second half of the nineteenth century. It was a time that, in many ways, was very like our own, especially in the conflicting demands that women were newly confronting: the opening up of new possibilities, the continuing grip of the old expectations. On the one hand, the old preindustrial order, with the father at the head of a self-contained family production unit, had given way to the dictatorship of the market, opening up new, nondomestic opportunities for working women; on the other, it also turned many of the most valued "female" skills—textile and garment manufacture, food processing—out of the home and over to the factory system.[66] In the new machine economy, the lives of middle-class women were far emptier than they had been before.

It was an era, too, that had been witnessing the first major feminist wave: In 1840, the World Anti-Slavery Conference had been held, at which the first feminists spoke loudly and long on the connections between the abolition of slavery and women's rights. 1848 saw the Seneca Falls Convention. In 1869, John Stuart Mill published his landmark work, "On the Subjection of Women." And in 1889, the Pankhursts formed the Women's Franchise League. But it was an era, too (and not unrelatedly, as I shall argue later) when the prevailing ideal of femininity was the delicate, affluent lady, unequipped for anything but the most sheltered domestic life, totally dependent on her prosperous husband, providing a peaceful and comfortable haven for him each day after his return from the labors of the public sphere.[67] In a now famous 1883 letter, Freud, criticizing John Stuart Mill, writes:

> It really is a still-born thought to send women into the struggle for existence exactly as men. If, for instance, I imagine my gentle sweet girl as a competitor it would only end in my telling her, as I did seventeen months ago, that I am fond of her and that I implore her to withdraw from the strife into the calm uncompetitive activity of my home.[68]

This is exactly what male doctors *did* do when women began falling ill, complaining of acute depression, severe headaches, weakness, nervousness, and self-doubt.[69] Among them were such noted feminists and social activists as Charlotte Perkins Gilman, Jane Addams, Elizabeth Cady Stanton, Margaret Sanger, leading English abolitionist Josephine Butler, and German suffragist Hedwig Dohm. "I was weary of myself and sick of asking what I am and what I ought to be," recalls Gilman, who later went on to write a fictional account of her mental breakdown in the chilling novella *The Yellow Wallpaper*. Her doctor, the famous female specialist S. Weir Mitchell, instructed her, as Gilman recalls, to "live as domestic a life as possible. Have your child with you all the time. . . . Lie down an hour every day after each meal. Have but two hours intellectual life a day. And never touch pen, brush or pencil as long as you live."[70]

Freud, who favorably reviewed Mitchell's 1887 book and who advised that psychotherapy for hysterical patients be combined with Mitchell's rest cure ("to avoid new psychical impressions"),[71] was as blind as Mitchell to the contribution that isolation, boredom, and intellectual frustration made in the etiology of hysteria. Nearly all of the subjects in *Studies in Hysteria* (as well as the later "Dora") are acknowledged to be unusually intelligent, creative, energetic, independent, and often highly educated. Freud even comments, criticizing Janet's notion that hysterics were "psychically insufficient," on the characteristic coexistence of hysteria with "gifts of the richest and most original kind."[72] Yet Freud never makes the connection (which Breuer had begun to develop)[73] between the monotonous domestic lives these women were expected to lead after their schooling was completed, and the emergence of compulsive daydreaming, hallucinations, dissociations, and hysterical conversions.

Charlotte Perkins Gilman does. In *The Yellow Wallpaper* she describes how a prescribed regime of isolation and enforced domesticity eventuates, in her fictional heroine, in the development of a full-blown hysterical symptom, madness, and collapse. The symptom, the hallucination that there is a woman trapped in the wallpaper of her bedroom, struggling to get out, is at once both a perfectly articulated expression of protest and a completely debilitating idée fixe that allows the woman character no distance on her situation, no freedom of thought, no chance of making any progress in leading the kind of active, creative life her body and soul crave.

So too for the anorexic. It is indeed essential to recognize in this illness a dimension of protest against the limitations of the ideal of female domesticity (the "feminine mystique," as Betty Friedan called it) that reigned in America throughout the 1950s and early 1960s—the era when most of their mothers were starting homes and families. This was, we should recall, the era of the return to "normalcy" following World War II, an era during which women had been fired en masse from the jobs they had held during the war and shamelessly propagandized back into the full-time job of wife and mother. It was an era, too, when the "fuller figure," as Jane Russell now calls it, came into fashion once more, a period of "mammary madness"[74] (or "resurgent Victorianism," as Lois Banner calls it),[75] that glamorized the voluptuous, large-breasted woman. This remained the prevailing fashion tyranny until the late 1960s and early 1970s.

But we must recognize that the anorexic's "protest," like that of the classical hysterical symptom, is written on the bodies of anorexic women, and *not* embraced as a conscious politics, nor, indeed, does it reflect any social or political understanding at all. Moreover, the symptoms themselves function to preclude the emergence of such an understanding: the idée fixe—staying thin—becomes at its farthest extreme so powerful as to render any other ideas or lifeprojects meaningless. Liu describes it as "all-encompassing" (*Solitaire*, p. 141). West writes that "I felt all inner development was ceasing, that all becoming and growing were being choked, because a single idea was filling my entire soul" ("EW," p. 257).

Paradoxically—and often tragically—these pathologies of female "protest" (and we must include agoraphobia here, as well as hysteria and anorexia)[76] actually function as if in collusion with the cultural conditions that produced them. The same is true for more moderate expressions of the contemporary female obsession with slenderness. Women may feel themselves deeply attracted by the aura of freedom and independence suggested by the boyish body ideal of today. Yet, each hour, each minute that is spent in anxious pursuit of that ideal (for it does not come "naturally" to most mature women) is *in fact* time and energy diverted from inner development and social achievement. As a feminist protest, the obsession with slenderness is hopelessly counterproductive.

It is important to recognize, too, that the anorexic is terrified and repelled, not only by the traditional female domestic role—which she associates with mental lassitude and weakness—but by a certain archetypal image of the female: as hungering, voracious, all-needing, and all-wanting. It is this image that shapes and permeates her experience of her own hunger for food as insatiable and out-of-control, which makes her feel that if she takes just one bite, she won't be able to stop.

Let's explore this image. Let's break the tie with food and look at the metaphor: Hungering. Voracious. Extravagantly and excessively needful. Without restraint. Always wanting. Always wanting too much affection, reassurance, emotional and sexual contact and attention. This is how many women frequently experience themselves, and, indeed, how many men experience women. "Please, please God, keep me from telephoning him," prays the heroine in Dorothy Parker's classic "The Telephone Call," experiencing her need for reassurance and contact as being as out of control and degrading as the anorexic experiences her desire for food. The male counterpart to this is found in someone like Paul Morel in Lawrence's *Sons and Lovers:* "Can you never like things without clutching them as if you wanted to pull the heart out of them?" he accuses Miriam as she fondles a flower, "Why don't you have a bit more restraint, or reserve, or something. . . . You're always begging things to love you, as if you were a beggar for love. Even the flowers, you have to fawn on them."[77] How much psychic authenticity do these images carry in 1980s America? One woman in my class provided a stunning insight into the connection between her perception of herself and the anxiety of the compulsive dieter: "You know," she said, "the anorexic is always convinced she is taking up too much space, eating too much, wanting food too much. I've never felt that way, but I've often felt that I was *too much*— too much emotion, too much need, too loud and demanding, too much *there,* if you know what I mean."[78]

The most extreme cultural expressions of the fear of woman-as-too-much—which almost always revolve around her sexuality—are strikingly full of eating and hungering metaphors. "Of woman's unnatural, *insatiable* lust, what country, what village doth not complain?" queries Burton in *The Anatomy of Melancholy.* "You are the true hiennas," says Walter Charleton, "that allure us with the fairness of your skins, and when folly hath brought us within your reach, you leap upon us and *devour* us."[79]

The mythology/ideology of the devouring, insatiable female (which, as we have seen, is the internalized image the anorexic has of her female self) tends historically to wax and wane. But not without rhyme or reason. In periods of gross environmental and social crisis, such as characterized the period of the witch-hunts in the fifteenth and sixteenth centuries, it appears to flourish.[80] "All witchcraft comes from carnal lust, which is in women *insatiable*," say Kramer and Sprenger, authors of the official witch-hunters' handbook, *Malleus Malificarum.* For the sake of fulfilling the "*mouth* of the womb . . . [women] consort even with the devil."[81]

Anxiety over women's uncontrollable hungers appears to peak, as well, during periods when women are becoming independent and asserting themselves politically and socially. The second half of the nineteenth century saw a virtual "flood" (as Peter Gay calls it) of artistic and literary images of the dark, dangerous, and evil female: "sharp-teethed, devouring" Sphinxes, Salomés, and Delilahs, "biting, tearing, murderous women." "No century," claims Gay, "depicted woman as vampire, as castrator, as killer, so consistently, so programmatically, and so nakedly as the nineteenth."[82] No century, too, was as obsessed with female sexuality and its medical control. Treatment for excessive "sexual excitement" and masturbation included placing leeches on the womb (*TS*, p. 38), clitoridectomy, and removing of the ovaries (also recommended for "troublesomeness, eating like a ploughman, erotic tendencies, persecution mania, and simple 'cussedness' ").[83]

It is in the second half of the nineteenth century, too, despite a flurry of efforts by feminists and health reformers, that the stylized "S-curve," which required a tighter corset than ever before, comes into fashion.[84] "While the suffragettes were forcefully propelling all women toward legal and political emancipation," says Amaury deRiencourt, "fashion and custom imprisoned her physically as she had never been before."[85] Described by Thorstein Veblen as a "mutilation, undergone for the purpose of lowering the subject's vitality and rendering her permanently and obviously unfit for work,"[86] the corset indeed did just that. In it, a woman could barely sit or stoop, was unable to move her feet more than six inches at a time, and had difficulty keeping herself from regular fainting fits. The connection was often drawn in popular magazines between enduring the tight corset and the exercise of self-restraint and control. The corset is "an ever present monitor," says one 1878 advertisement, "of a well-disciplined mind and well-regulated feelings."[87] Today, of course, we diet to achieve such control.

It is important to emphasize that, despite bizarre and grotesque examples of gross physical manipulation and external control (clitoridectomy, Chinese foot binding, the removal of bones from the rib cage in order to fit into the tight corset), such control plays a relatively minor role in the maintenance of gender power relations. For every historical image of the dangerous, aggressive woman, there is a corresponding fantasy—an ideal femininity, from which all threatening elements have been purged—that women have mutilated themselves *internally* to attain. In the Victorian era, at the same time as operations were being performed to control female sexuality, William Acton, Krafft-Ebing, and others were proclaiming the official scientific doctrine that women are naturally passive and "not very much troubled with sexual feelings of any kind."[88]

Corresponding to this male medical fantasy was the popular artistic and moral theme of woman-as-ministering-angel: sweet, gentle, domestic, without intensity or personal ambition of any sort.[89] Peter Gay suggests, correctly, that these ideals must be understood as a reaction-formation to the era's "pervasive sense of manhood in danger,"[90] and argues that few women actually fit the "insipid goody" (as Kate Millett calls it)[91] image. What Gay forgets, however, is that most women *tried*—lower classes as well as middle were affected by the "tenacious and all-pervasive" ideal of the perfect lady[92]—and that many women did manage to achieve depressingly effective results.

On the gender/power axis the female body appears, then, as the unknowing medium of the historical ebbs and flows of the fear of woman-as-too-much. That, as we have seen, is how the anorexic experiences her female, bodily self: as voracious, wanton, needful of forceful control by her male will. Living in the tide of cultural backlash against the second major feminist wave, she is not alone in these images. Christopher Lasch, in *The Culture of Narcissism*, speaks of what he describes as "the apparently aggressive overtures of sexually liberated women" that "convey to many males the same message—that women are *voracious, insatiable*," and call up "early fantasies of a possessive, suffocating, *devouring* and castrating mother" (emphasis added).[93]

Our contemporary beauty ideals, on the other hand, seem purged, as Kim Chernin puts it, "of the power to conjure up memories of the past, of all that could remind us of a woman's mysterious power" (*TS*, p. 148). The ideal, rather, is an "image of a woman in which she is not yet a woman": Darryl Hannah as the lanky, newborn mermaid in *Splash;* Lori Singer (appearing virtually anorexic) as the reckless, hyper-kinetic heroine of *Footloose;* The Charlie Girl; "Cheryl Tiegs in shorts, Margaux Hemingway with her hair wet, Brooke Shields naked on an island";[94] the dozens of teen-age women who appear in Coke commercials, in jeans commercials, in chewing gum commercials.

The images suggest amused detachment, casual playfulness, flirtatiousness without demand, and lightness of touch. A refusal to take sex, death, or politics too deadly seriously. A delightfully unconscious relationship to her body. The twentieth century has seen this sort of feminine ideal before, of course: When, in the 1920s, young women began to flatten their breasts, suck in their stomachs, bob their hair, and show off long, colt-like legs, they believed they were pursuing a new freedom and daring that demanded a carefree, boyish style.[95] If the traditional female hourglass suggested anything, it was confinement and immobility.

Yet the flapper's freedom, as Mary McCarthy's and Dorothy Parker's short stories brilliantly reveal, was largely an illusion—as any obsessively cultivated sexual style must inevitably be. Although today's images may suggest androgynous independence, we need only consider who is on the receiving end of the imagery in order to confront the pitiful paradox involved.

Watching the commercials are thousands of anxiety-ridden women and adolescents (some of whom are likely the very ones appearing in the commercials) with anything *but* an unconscious relation to their bodies. They are involved in an absolutely contradictory state of affairs, a totally no-win game: caring desperately, passionately, obsessively about attaining an ideal of coolness, effortless confidence, and casual freedom. Watching the commercials is a little girl, perhaps ten years old, who I saw in Central Park, gazing raptly at her father, bursting with pride: "Daddy, guess what? I lost two pounds!" And watching the commercials is the anorexic, who associates her relentless pursuit of thinness with power and control, but who in fact destroys her health and imprisons her imagination. She is surely the most startling and stark illustration of how cavalier power relations are with respect to the motivations and goals of individuals, yet how deeply they are etched on our bodies, and how well our bodies serve them.

Notes

This essay, like all intellectual projects, has been a collaborative enterprise. All of the many students, friends, and colleagues who have discussed its ideas with me, suggested articles and resources, commented on earlier versions, shared personal experiences, or allowed me to glimpse their own fears and angers have collaborated with me on this project, have made its development possible. In particular, I owe a large debt to the students of my metaphysics and "Gender, Culture, and Experience" classes, whose articulate and honest journals I have drawn on in these pages, and whose work often pushed forward my own. Here, I would single out Christy Ferguson, Vivian Conger, and Nancy Monaghan, whose research on Victorian and early twentieth-century ideals of femininity contributed insights and information that proved significant to this paper. Although many people have commented on earlier drafts, Lynne Arnault, Mario Moussa, and Nancy Fraser were especially helpful in providing systematic and penetrating criticisms and editorial suggestions for the final version.
Since this essay first appeared in 1985, there has been an explosion of published material, media attention, and clinical study devoted to eating disorders. At the same time, my own thinking on the subject has evolved, as the essay itself has evolved into further essays and ultimately into a book, *Food, Fashion and Power*, currently in progress. I have not incorporated new statistics or studies into this piece, although many of them strongly bear out observations and interpretations offered here. Nor have I

attempted to revise the essay in light of changes in my own perspective. Instead, I have chosen to let the essay stand in its original form, as an initial mapping of a complex, culturally live domain, about which we are learning new things all the time.

1. Jules Henry, *Culture Against Man* (New York: Knopf, 1963).
2. Throughout this paper, the term "anorexia" will be used to designate a general class of eating disorders within which intake-restricting (or abstinent) anorexia and bulimia/anorexia (characterized by alternating bouts of gorging and starving and/or gorging and vomiting) are distinct subtypes (see Hilde Bruch, *The Golden Cage: The Enigma of Anorexia Nervosa* [New York: Vintage, 1979], p. 10 [cited parenthetically in the text as *GC*]; Steven Levenkron, *Treating and Overcoming Anorexia Nervosa* [New York: Warner Books, 1982], p. 6 [cited parenthetically in the text as *TO*]; R. L. Palmer, *Anorexia Nervosa* [Middlesex, U.K.: Penguin, 1980], pp. 14, 23–24; Paul Garfinkel and David Garner, *Anorexia Nervosa: A Multidimensional Perspective* [New York: Brunner/Mazel, 1982], p. 4). Although there are striking and fascinating differences in personality traits and personal history characteristic of these two subgroups of anorexics (see Levenkron, pp. 65–66; Garfinkel and Garner, pp. 40–55), I will concentrate on those images, concerns, and attitudes largely common to both. Where a difference seems significant in terms of the themes of this essay, I will indicate the relevant difference in a note rather than overcomplicate the main argument of the text. This procedure is not to be taken as belittling the importance of these differences in the understanding and treatment of eating disorders. Rather, separate and extended discussion of such differences will appear elsewhere in my work.
3. Although throughout history there have been scattered references to patients who sound as though they may have been suffering from self-starvation, the first medical description of anorexia as a discrete syndrome was made by W. W. Gull in an 1868 address at Oxford. Six years later, Gull began to use the term "anorexia nervosa"; at the same time, E. D. Lesegue independently described the disorder (Garfinkel and Garner, pp. 58–59). Although cases have been recorded ever since then, researchers are in almost universal agreement that the evidence suggests a striking increase in frequency over the last twenty years (see Garfinkel and Garner, p. 100, for an exhaustive list of studies suggestive of this; also Bruch, p. vii; Levenkron, p. xvi). So startling is the increase in rate of occurrence, and so rare was it formerly, that Bruch, in 1978, suggests it can in a sense be regarded as "a new disease."
4. Ludwig Binswanger, "The Case of Ellen West," in *Existence*, ed. Rollo May (New York: Simon and Schuster, 1958), p. 288 (cited parenthetically in the text as "EW"). Hilde Bruch, *Eating Disorders* (New York: Basic Books, 1973), p. 4 (cited parenthetically in the text as *ED*).
5. Susan Squire, "Is the Binge-Purge Cycle Catching?" *Ms.*, October 1983; *Anorexia/Bulimia Support*, Syracuse, New York.
6. Dinitia Smith, "The New Puritans," *New York*, June 11, 1984, p. 28.
7. Kim Chernin, *The Obsession: Reflections on the Tyranny of Slenderness* (New York: Harper and Row, 1981), pp. 63, 62 (cited parenthetically in the text as *TS*).
8. Garfinkel and Garner, *Anorexia Nervosa*, pp. 186–213.
9. Anorexics characteristically suffer from a number of physiological disturbances, including amenorrhea (cessation of menstruation) and abnormal hypothalamic function (see Garfinkel and Garner, pp. 58–89, for an extensive discussion of these and other physiological disorders associated with anorexia; also, Eugene Garfield, "Anorexia Nervosa: The Enigma of Self-Starvation," *Current Contents*,

August 6, 1984, pp. 8–9). Researchers are divided, with arguments on both sides, as to whether hypothalamic dysfunction may be a primary cause of the disease, or whether these characteristic neuroendocrine disorders are the result of weight loss, caloric deprivation, and emotional stress. The same debate rages over abnormal vasopresin levels discovered in anorexics, recently touted in tabloids all over the United States as the "explanation" of anorexia and key to its cure. Apart from such debates concerning a possible biochemical predisposition to anorexia, research continues, as well, exploring the role of biochemistry as possibly contributing to the self-perpetuating nature of the disease, and the relation of the physiological effects of starvation to particular experiential symptoms, such as the anorexic's preoccupation with food (see Bruch, *The Golden Cage*, pp. 7–12; Garfinkel and Garner, *Anorexia Nervosa*, pp. 10–14).

10. Garfinkel and Garner, *Anorexia Nervosa*, p. 189.

11. Initially, anorexia was found to predominate among upper-class white families. There is, however, widespread evidence that this is now rapidly changing (as we might expect; no one in America is immune to the power of popular imagery). The disorder has become more equally distributed in recent years, touching populations (e.g., blacks and East Indians) previously unaffected, and all socioeconomic levels (Garfinkel and Garner, *Anorexia Nervosa*, pp. 102–3). There remains, however, the overwhelming disproportion of women to men (ibid., pp. 112–13).

12. Kim Chernin's book *The Obsession*, whose remarkable insights inspired my interest in anorexia, was the first outstanding exception to the lack of cultural understanding of eating disorders. Since the writing of this essay, Chernin's second book on eating disorders, *The Hungry Self* (New York: Harper and Row, 1985) and Susie Ohrbach's *Hunger Strike* (New York: W. W. Norton, 1986) have appeared. Both contribute significantly to our cultural understanding of anorexia.

13. Chernin, *The Obsession*, pp. 36–37. My use of the term "our culture" may seem overly homogenizing here, disrespectful of differences among ethnic groups, socioeconomic groups, subcultures within American society, etc. It must be stressed here that I am discussing ideology and images whose power is *precisely* the power to homogenize culture. Even in pre–mass media cultures, we see this phenomenon: the nineteenth-century ideal of the "perfect lady" tyrannized even those classes who couldn't afford to realize it. With television, of course, a massive deployment of images becomes possible, and there is no escape from the mass shaping of our fantasy lives. Although they may start among the wealthy and elite ("A woman can never be too rich or too thin"), media-promoted ideals of femininity and masculinity quickly and perniciously "trickle down" to everyone who owns a TV or can afford a junk magazine or is aware of billboards. Recent changes in the incidence of anorexia among lower-income groups (see note 11) bear this out.

14. Until very recently, this dimension was largely ignored or underemphasized, with a very few notable exceptions. Kim Chernin and Susie Ohrbach *(Fat is a Feminist Issue)* were ground-breakers in exploring the connections between eating disorders and images and ideals of femininity. Robert Seidenberg and Karen DeCrow *(Women Who Marry Houses: Panic and Protest in Agoraphobia)* provide a very brief, interesting discussion, the value of which is marred, however, by some fundamental errors concerning the typical pattern of the disorder. Hilde Bruch touches these issues, but only barely, in her otherwise excellent work on eating disorders. Lately, however, there has been a veritable explosion of creative work, both theoretical and therapeutic, confronting the connections between eating disorders and the situation of women. Shortly after this paper was completed, I attended the Third Annual Conference of the Center for the Study of Anorexia and Bulimia (New

York, November 17–18, 1984), which was devoted entirely to the theme of "The Psychology of Women and the Psychotherapy of Eating Disorders." Institutes such as The Women's Therapy Institute in New York have developed techniques of treatment that are specifically grounded in a feminist reconstruction of object-relations theory (see Luise Eichenbaum and Susie Ohrbach, *Understanding Women: A Feminist Psychoanalytic Approach* [New York: Basic Books, 1983]). And new perspectives are emerging all the time, from ideological quarters as diverse as experimental psychology and Jungian analysis (see, for example, Angelyn Spignesi, *Starving Women* [Dallas, Tex: Spring Publications, 1983]).

15. Christopher Lasch, *The Culture of Narcissism* (New York: Warner Books, 1979), p. 88.

16. I choose these three primarily because they are where my exploration of the im-agery, language, and metaphor produced by anorexic women led me. Delivering earlier versions of this essay at colleges and conferences, I discovered that one of the commonest responses of members of the audiences was the proffering of further axes; the paper presented itself less as a statement about the ultimate "meaning" or causes of a phenomenon than as an invitation to continue my "unpacking" of anorexia as a crystallizing formation. Yet the particular axes chosen have more than a purely autobiographical rationale. The dualist axis serves to identify and articulate the basic body imagery of anorexia. The control axis is an exploration of the question "Why Now?" The gender/power axis continues this exploration, but focuses on the question "Why Women?" The sequence of axes takes us from the most general, most historically diffuse structure of continuity—the dualist experience of self—to ever narrower, more specified "arenas" of comparison and connection. At first, the connections are made without regard to historical context, drawing on diverse historical sources to exploit their familiar coherence in an effort to sculpt the "shape" of the anorexic experience. In this section, too, I want to suggest that the Greco-Christian tradition provides a particularly fertile soil for the development of anorexia. Then, I turn to the much more specific context of American fads and fantasies in the 1980s, considering the contemporary scene largely in terms of popular culture (and therefore through the "fiction" of homogeneity), without regard for gender difference. In this section, the connections drawn point to a historical experience of self common to both men and women. Finally, my focus shifts to consider not what connects anorexia to other general cultural phenomena, but what presents itself as a rupture from them, and what forces us to confront how ultimately opaque the current epidemic of eating disorders remains unless it is linked to the particular situation of women.

The reader will notice that the axes are linked thematically as well as through their convergence in anorexia: e.g., the obsession with control is linked with dual-ism, and the gender/power dynamics discussed implicitly deal with the issue of control (of the feminine) as well. Obviously the notion of a "crystallizing formation" requires further spelling out: e.g., more precise articulation of the relation of cultural axes to each other and elaboration of general principles for the study of culture suggested by this sort of analysis. I have chosen not to undertake this project within this essay, however, but to reserve it for a more extended treatment of the relationship between psychopathology and culture. The inevitable complexity of such a theoretical discussion would divert from the concrete analysis that is the focus of the essay.

17. Michel Foucault, *The History of Sexuality*, vol. 1 (New York: Vintage Books, 1980), p. 155.

18. Ibid., pp. 47–48.

19. Hubert L. Dreyfus and Paul Rabinow, *Michel Foucault: Beyond Structuralism and Hermeneutics* (Chicago: University of Chicago Press, 1983), p. 112.

20. Foucault, *History of Sexuality*, p. 95.

21. Michel Foucault, *Discipline and Punish* (New York: Vintage Books, 1979), p. 26.

22. Plato, *Phaedo*, in *The Dialogues of Plato*, trans. Benjamin Jowett, 4th ed. rev. (Oxford: Clarendon Press, 1953), 83d.

23. St. Augustine, *The Confessions*, trans. R. S. Pine-Coffin (Middlesex, U.K.: Penguin Books, 1961), p. 164.

24. *Phaedo*, 81d.

25. *Phaedo*, 66c. For Descartes on the body as a hindrance to knowledge, see *Conversations with Burman*, trans. John Cottingham (Oxford: Clarendon Press, 1976), p. 8, and *Passions of the Soul* in *Philosophical Works of Descartes*, trans. Elizabeth Haldane and G. R. T. Ross (Cambridge: Cambridge University Press, 1969), Vol. 1, p. 353.

26. *Phaedo*, 80a.

27. Indeed, the Cartesian "rules for the direction of the mind," as carried out in the *Meditations* especially, are actually rules for the transcendence of the body—its passions, its senses, the residue of "infantile prejudices" of judgment lingering from that earlier time when we were "immersed" in body and bodily sensations.

28. Alan Watts, *Nature, Man and Woman* (New York: Vintage, 1970), p. 145.

29. Entry in student journal, 1984.

30. Augustine, *Confessions*, p. 164.

31. Entry in student journal, 1984.

32. Aimée Liu, *Solitaire* (New York: Harper and Row 1979), p. 141 (cited parenthetically in the text as *Solitaire*).

33. Jennifer Woods, "I Was Starving Myself to Death," *Mademoiselle*, May 1981, p. 200.

34. Why they should emerge with such clarity in the twentieth century and through the voice of the anorexic is a question answered, in part, by the following two axes.

35. Augustine, *Confessions*, p. 165.

36. Entry in student journal, 1983.

37. Woods, "Starving Myself," p. 242.

38. "I equated gaining weight with happiness, contentment, then slothfulness, then atrophy, then death." (From case notes of Binnie Klein, MSW, to whom I am grateful for having provided parts of a transcript of her work with an anorexic patient.) See also Binswanger, "The Case of Ellen West," p. 343.

39. Klein, case notes.

40. Cherry Boone O'Neill, *Starving for Attention* (New York: Dell, 1982), p. 131.

41. Ibid., p. 49.

42. A Minnesota study of high school students determined that one in every ten anorexics was a victim of sexual abuse. Comments by and informal discussion with therapists at the Third Annual Conference for the Study of Anorexia and Bulimia bear these findings out; therapist after therapist remarked on the high incidence of early sexual violence and incest in anorexic patients.

43. Bruch, *The Golden Cage*, p. 73. The same is not true of bulimic anorexics, who tend to be sexually active (Garfinkel and Garner, *Anorexia Nervosa*, p. 41). Bulimic anorexics, as seems symbolized by the binge/purge cycle itself, stand in a somewhat more ambivalent relationship to their hungers than do abstinent anorexics.

44. Liu, *Solitaire*, p. 46. In one study of female anorexics, 88% of the subjects questioned reported that they lost weight because they "liked the feeling of will power

and self-control" (G. R. Leon, "Anorexia Nervosa: The Question of Treatment Emphasis," in M. Rosenbaum, C. M. Franks, and Y. Jaffe, eds., *Perspectives on Behavior Therapy in the Eighties* [New York: Springer, 1983], pp. 363–77). For an insightful and stimulating discussion of the contemporary conception of health as linked to self-control, discipline, and self-denial, see Robert Crawford, "A Cultural Account of 'Health'—Self-Control, Release, and the Social Body," in John B. McKinlay, ed., *Issues in the Political Economy of Health Care* (New York: Tavistock, 1984).

45. Smith, "The New Puritans," p. 24.

46. Entry in student journal, 1984.

47. Entry in student journal, 1984.

48. Trix Rosen, *Strong and Sexy* (New York: Putnam, 1983), p. 108.

49. Ibid., pp. 62, 14, 47, 48.

50. Smith, "The New Puritans," pp. 27, 26.

51. Rosen, *Strong and Sexy*, pp. 61–62.

52. Ibid., p. 72.

53. Ibid., p. 61. This fantasy is not limited to female bodybuilders. John Travolta describes his experience training for *Staying Alive:* "[It] taught me incredible things about the body . . . how it can be reshaped so you can make yourself over entirely, creating an entirely new you. I now look at bodies almost like pieces of clay that can be molded." ("Travolta: 'You really can make yourself over,' " *Syracuse Herald*, Jan. 13, 1985.)

54. Smith, "The New Puritans," p. 29.

55. Durk Pearson and Sandy Shaw, *Life Extension* (New York: Warner, 1982), p. 15.

56. Sidney Journard and Paul Secord, "Body Cathexis and the Ideal Female Figure," *Journal of Abnormal and Social Psychology* 50: 243–46; Orland Wooley, Susan Wooley, and Sue Dyrenforth, "Obesity and Women—A Neglected Feminist Topic," *Women's Studies Institute Quarterly* 2(1979):81–92. Student journals and informal conversations with women students certainly have borne this out. See also Garfinkel and Garner, *Anorexia Nervosa*, pp. 110–15.

57. "Feeling Fat in a Thin Society," *Glamour*, February 1984, p. 198.

58. The same trend is obvious when the measurements of Miss America winners are compared over the last fifty years (see Garfinkel and Garner, *Anorexia Nervosa*, p. 107). Recently, there is some evidence that this tide is turning, and that a more solid, muscular, and athletic style is emerging as the latest fashion tyranny.

59. Entry in student journal, 1984.

60. This is one striking difference between the abstinent anorexic and bulimic anorexic: In the binge-and-vomit cycle, the hungering female self refuses to be annihilated, is in constant protest (to the great horror, of course, of the male self, who must negate every indulgence with a cleansing purge).

61. Entry in student journal, 1983.

62. Entry in student journal, 1983.

63. Bruch, *The Golden Cage*, p. 72; Bruch, *Eating Disorders*, p. 277. Others have fantasies of androgyny: "I want to go to a party and for everyone to look at me and for no one to know whether I was the most beautiful slender woman or handsome young man" (as reported by therapist April Benson, panel discussion, "New Perspectives on Female Development," Third Annual Conference of the Center for the Study of Anorexia and Bulimia, New York, 1984.)

64. See, for example, Levenkron's case studies; O'Neill, *Starving for Attention*, p. 107; Susie Ohrbach, *Fat is a Feminist Issue* (New York: Berkley, 1978), pp. 174–75.

65. Klein, case study.

66. See, among many other works on this subject, Barbara Ehrenreich and Deirdre English, *For Her Own Good* (Garden City, N.Y.: Doubleday, 1979), pp. 1–29.

67. See Martha Vicinus, ed., *Suffer and Be Still* (Bloomington: Indiana University Press, 1972), pp. x–xi.

68. Ernest Jones, *Sigmund Freud: Life and Work* (London: Hogarth Press, 1956), vol. 1, p. 193.

69. On the nineteenth-century epidemic of female invalidism and hysteria, see Ehrenreich and English, *For Her Own Good;* Carroll Smith-Rosenberg, "The Hysterical Woman: Sex Roles and Conflict in Nineteenth-Century America," *Social Research* 39, no. 4 (Winter 1972): 652–78; Ann Douglas Wood, "The 'Fashionable Diseases': Women's Complaints and Their Treatment in Nineteenth Century America," *Journal of Interdisciplinary History*, 4 (Summer 1973): 25–52.

70. Ehrenreich and English, *For Her Own Good*, pp. 2, 102.

71. Sigmund Freud and Joseph Breuer, *Studies on Hysteria* (New York: Avon, 1966), p. 311.

72. Ibid., p. 141; see also p. 202.

73. See especially ibid., pp. 76 (Anna O.), 277, 284.

74. Marjorie Rosen, *Popcorn Venus* (New York: Avon, 1973).

75. Lois Banner, *American Beauty* (Chicago: University of Chicago Press, 1983), pp. 283–85. Christian Dior's enormously popular full skirts and cinch-waists, as Banner points out, are strikingly reminiscent of Victorian modes of dress.

76. On the protest dimension in anorexia, see Chernin, *The Obsession*, pp. 102–3; Seidenberg and DeCrow, *Women Who Marry Houses*, pp. 88–97; Bruch, *The Golden Cage*, p. 58; Ohrbach, *Hunger Strike*, pp. 97–115. For an examination of the connections between hysteria, agoraphobia, and anorexia, see Susan Bordo, "The Body and the Reproduction of Femininity," in Alison Jaggar and Susan Bordo, eds., *Gender/Body/Knowledge: Feminist Reconstructions of Being and Knowing* (New Brunswick, N.J.: Rutgers University Press, 1988).

77. D. H. Lawrence, *Sons and Lovers* (New York: Viking, 1958), p. 257.

78. This experience of oneself as "too much" may be more or less emphatic, depending on variables such as race, religion, socioeconomic class, sexual orientation, etc. Eichenbaum and Ohrbach *(Understanding Women: A Feminist Psychoanalytic Approach)* emphasize, however, how frequently their clinic patients, non-anorexic as well as anorexic, "talk about their needs with contempt, humiliation, and shame. They feel exposed and childish, greedy and insatiable" (p. 49). Eichenbaum and Ohrbach trace such feelings, moreover, to infantile experiences that are characteristic of all female development, given a division of labor within which women are the emotional nurturers and physical caretakers of family life. Briefly (and this sketch cannot begin to do justice to their rich and complex analysis): mothers unwittingly communicate to their daughters that feminine needs are excessive, bad, and must be contained. The mother will do this out of a sense that her daughter will have to learn this lesson in order to become properly socialized into the traditional female role of caring for others— of feeding others, rather than feeding the self—and also because of an unconscious identification with her daughter, who reminds the mother of the "hungry, needy little girl" in herself, denied and repressed through the mother's *own* "education" in being female: "Mother comes to be frightened by her daughter's free expression of her needs, and unconsciously acts toward her infant daughter in the same way she acts internally toward the little-girl part of herself. In some ways the little daughter becomes an external representation of that part of herself that she has come to dislike and deny. The complex of emotions that results from her own deprivation

through childhood and adult life is both directed inward in the struggle to negate the little-girl part of herself and projected outward onto her daughter" (p. 44). Despite a real desire to be totally responsive toward her daughter's emotional needs, the mother's own anxiety limits her capacity to respond. The contradictory messages she sends out convey to the little girl "the idea that to get love and approval she must show a particular side of herself. She must hide her emotional cravings, her disappointments and her angers, her fighting spirit. . . . She comes to feel that there must be something wrong with who she really is, which in turn must mean that there is something wrong with what she needs and what she wants. . . . This soon translates into feeling unworthy and hesitant about pursuing her impulses" (pp. 48–49). Once she has grown up, of course, these feelings are reinforced by cultural ideology, further social "training" in femininity, and the likelihood that the men in her life will regard her as "too much" as well, having been schooled by their own training in masculine detachment and autonomy.

(With boys, who do not stir up such intense identifications in the mother and who she knows, moreover, will grow up into a world that will meet their emotional needs [i.e., the son will eventually grow up to be looked after by his future wife, well-trained in the feminine arts of care], mothers feel much less ambivalent about the satisfaction of needs, and behave much more consistently in their nurturing. Boys therefore grow up, according to Eichenbaum and Ohrbach, with an experience of their needs as legitimate, appropriate, worthy of fulfillment.)

The male experience of the "woman-as-too-much" has been developmentally explored, as well, in Dorothy Dinnerstein's much-discussed *Mermaid and the Minotaur* (New York: Harper and Row, 1970). Dinnerstein argues that it is the woman's capacity to call up memories of helpless infancy, primitive wishes of "unqualified access" to the mother's body, and "the terrifying erotic independence of every baby's mother" (p. 62) that is responsible for the male fear of what he experiences as "the uncontrollable erotic rhythms" of the woman. Female impulses, a reminder of the autonomy of the mother, always appear on some level as a threatening limitation against his own. This gives rise to a "deep fantasy resentment" of female impulsivity (p. 59) and, on the cultural level, "archetypal nightmare visions of the insatiable female" (p. 62).

79. Quoted in Brian Easlea, *Witch-Hunting, Magic and the New Philosophy* (Atlantic Highlands, N.J.: Humanities Press, 1980), p. 242.
80. See Peggy Reeve Sanday, *Female Power and Male Dominance* (Cambridge: Cambridge University Press, 1981), pp. 172–84.
81. Easlea, *Witch-Hunting*, p. 8.
82. Peter Gay, *The Bourgeois Experience*, vol. 1, *Education of the Senses* (New York: Oxford University Press, 1984), pp. 197–201, 207.
83. Ehrenreich and English, *For Her Own Good*, p. 124.
84. Banner, *American Beauty*, pp. 86–105, 149–50. It is significant that these efforts failed, in large part, because of their association with the woman's rights movement. Trousers, such as those proposed by Amelia Bloomer, were considered a particular badge of depravity and aggressiveness, the *New York Herald* predicting that bloomer women would end up in "lunatic asylums or perchance in the state prison" (p. 96).
85. Amaury deRiencourt, *Sex and Power in History* (New York: David McKay, 1974), p. 319. The metaphorical dimension here is as striking as the functional, and it is a characteristic feature of female fashion: the dominant styles always decree, to one degree or another, that women *should not take up too much space*, that the territory we occupy should be limited. This is as true of cinch-belts as it is of foot-binding.

86. Quoted in deRiencourt, *Sex and Power in History*, p. 319.
87. Christy Ferguson, "Images of the Body: Victorian England" (philosophy research project, LeMoyne College, 1983).
88. Quoted in E. M. Sigsworth and T. J. Wyke, "A Study of Victorian Prostitution and Venereal Disease," in Vicinus, *Suffer and Be Still*, p. 82.
89. See Kate Millett, "The Debate Over Women: Ruskin vs. Mill," and Helen E. Roberts, "The Painter's View of Women in the First Twenty-five Years of Victoria's Reign," in Vicinus, *Suffer and Be Still*.
90. Gay, *Education of the Senses*, p. 197.
91. Vicinus, *Suffer and Be Still*, p. 123.
92. Ibid., p. x.
93. Lasch, *The Culture of Narcissism*, p. 343.
94. Charles Gaines and George Butler, "Iron Sisters," *Psychology Today*, November 1983, p. 67.
95. Some disquieting connections can be drawn, as well, between the anorexic and the flapper, who, according to Banner, *American Beauty*, expressed her sensuality "not through eroticism but through constant vibrant movement." The quality that marked the sex appeal of the 1920s—the "It" made famous by Clara Bow— was characterized by "vivacity, fearlessness and a basic indifference to men" (p. 279), qualities high on the list of anorexic values.

Kathleen B. Jones

On Authority: Or, Why Women Are Not Entitled to Speak

The standard analysis of authority in modern Western political theory begins with its definition as a set of rules governing political action, issued by those who are entitled to speak. Descriptions of those who act as public authorities, and of the norms and rules that they articulate, generally have excluded females and values associated with the feminine. This seems to be an unexceptional observation. After all, few women have been rulers in any political system of any epoch. But

The author gratefully acknowledges the support of the National Endowment for the Humanities Summer Seminar Program, and the critical comments of Terence Ball, William Connolly, Tom Dumm, Richard Flathman, Jane Jaquette, Kingsley Widmer, and the editors of NOMOS.

what if we argue that the very definition of authority as a set of practices designed to institutionalize social hierarchies lies at the root of the separation of women qua women from the process of "authorizing"?[1] If we argue further that the dichotomy between compassion and authority contributes to the association of the authoritative with a male voice, then the implication is that the segregation of women and the feminine from authority is internally connected to the concept of authority itself. It is this structural implication that I want to explore.

Feminist scholars have argued that the roots of the dichotomy experienced by women between being in authority and being subject to it stem from the separation of public life and political authority from private life and the passions. As a corollary, they claim that the discourse of political theory identifies women with the private sphere and affective life.[2] Since women are excluded from the public realm, they do not learn how to lead others in authoritative ways. They are not originators of orders, or high in the hierarchy of commands, ritualistic or real.

To a certain extent these arguments have merit. Feminist scholars have revealed how the practice of authority depends in many ways on patterns of socialization established in the private sphere, and that these patterns educate women in subordination. They have clarified how conceptual analyses of power have excluded women systematically by rendering female power invisible, either because it is different from male power, or because it is wielded in the private sphere. They have not, however, extended this criticism to the idea of authority. Indeed, all too frequently they have allowed power to stand for authority, despite the fact that political thought has long recognized not only a distinction between power and authority but, at times, a fundamental antithesis.

While building on their work, I will argue that the feminist critique of authority as a specific form of male privilege has not focused enough on the limitations of traditional concepts of authority. When these scholars argue that women have not learned how to be in authority, they accept the adequacy of the concept of authority itself. In contrast, I would suggest that authority currently is conceptualized so that female voices are excluded from it. Following the genealogical method of Michel Foucault, we may see how the dominant discourse on authority silences those forms of expression linked metaphorically and symbolically to "female" speech. It is my claim that this discourse is constructed on the basis of a conceptual myopia that normalizes authority as a disciplinary, commanding gaze.[3] Such a discourse secures authority by opposing it to emotive connectedness or compassion. Authority orders existence through rules. Actions and actors are defined by these rules. Compassion cuts through this orderly universe with feelings that connect us to the specificity and particularity of actions and actors. Authority's rules distance us from the person. Compassion pulls us into a face-to-face encounter with another. If it is legitimate to contend, as Carol Gilligan has in her studies of women's moral development,[4] that women approach ethical dilemmas and make decisions with a fundamentally different language and logic, then the female voice of would-be authority may speak in compassionate tones inaudible to listeners attuned to harsher commands. Hence, in the dominant discourse, much of compassion is taken as nonauthoritative, marginal pleadings for mercy—gestures of the subordinate.

With this issue, we might follow the course of what Foucault has called the project of genealogy. Its purpose is to explore the constraints and discipline involved in traditional constructions of authority. It is meant to be subversive, substantive, in a literal way: it looks below the dominant meanings of texts to consider meanings and knowledge hidden or disqualified. To deconstruct authority is to discover the ways that a particular conceptual framework restricts our knowledge of it. For example, an overemphasis on the "rationality" of authority, i.e., the radical separation of the realm of cognition from the realm of belief and feeling, arbitrarily restricts authority to formal rules. In addition, the logic of defining authority as a system of "conflict resolution" sees decision making less as consensus building and more as a process of adjudicating competing private claims of self-interest. Moreover, since adjudication requires some "surrender of private judgment," traditional notions of authority incorporate an acceptance of an internal conflict between authority and personal autonomy. Finally, the norms that constitute authority as an association of inequality and control are understood to be unmodified by emotive connectedness or compassion. Authority, like judgment, is necessarily hierarchical and dispassionate.

Each of these aspects of authority helps define it as a system of rules for social control within the context of social hierarchies. To the extent that authority is understood to order social behavior, making it predictable and manageable because it is rule-governed, then even those social relationships that seem to operate more arbitrarily—as in the case of parenting and the judgments of juries—gain authority insofar as the actions of those in authoritative positions are explicable in relation to rules. In the Anglo-American tradition, a jury responds with mercy toward a defendant, in the legal sense, because the defendant's behavior fits the category of excuses for crimes established by statutory and case law. Or they excuse a particular defendant because the individual lacks the mental capacity to behave in conformity with the law, also as defined by statutory and case law.[5] Even parenting is a relationship of authority to the extent that the parent's judgments have more than mere compulsion or whim to rationalize them. Consider the case of the state operating as protector and legitimate authority *in loco parentis* in instances where the actual parents have reduced their authoritative claims to rule over the child to power relations, as in cases of child abuse.

But this definition of authority as rules normalizes an androcentric view of authority. Although it comes to be associated with systems of rule that are themselves genderless, this form of sociality is at least arguably male. "Male hegemony in the culture," writes Jessica Benjamin, "is expressed by the generalization of rationality and the exclusion of nurturance, the triumph of individualistic, instrumental values in all forms of social interaction."[6] Even when the attempt to make authority compatible with agency modifies this view, the ideal of autonomy and participation in rational discourse excludes certain forms of expression, linked metaphorically and symbolically to "female" speech, from those which make authority coherent. For example, sociolinguists recently have argued that female patterns of speech reveal a different expressiveness than do male patterns. Rhythms, nuance, emphasis, and assertiveness, in tone and syntax, appear to vary with gender. Nevertheless, we define the masculine mode of self-assured, self-assertive, unqualified declarativeness as the model of authoritative speech. "Female" hesitancy and other-oriented language patterns, considered as the marks of uncertainty or confusion, are derogated.[7] Consequently, we purchase the distinction between authority, coercion, and persuasion at the expense of recognizing certain dimensions of human action and speech that would make authority more humane, although more ambiguous.

Following Thomas Hobbes, the standard view of authority is of a mode of discourse that gives expression to rank, order, definition, and distinction, and hides dimensions of human reality that disorient and disturb. The problem here is to consider the ways that the subject of authority is constituted so that "female" bodies, gestures, and behaviors are hidden by authority's gaze.[8] Can it be that the exclusion of the "female" from the practice of authority contributes to the tendency to identify authority with rationalized compulsion?

In Western political philosophy it is common to regard authority as a distinctive type of social control or influence.[9] Sometimes the differentiation between authority and force is not clear.[10] But generally, theorists have attempted to distinguish authority as a peculiar form of getting people to obey social prescriptions short of compulsion.[11]

Most theorists of authority also would agree that some sort of surrender of private judgment—at least in the weak sense of submitting to the judgment of another without making conduct dependent on one's assessment of the merits of the command—is entailed in any concept of authority.[12] For them, recognition of authority is sufficient for accepting the prescriptions produced by authority systems. Put differently, if authority is defined as a "mutually recognized normative relationship giving the one the right to command or speak and the other the duty to obey,"[13] then any justification of authority depends only on clarification of the criteria whereby authority is recognized in the first place. One does not have to be persuaded to particular obedience to those in authority, nor is one coerced into obeying. One obeys those in authority because they are, in general, entitled to obedience.

This notion of authority seems to separate the obligation to obey from any judgment about the substantive merits of specific acts one is required to perform.[14] But the particular act of recognition that establishes authority in the first place can neither originally nor over time be dissociated from the network of common beliefs that constitutes the identity of those in authority, or those subject to it. Although many political theorists concede that communal beliefs establish the criteria for recognizing authority originally, they contend that the idea of authority requires that subjects suspend disbelief once a leader's right to rule is established. But this conceptual stress on the rationality of deferential obedience hides the ambiguous and contentious ground out of which obedience springs. The idea of authority as traditional hierarchy makes sense so long as we accept on faith that the need for an ordered, efficient social system takes precedence over any other form of social organization. But this may be a variable condition. The identification of authority with some form of hierarchy is based, although not intentionally, on what Carol Gilligan has called a peculiarly male approach to decision making: the willingness to sacrifice relations to others in the face of established rules; or, to put it differently, to exchange the uncertainty of human relationship for the certainty of rules. It may be interesting to consider the ways that a "female" stress on relationship over rules or abstract rights modifies the ways that authority is constituted and practiced.

Recall that in conventional rule-oriented definitions, the need for authority is made identical with the need for some hierarchical system of decision making that defines social cooperation within the context of necessarily stratified relations. To institutionalize authority is to institutionalize vertical hierarchies of differential rights, privileges, and duties in order to facilitate the accomplishment of some common project. This conception of authority depends upon an instrumentalist view of political life and political action. Heavily influenced by some variant of the Hobbesian view of human nature ("the war of all against all"), authority, from this perspective, stabilizes social interaction, marking human action by tolerable, rule-governed levels of sociality. Since, in Hobbes's view, "every man has a right to every thing," human social behavior is intrinsically bellicose and, ironically, in the state of nature, it appears inherently antisocial. Authority enables groups of individuals, necessarily in conflict with one another, to resolve their conflicts by appealing to the rules that specify priorities of rights. The rules of authority systems provide sanctuary from the dangers of social intercourse. Hobbes's metaphor, in *Leviathan*, of the Sovereign as an artificial man and his definition of the commonwealth as a society created by convention become literal descriptions of the perspective on community reflected in nominalist discourse on authority. The community *is* an artifice: a mask of rules and roles that covers the face of *real* humanity—the autonomous Self.

This instrumental view of human community, and the identification of authority with hierarchy, may be based on peculiarities of masculine need. In her study of the psychodynamics of sex roles in modern Western societies, Dorothy Dinnerstein has suggested that the sexual division of roles in the family, and the consequent fact that women monopolize early child rearing, explain the identification of authority with male-dominated systems of rule. Dinnerstein argues that "our earliest and profoundest prototype of absolute power" occurs in infancy. This power is wielded virtually exclusively by the female sex through their monopolization of early child care, making later male dominion "an inexorable emotional necessity."[15] The power of the mother is experienced as absolute because it is she who both satisfies our deepest needs for comfort and security and stirs our deepest fears of rejection and separation. It is the memory of the mother's body that reawakens a primordial desire that Freud called the "oceanic feeling," a desire to be in blissful union with the world, but which our existence as mortal, individual selves requires that we overcome. Both sexes, although with different consequences, then accept paternal authority as a model for ruling the world because, under prevailing social conditions, it provides sanctuary from maternal authority.[16]

In a related argument, Nancy Chodorow uses this paradigm to analyze the structuring of patterns of male and female personality characteristics.

She argues that current patterns of child rearing in Western industrial society—women's mothering occurs in the context of the isolated nuclear family—create specific personality types and structure gender-differentiated affective patterns. Nurturing activities become normatively female, and instrumental activities become normatively male. The consequence is that for women, intimacy and relation to others become part of the development of the female self. For men, the self is defined in isolation from others, with the consequence that intimacy is more fundamentally threatening to the male.[17]

Both of these accounts point to the importance of the meaning of the memory of the mother—the recognition of woman's body and gestures through the remembered fear of rejection—in the reading of the signs of authority. Why authority means rules may be connected to the sense of instability and discontinuity "most intimately related to our bodies and our everyday behavior."[18] But because this sense of instability is structured differentially for men and women, acceptance of the idea of authority as rules may be more consonant with a male orientation to the world.

Recent feminist criticism has returned to the concept of gender differences to argue, from a nonessentialist stance, that the history of women's experiences and women's voices about those experiences leads to the development of alternative ways of knowing and seeing.[19] If we are searching for a model that moves away from defining authority exclusively as a form of problem solving, and toward a metaphor that emphasizes that authority is a contextual, relational process of communication and connection, then it may be that examining "female" experience will provide us with such an alternative. I would like to consider the ways that the role of nurturing—a role not necessarily gender-defined, but one that has been associated historically with women—provides such a model.[20]

Carol Gilligan's work on women's moral development offers some suggestive, though underdeveloped, hypotheses about how to proceed. Commenting on her interpretation of the ways females reach decisions about complex moral dilemmas compared with males, and on the prevalence of images of relationship in girls' fantasies about dangerous situations, Gilligan remarks that women appear to perceive the fracture of human connections as violent, whereas men see connection itself as threatening. Since women seem to tie the rupture of relationship to aggression, "then the activities of care, as their fantasies suggest, are the activities that make the world safe, by avoiding isolation and preventing aggression rather than by seeking rules to limit its extent."[21] For men, rule-bound situations, with clear boundaries and limits to aggressiveness, are safe: whereas for women, it is precisely this inability to connect, or to affiliate, that represents the dominance of aggression. If we now accept the idea, as indicated earlier, that authority is opposed to power and domination, then it would appear that what constitutes authority for women is exactly what is most feared by men: sustained connections, or what Freud called the altruistic urge for union in relationship to others.[22]

Sophocles' *Antigone* can be read as a commentary on this ethic of care as authority. Upon hearing of Antigone's willful defiance of his edict forbidding the burial of Polyneices, Creon explains his condemnation of her to Haemon, his son: "The man the state has put in place must have obedient hearing to his least command when it is right, and even when it's not."[23] Haemon replies that the community speaks its discontent with Creon's judgment, though Creon's "presence frightens any common man from saying things [Creon] would not care to hear." Creon denies that he should be moved by the speech of his subjects or his son: "At my age I'm to school my mind by his? . . . This boy instructor is my master, then? . . . Is the town to tell me how I ought to rule? . . . Am I to rule by other mind than mine?"[24] But Haemon replies that "no city is the property of a single man," and warns that Creon wishes to speak but never wishes to hear.[25] Creon's insistence that his commands be heard is countered by Haemon's insistence that speech is communicative dialogue, not monologue. Antigone's actions speak compellingly to the community because they remain connected to the fabric of its life. Her being silenced by the authority of the state reminds us of what connections are lost in Creon's (male) view of authority: Antigone was burying the dead.

Contrary to the restricted understanding of authority as contingent on conflicting individual (and primarily male) wills, authority is seen here as the construction of a meaningful world. Apart from the problem solving that authority permits, its essence is the vitalizing of community itself. As Hannah Arendt reminds us, authority is derived, etymologically, from the verb *augere*, "to augment."[26] Authority adds meaning to human action by connecting that action to a realm of value and to justifications for action beyond criteria of efficiency or feasibility. If we define authority as expressing and enabling political action in community—interaction among equals—then authority would be represented as a horizontal rather than a vertical relationship and as male/female rather than primarily male.

This alternative view accepts authority as an essential feature of human social behavior because that behavior is a type of interaction that involves "speech, communication, and mutual understanding."[27] Since being in community is given ontological priority, then authority as a system of rules for securing private rights, structuring individual obligations, or protecting autonomy through reciprocal duties gives way to authority as a way of cohering and sustaining connectedness. Much of the fabric of communal connectedness is lost in the male-rule, instrumental model. In this female perspective, the quest for authority becomes the search for contexts of care that do not deteriorate into mechanisms of blind loyalty.

Gilligan notes that female caring traces a path of "deprivation followed by enhancement in which connection, though leading through separation, is in the end maintained or restored." The female self in connection with others "appears neither stranded in isolation screaming for help nor lost in fusion with the entire world as a whole, but bound in an indissoluble mode of relationship that is observably different but hard to describe."[28] Some myths contain the dramatic-poetic discourse on authority as the augmentation of community that is obscured in the rule-dominant mode. For example, this pattern emerges clearly in the Demeter-Persephone myth. Persephone, daughter of Demeter, while playing in the fields one day, admires the narcissus. As she picks it, the earth opens, and Persephone disappears into the underworld. Angered at the loss of her daughter, Demeter, goddess of agriculture, refuses to allow the fields to grow until she is returned. The earth lies fallow until Zeus agrees to release Persephone from his brother Hades' control. Once Persephone is reunited with Demeter, the fields again are productive. But Persephone is required, as part of the agreement between Zeus and Demeter, to return annually to the underworld. And so, in Greek myth, is the origin of the seasons explained.

In interpreting this myth, David McClelland argues that it suggests an alternate interpretation of power, and, I would add, of authority. Whereas power is often conceptualized as the willful assertion of control over another—the power of taking—this "female" myth, which invokes "interdependence, building up resources, and giving," contains different understandings of the resources of power.[29] Demeter's authority seems to stand in a more literal relationship to the activity of augmenting that authority connoted originally. Her augmentation of the life of the world is born of the restoration, albeit on a constantly changing basis, of her intimate connection with her daughter.

What remains troubling about the idea of authority as an augmentation is that we are aware that every search for harmonious connectedness contains choices and, therefore, losses and limits. Antigone loses her life, Demeter loses her relationship to her daughter, and Persephone is limited by the requirement that she regularly return to the underworld. We perceive these limits as threats to the self and fear the authority that constructs them. In part this is because the dominant notion of autonomy is a disembodied one that abstracts human will and agency from the meaning of living as mortals in a world filled with those who are different from us. The refusal to consider the internal connection between authority and caring leads us to search for a spaceless and timeless order through rules and, paradoxically, to the embrace of domination and bondage to those authorities whom we want most to reject.[30]

The inability to reconcile authority with human agency is the result, in part, of a conception of the self in isolation from others as opposed to a self in connection with others. Authority does not have to be conceptualized in opposition to personal autonomy so long as autonomy does not deny the critical function of nurturance and its relation to the humanization of authority. Richard Sennett notes that the dominant forms of authority in our lives are destructive precisely because they lack nurturance and compassion. These emotions are what enable us to "express a full awareness of one another," and, consequently, "to express the moral and human meaning of the institutions in which we live."[31] It is out of this emotive connectedness to others that genuine authority as an augmentation of the texture of daily life emerges.

But there may be reasons to fear the establishment of compassionate authority. In *On Revolution* Hannah Arendt argued that it was the substitution of compassion for the masses by authoritative decision making that accounted for the destructiveness and violence of revolutionary authority. Virtue, Arendt contended, can be embodied in lasting institutions: compassion cannot. Virtue facilitates political action. It operates in the sphere of choice and knows the limits of human existence. Compassion precludes political action. It knows only force and violence. By overwhelming the political world with "the cares and worries which actually [belong] to the household" compassion makes a lawful civil society impossible. It substitutes power for authority, and will—the force of the multitude—for consent, or the considered opinion of several, particular interests. If virtue is rational and its mode of expression is argumentative speech or persuasion, compassion speaks only the language of emotive gestures. Its presence in the political realm triggers the release of the "force of delirious rage."[32] To base authority on compassion makes the idea that violence is a legitimate form of conflict resolution compelling.

To make compassion the foundation of authority would permit an "irresistible and anonymous stream of violence [to replace] the free and deliberate action of men."[33]

But is it possible to reconcile freedom and rational discourse with compassion, and still distinguish political authority from compulsion? What Arendt translates as the "barbarian vice of effeminacy" and rejects as a principle of authority may provide an important way to make authority more compatible with autonomy.

In Arendt's terms, human understanding is understanding the limitedness of human action in the world. It is living in a world in which one has to make choices and suffer the consequences. But authority seems to lift one beyond one's emotions, beyond "merely" private, "merely" personal feelings. Authority is embodied in the judge who orders the sentence of death despite sympathy for the accused. It is Arendt's interpretation of Captain Vere in Herman Melville's *Billy Budd* that best represents her view here. Arendt argues that Vere must condemn Budd, even though he knows that Budd is innocent in some larger sense of the term. Authority cannot be modified by compassion in this instance. To allow compassion to rule would be to allow unreflective immediate action to be substituted for the processes of persuasion, negotiation, and compromise. It would substitute faith for reason.[34]

Budd cannot defend himself. He lacks the capacity for predictive or argumentative speech. Compassion, says Arendt, "speaks only to the extent that it has to reply directly to the sheer expressionist sound and gesture through which suffering becomes audible and visible in the world."[35] And it is the very directness of the compassionate response, according to Arendt, that removes it from the realm of politics, and hence the realm of lasting institutions.

But Vere's response to Budd is not unmediated, as Arendt claims. Nor is his compassion for Budd the result merely of the "belief" in Budd's innocence. Both he and his officers know that Budd is innocent since Budd "purposed neither mutiny nor homicide."[36] Most importantly, Vere's response to Budd is mediated by his relationship to Budd as a father to a son. Although Arendt is correct that this sort of connection, born of compassion and caring, is particularized, it is not without its own rules of recognition. Vere's caring for Billy Budd provides him with the knowledge that the law he is required to apply is more barbaric than the act it thereby punishes. But the discourse of authority subjugates this knowledge through an imperious gaze that focuses attention on disembodied agents whose intentions are read by the effects of their acts.

As an ironic commentary on Arendt's interpretation that following the rule of law secures the public space for rational, persuasive discourse, Vere declares that among his reasons for condemning Billy is that the people, "long molded by arbitrary discipline, have not the kind of intelligent responsiveness that might qualify them to comprehend and discriminate."[37] Finally, too, the death of Billy, while ostensibly carrying out the "measured forms" of politics, achieves no positive, nurturing, political value.

The importance of connecting compassion and authority is that it reminds us that the order authority imposes "does not correspond to the world in all its complexity."[38] Compassion can respond to the gesture of those who are inarticulate, thereby helping "that which is subordinate to find its own voice and, perhaps, to expand the space in which [the subordinate] can be for itself rather than only for the order."[39] In the compassionate view, Budd's last words are not mere gestures, as Arendt characterizes them. They, like Jesus' embrace of the Grand Inquisitor in *The Brothers Karamazov*, represent acts of resistance to repression, because, as Sennett suggests, they are a response outside the terms of repression.[40]

Without consideration of the meanings of words and gestures outside the realm of past dominant discourse, the logic of any theory of authority as the rational practice of freedom is dubious. Many voices speak to us from different perspectives. This does not make what they communicate "mere" gesture. The rational modes of speech taken to be constitutive of authority exclude certain critical human dimensions, voices, and "interests" from the public realm. Indeed, the structure of authority in the public realm is connected internally to this exclusion. These dimensions, voices, and interests cannot be translated simply into the language of dispassionate, discursive speech. Nevertheless, their expressiveness is essential to understanding the nuances of meaning, and the recognition of what is silenced, by the speech of political actors.

For example, Sara Ruddick describes the ways that the mother's interest in the growth and preservation of her child—an interest oriented toward the particularity of each child's person—leads her to a dramatically different orientation to the child's needs than that required by the culture's imperative of "acceptability." This imperative constrains the mother's attention to the child, a particularized attention with a more ambiguous, flexible set of rules, in favor of regimenting the child to fit the culture's desiderata. From the perspective of "maternal thinking," the raising of girls for self-abnegating roles in our culture, and the raising of boys for military service, is irrational. It violates the mother's interest in protecting the child. But the subordination of this interest in favor of the "rationality" of acceptability makes the mother's "knowledge" of her child's needs appear irrational.[41]

The dominant discourse on authority places strict limits on the publicly expressible, and limits critical reflection about the norms and values that structure "private" life and which affect the melodies of public speech.[42] By rejecting the ambiguities that our feelings introduce, we reject a mode of compassionate authority that would remind us that the construction of a harmonious world is always an "ambiguous achievement: it excludes and denigrates that which does not fit into its confines."[43] Nevertheless, accepting the concept of compassionate authority does not permit one to use it as a cover for maudlin sentimentality. Nor does it permit one to so overbroaden the concept of authority as to render it meaningless. The difficult task of distinguishing authority in this looser sense from other types of political action remains. Compassion has the potential for humanizing authority. If women do not speak authoritatively, perhaps their hesitancy reveals the ambiguity, and the choices, behind all rule systems. By reminding us of this ambiguity, the voice and gesture of compassion shocks us into a memory of what has been hidden by the ordered discourse of authority.

Notes

1. Initially this exclusion extended to the denial that even individual women could enter into the establishment of the "social contract." Even as liberalism was modified to include more and more persons, the exclusion of specific forms of "authorizing" remained gender-specific. See Teresa Brennan and Carole Pateman, "Mere Auxiliaries to the Commonwealth: Women and the Origins of Liberalism," *Political Studies* 27 (1978):191; and Irene Diamond and Nancy Hartsock, "Beyond Interests in Politics: A Comment on Virginia Sapiro's 'When Are Interests Interesting? The Problem of the Political Representation of Women,' " *American Political Science Review* 75 (1983):191.

2. See Jean Bethke Elshtain, *Public Man/Private Woman* (Princeton, N.J.: Princeton University Press, 1982); Dorothy Dinnerstein, *The Mermaid and the Minotaur* (New York: Harper and Row, 1976); Nancy Chodorow, *The Reproduction of Mothering* (Berkeley: University of California Press, 1978); and Susan Okin, *Women in Western Political Thought* (Princeton, N.J.: Princeton University Press, 1979).

3. See Michel Foucault, *Power/Knowledge: Selected Interviews and Other Writings, 1972–1977,* ed. Colin Gordon (New York: Pantheon, 1980), especially chapters 6 and 8. See also E. Ann Kaplan, "Is the Gaze Male?" in Ann Snitow et al., eds., *Powers of Desire: The Politics of Sexuality* (New York: Monthly Review Press, 1983), pp. 309–27.

4. Carol Gilligan, *In a Different Voice* (Cambridge, Mass.: Harvard University Press, 1982).

5. See the general discussion of excuse and justification in law in George Fletcher, *Rethinking Criminal Law* (Boston: Little, Brown, 1978), and "The Individualization of Excuse," *Southern California Law Review* 47 (1974): 1269–1304. See also my discussions of the implications of this for a theory of criminal responsibility in "The Irony of the Insanity Plea: A Theory of Relativity," *Journal of Psychiatry and Law* (Fall 1982): 285–308.

6. Jessica Benjamin, "Master and Slave: The Fantasy of Erotic Domination," in Snitow, *Powers of Desire*, p. 295.

7. See Ivan Illich's review of research on gendered speech in his *Gender* (New York: Pantheon, 1982), pp. 132–39.

8. I am not using the term "female" only in the biological sense. I mean to suggest that the social construction of femaleness has contributed to the reading of the meaning of female bodies, etc., in ways that are hidden by the language of authority, and seem to be irrelevant to it.

9. R. S. Peters, "Authority," in Anthony Quinton, ed., *Political Philosophy* (Oxford: Oxford University Press, 1967); Richard B. Friedman, "On the Concept of Authority in Political Philosophy," in Richard Flathman, ed., *Concepts in Social and Political Philosophy* (New York: Macmillan, 1973); and R. F. Kahn, "A Note on the Concept of Authority," in Gehan Wijeyewardene, ed., *Leadership and Authority* (Singapore: University of Malaya Press, 1968).

10. Friedman, "On the Concept of Authority," p. 127.

11. Hannah Arendt is a theorist who dissents from the classification of authority as a subset of what Max Weber called imperative coordination. But the degree to which her model of authority succeeds in breaking out of the classification of authority as a type of hierarchical relationship will be examined below.

12. See Friedman, "On the Concept of Authority," p. 127.

13. Ibid., p. 134.

14. See Joseph Raz, *Practical Reasons and Norms* (London: Hutchinson, 1975), for an extreme formulation of the separation of moral judgments and the obligation to obey.

15. Dinnerstein, *The Mermaid and the Minotaur*, pp. 166, 177.

16. Ibid., p. 176.

17. Chodorow, *The Reproduction of Mothering*, pp. 180–81.

18. Foucault, *Power/Knowledge*, p. 80.

19. See Evelyn Fox Keller, *Gender and Science* (Cambridge: Harvard University Press, 1985), Carol MacMillan, *Women, Reason, and Nature* (Princeton, N.J.: Princeton University Press, 1982), and Sara Ruddick, "Maternal Thinking," in Joyce Trebilcot, ed., *Mothering: Essays in Feminist Theory* (Totowa, N.J.: Rowman and Allanheld, 1984).

20. Jean Elshtain, "Antigone's Daughters," *democracy* 2 (1982): 51.

21. Gilligan, *In a Different Voice* p. 43.

22. At this juncture it must be reiterated that the apparently cavalier use of "women" and "men" in no way is meant to imply derivation from biology or to ignore real differences for men and women of different races, classes, etc., as well as individual differences.

23. Sophocles, *Antigone*, in David Grene and Richmond Lattimore, eds., *Greek Tragedies* (Chicago: University of Chicago Press, 1960), vol. I, p. 204.

24. Ibid., p. 206.

25. Ibid.

26. Hannah Arendt, "What Is Authority?" in Arendt, *Between Past and Future* (New York: Viking Press, 1961), p. 121.
27. Friedman, "On the Concept of Authority," pp. 98–99.
28. Gilligan, *In a Different Voice*, pp. 48, 47.
29. David McClelland, *Power: The Inner Experience* (New York: Irvington, 1975), pp. 96–99.
30. See Richard Sennett's discussion in *Authority* (New York: Vintage, 1981).
31. Ibid., p. 6.
32. Hannah Arendt, *On Revolution* (New York: Viking Press, 1963), pp. 86, 107.
33. Ibid., p. 109.
34. Ibid., p. 82.
35. Ibid.
36. Herman Melville, *Billy Budd and Other Tales* (New York: Signet, 1961), p. 70.
37. Ibid., pp. 68–69.
38. William Connolly, "Modern Authority and Ambiguity" (Amherst: University of Massachusetts, unpublished manuscript, 1984), p. 21.
39. Ibid., p. 22.
40. Sennett, *Authority*, p. 198. See also my discussion of George Orwell's images of women, in "Women, Compassion and Rationality: Rethinking the Power/Authority Distinction," *Papers in Comparative Studies* 4 (1985): 81–90.
41. Ruddick, "Maternal Thinking."
42. For an interesting discussion of the consequent reduction of the meaning of human communication, see Oliver Sacks's exploration of the world of "idiots savants" in "The Twins," *New York Review of Books* 32 (1985): 16–20.
43. Connolly, p. 18.

Mary Lydon

Foucault and Feminism: A Romance of Many Dimensions

> I hate that confession when I used to go to Father Corrigan
> he touched me father and what harm if he did where and I
> said on the canal bank like a fool but whereabouts on your
> person my child . . .
>
> —*James Joyce*

This vignette, a piece of flotsam surfacing on the flux of Molly Bloom's reminiscences, puts the question of sexuality as raised in *La Volonté de Savoir (The Will to Knowledge)*[1] in a nutshell. The lover's tact yields to the confessor's probing—spuriously tactful ("and what harm if he did"), shockingly pointed ("where"). Molly artlessly or artfully parries the thrust but only gains a reprieve. The inquisitorial gaze, fleetingly deflected onto the grassy borders of the canal, swivels immediately back to its favored object of scrutiny, the woman's body, or as Father Corrigan more circumspectly puts it, "person." We are witnessing the transformation of sexuality into discourse, to use Michel Foucault's formula; moreover, Molly's experience in the confession box serves to confirm Foucault's skepticism regarding what he calls the repressive hypothesis. According to the latter, sexuality had been a forbidden topic from the seventeenth century up to our present era of sexual liberation. On the contrary, Foucault claims, people have been endlessly prodded to avow their sexual practices and desires, and one of the earliest, most effective, and most influential instruments of this inquisition was the confessional.

Now if the repressive hypothesis were to hold good anywhere, it ought to be in Ireland, that Galapagos of sexual life where the Jansenist species reportedly still survives. But Molly's exchange with Father Corrigan (and it may be taken as typical) is evidence to the contrary. Even in Ireland (and therefore one should perhaps say especially in Ireland) sex, far from being condemned to silence, has been talked about at length and in detail in circumstances fostered and controlled by the only power the Irish have acknowledged consistently throughout centuries of revolution—the Catholic church. (Indeed, new perspectives on the complex relationship between Irish nationalism and sexuality are opened by Foucault's discourse.) Thus a few years ago the Irish bishops were moved to give a public and detailed description of the minute daily changes in their vaginal secretions that women would have to monitor if they were successfully to practice the Billings method of contraception, the only method countenanced by the church. As I remember, the bishops drew an analogy with egg white and made a fine distinction between its consistency in its virgin state and after it had been lightly beaten. The response of most women was one of astonishment. They had not been accustomed to turn such a clinical gaze on their bodily functions.

But the bishops' pronouncements are a remarkable example of the productive as opposed to the repressive nature of the sexual ethos, of power as a positive as well as a negative force. Thus confession produces the discourse of sexuality, which in turn adds another twist to the spiral of power. Is it not curious that the same field of relationships which produced the women's self-help clinics of the 1960s in the United States gave rise to the bishops' intervention in Ireland? The result of this was that rural Irish women, for whom such clinics would have been inconceivable, could learn the truth of their reproductive systems from their bishops, themselves no doubt goaded into speech by the women's own murmurings in the confessional.

Through confession the flesh becomes word by virtue of an elaborate process of classification and reduction that operates simultaneously on the institution of confession itself and on the penitent and her sins. Thus as confessional techniques become increasingly refined, so is the flesh melted down to the pure gold of sex, which then appears to be the nugget of truth at the heart of the human mystery. Let me illustrate this point with a story that is particularly, though not exclusively, Irish in its apocalyptic vision of sexuality.

It is the day of the Last Judgment. Every human being who has ever lived is present waiting to be judged. Christ appears in his majesty, accompanied by the recording angel. He speaks to those people in his immediate vicinity and at once a great shout of jubilation goes up. Those further away are filled with curiosity and impatience to hear what he has said. The message is slowly and tediously relayed back through all the hundreds of thousands of people. As each new group hears the news they raise the same wild cheer. Finally, it reaches those on the very border of the crowd. "What did he say?" they cry impatiently. "What's all the cheering about?" The answer comes back, succinct and entirely satisfactory: "Fucking doesn't count."

The economic metaphor is not the least interesting aspect of this anecdote, but its chief value in the present context is the oblique light it sheds on Foucault's postulate that the practice of confession, prompted by the will to knowledge, produces a truth that is assimilated to the secret of the individual's sex.

The French word *aveu*, which recurs throughout *The Will to Knowledge*, carries with it a resonance that the English "confession" or even "avowal" lacks. Historically it meant the document by which the vassal was enfeoffed to the feudal lord, the record of his engagement of himself in return for the land he had received. To be "sans aveu" (without *aveu*) was therefore to owe no fealty to any lord, but by the same token it was to be without protection. A person in this situation is literally displaced, "sans feu ni lieu," without hearth or home. Confession therefore, in a certain sense, has the positive value of guaranteeing the speaker a place in the scheme of things. It is a normalizing process by which one is classified, situated in the great table of resemblances, grounded. The aggressive electric charge of difference is thus rendered harmless, its energy diverted into and diffused throughout the body politic. It follows that to refuse to confess, either by remaining silent or by dodging the question, may be dangerous. The subversiveness of Molly Bloom's equivocation is not entirely compensated for by her appeal to stupidity— or is it to innocence?—"and I said on the canal bank like a fool," and it causes her interrogator to narrow his range: "but whereabouts on your person my child," limiting her space to maneuver. True to her name, Molly had refused the herbarium of desiccated sexual pleasures within whose leaves the confessor would have pressed her body for her own narcissistic contemplation. Instead she had chosen that living garden of delights which is the site of an encounter with the other. Like her name-sake, the fabulous herb moly, which preserved Odysseus from being turned into one of Circe's swine, Molly, I suggest, might be taken as a specific, a medicine to protect women from imprisonment in the *real* of their own sexuality, in the image of the mother's body, cut off from the heterotopia of the symbolic.

In this era of ostensible liberation for women, of the inauguration of women's studies programs at many universities, of the proliferation of reviews devoted to feminist criticism, of preoccupation with "images" of women, Molly Bloom's response to Father Corrigan's question has a strategic importance for women scholars that Michel Foucault's discursive practice both reflects and discloses.

Within the last decade we have witnessed the birth of Woman. I mean Woman as an effect of discourse, secreted by power in the same way that her predecessor Man had been produced not very much earlier, in Foucault's account. The impulse to hail the advent of Woman as a victory for women in their struggle for recognition may have been precipitate, though understandable. Thus when women scholars are summoned to the podium to account for themselves, not as pale imitations of men but as specimens of difference, the impulse to confess is strong. To claim essential womanhood, to assert oneself as subject, to demand the freedom to write "like a woman," to reclaim women's history, to speak their sexuality is a powerful temptation. Yet it must be resisted, I would argue, taking a leaf from Foucault's book. However inviting the mirror, we must look behind it, like Alice, or whatever the consequences, away from it, like the Lady of Shalott, but in any case we must look elsewhere, like Molly Bloom, away from our own bodies insofar as they are ready-made reflections that promise a false identity.

When we are invited to represent women, to give the woman's per-spective, to reveal her truth, we should perhaps remember Nietzsche's warning that

We still do not know where the urge for truth comes from; for as yet we have heard only of the obligation imposed by society that it should exist: to be truthful means using the customary metaphors—in moral terms: the obligation to lie according to fixed convention, to lie herd-like in a style obligatory for all. . . .[2]

When we urge, or ourselves attempt, a feminist practice, whether aesthetic, scholarly, or overtly political, it becomes urgent to interrogate the notion of woman to which such practices would conform. Was not that notion itself secreted by the circulatory system of power? I use the word "secreted" for its value as a double entendre: its capacity to produce and conceal at the same time. Hence to bring to light and to identify with an occulted or allegedly repressed image of woman is not an enterprise to be undertaken naively. When we are offered the role of Woman, to "strut and fret [our] hour upon the stage," it may be strategically necessary to accept it for the place it offers us from which to speak, but we should maintain our reserve.

Thus even as we engage ourselves, making the *aveu* that allows us to enter discourse, it might be well to keep an ironic distance, bring humor into play, subverting simultaneously from above and below the discourse within which we are produced. A well-known feminist text of the 1970s was called *Man's World, Woman's Place*.[3] It is important for us perhaps not to know our place, not to rush to occupy it when we are being ushered into it, as with the establishment of women's studies programs, the contemporary equivalent of the gyneceum. Let us borrow from Foucault the word *esquive*, and the strategy it implies, from *esquiver*, "to dodge or to feint," as in fencing, the reflexive form of which, *s'esquiver*, means "to slip away," delightfully rendered by *Harrap's New Standard Dictionary* as "to take French leave." That is what Molly Bloom does, slipping out from under Father Corrigan's demand to show and tell, away from the closeted space of the confessional out of the confines of her own body, to the canal bank.

Philosophy for the feminist scholar may well consist in a version of what Foucault calls, writing of Deleuze, a "de-throned para-Platonism," which is to be effected by "a small lateral leap," *une esquive*.[4] Thus, whoever would speak of woman, her ideal, her essence, her image, should simultaneously invoke the legend "This is not a woman," borrowing the strategy of Magritte's *Ceci n'est pas une pipe* (This is not a pipe), in which the phrase, written in a calligraphic hand, accompanies a hyper-realistic image of a pipe. "Magritte's text is doubly paradoxical," Foucault has written:

> It undertakes to name what obviously has no need to be named (the shape is too well known, the name too familiar). And so at the very moment when he should give the name, he gives it but in doing so he denies that it is the name.[5]

Just as madness in Foucault's account has been the condition of reason, the silence of women, it might be argued, has been the condition of Western philosophy. "Among women the greatest glory is hers who is least talked about among the men, whether for good or for bad." Given the celebrated Greek penchant for talk, this quotation from Pericles' funeral speech is significant. Invited some twenty-four hundred years later to appear on the agora, women can hardly afford deconstruction for its own sake, but they must equally take care to avoid the adoption of a ready-made essence. The struggle to attain the status of subject must incorporate a critique of the notion of subjectivity. To be a subject, as Foucault demonstrates, is a knife that cuts both ways, since it implies being subjected *to*. "To what are we subjected when we would assume the role of authentic womanhood?" is the question that feminist theory must address. Here the strategy of Magritte's double paradox could prove invaluable by providing a blueprint for the difficult task of establishing an identity and criticizing it at the same time. Women have been *sans aveu* for too long to treat the offer of a fief lightly, but their act of engagement might legitimately consist in asking with Virginia Woolf:

> What is this "civilisation" in which we find ourselves? What are these ceremonies and why should we take part in them? What are these professions and why should we make money out of them? Where in short is it leading, the procession of the sons of educated men?[6]

It is significant, I believe, that women are appearing in acadame in their greatest numbers at the very moment when that world is in crisis if not actually in decay. Chairperson replaces chairman just as the very notion of a "chair" at a "seat" of learning becomes chimeric for a whole generation of scholars. The increasingly widespread practice of hiring young professors on three-year and sometimes even one-year contracts with no prospect of renewal is rapidly turning the present generation of academics into migrant workers. The enthusiasm and energy of their best years are tapped by the universities, who then discard them to wander where they may, *sans feu ni lieu*.

In spite of this grim picture, women, especially mature women, are pouring into the classrooms. The 1970s and 1980s may become known as the era of the "returning" woman student. What can this mean, if not a radical re-vision on their part of *La volonté de savoir*, the will to knowledge? Sexual curiosity satisfied, they are asking, like Colette's mettlesome young bride in *Mes apprentissages*, "And is that all?"[7] What they are seeking, what in some instances they are re-creating, is the pedagogical relationship that Foucault attributes to the Greeks: "In Greece," he writes, "truth and sex were linked, in the form of pedagogy, by the transmission of a precious knowledge from one body to another; sex served as a medium for initiation into learning"; whereas "for us," he adds, "it is in the confession that truth and sex are joined, through the obligatory and exhaustive expression of an individual secret" (*HS*, p. 61).

Women scholars, I would argue, both professors and students, are on the brink of re-creating pedagogy as an *ars erotica*, but differently. They will succeed in doing so in my view precisely to the degree that they resist the confessional impulse, espousing in its place what I call a Nietzschean "forgetting" of femininity. Let the classroom in women's studies programs not become the confession box translated. For, as Foucault has pointed out:

in this "question" of sex (in both senses: as interrogation and problematisation, and as the need for confession and integration into a field of rationality), two processes emerge, the one always conditioning the other: we demand that sex speak the truth (but, since it is the secret and is oblivious to its own nature, we reserve for ourselves the function of telling the truth of its truth, revealed and deciphered at last), and we demand that it tell us our truth, or rather the deeply buried truth of that about ourselves which we think we possess in our immediate consciousness. We tell it its truth by deciphering what it tells us about that truth; it tells us our own by delivering up that part of it that escaped us. From this interplay there has evolved over several centuries, a knowledge of the subject; a knowledge not so much of his form, but of that which divides him, determines him perhaps, but above all causes him to be ignorant of himself. As unlikely as this may seem, it should not surprise us when we think of the long history of the Christian and juridical confession, of the shifts and transformations this form of knowledge-power, so important in the West, has undergone: the project of a science of the subject has gravitated, in ever narrowing circles, around the question of sex. [*HS*, pp. 70–71]

The new erotic pedagogy that I would hope for would neither duplicate the homosexuality of the Greek system nor reproduce the reductive effects of a confession that would join sex with truth. It would rather reestablish the *amator*, a word that is so revealingly traduced by its current form: amateur.

I have begun to cherish the theory that the real scholars of today may be the "returning" women students, many of whom enjoy some financial independence (even if it is provided by Welfare), who are not therefore in immediate pursuit of a career-oriented education, who (seeing the plight of young academics) have few illusions about careers within the university, but who nonetheless pursue learning for the love of it. A good number, being divorced, owe no fealty to any lord; they are displaced, finding themselves in classrooms with students frequently not much older than their own children; but as anyone who has taught such women knows, theirs is "the ecstasy of interest," as Hopkins so marvelously puts it, speaking of another mystery, "their minds swinging, poised, but on the quiver."

Striking proof of the positive aspect of knowledge-power, women teachers and students are appearing in the interstices of the system. Perhaps it is as *events* that such women should be studied: in Foucault's terms they should perhaps be regarded as "point[s] without thickness or substance of which someone speaks and which [roam] the surface of things" (*TP*, p. 174). That is exactly how women are portrayed in that curious text, *Flatland: A Romance of Many Dimensions*, with illustrations by the Author, a Square (in real life the Victorian theologian and mathematician Edwin A. Abbot). In Flatland the women are straight lines, but because Flatland is a space that knows only two dimensions, a straight line looked at endways appears only to be a point; thus women have the capacity to become practically invisible at will. "Woman," writes the author, "is a needle; being, so to speak, all point, at least at the two extremities," adding "what can it be to run against a Woman, except absolute and immediate destruction?"[8] I juxtapose Foucault:

> We should not restrict meaning to the cognitive core that lies at the heart of a knowable object; rather, we should allow it to reestablish its flux at the limit of words and things, as what is said of a thing (not its attribute or the thing itself) and as something that happens (not its process or its state). Death supplies the best example, being both the event of events and meaning in its purest state. Its domain is the anonymous flow of speech; it is that of which we speak as always past or about to happen and yet it occurs at the extreme point of singularity. [*TP*, p. 174]

Perhaps we ought to consider woman as event, "a phantasm that cannot be reduced to a primordial fact through the intermediary of perception or an image, but that arises between surfaces where it assumes meaning . . . in . . . its 'incorporeal materiality' " (*TP*, p. 169).

Recently a "returning" woman student wrote the following for one of my classes:

> Socks were strung out on a line like fishes caught. They floated in the fountain, a very practical construction as fountains go. One with no flourishes, it was pure

utility and it drew no guests, only one user. In the evenings she came and did her laundry, that lady who haunts the East-side streets, gaunt, wiry, always in fashionable rags.

She can almost read my mind. As she passes me she is knowing. She reads soul, is punished and punishes by the attitude of her person. She dresses like me only more psychotically, or bummy if you prefer. She is the lady bum (like a lady clown). I imagine her to be brilliant behind her roaming facade. In glazed determination she walks on, passing by in bright purples, in lavish rags.

Other bums also have the ability to see into souls. There is a certain chemistry, a contact with our secret selves that they make with us.[9]

Jean's recognition of herself in the other woman is arresting. Could it be that we are witnessing the end of the great confinement of women? That it is the same seismic flutter in the force field of power that fills the universities with returning women students and the streets with bag ladies? What if, as Jean implies, they are really the same underneath, the bag lady a ragged copy of the intellectual, a prophetic figure, perhaps, in this era of the itinerant scholar?

"She . . . is punished and punishes by the attitudes of her person," Jean writes of her alter ego. "Whereabouts on your person my child," Father Corrigan asks Molly. Feminists, naively some might think, have sought to substitute "person" for the word "man." But "person" derives from the Latin *persona*, meaning mask, the word that gives *personne* in French: nobody. Roaming the surface of things from the canal bank to one's person might be to run parallel to the trajectory from Erewhon to Nemo, the space within which Michel Serres plots Foucault's path, a path he revealingly describes as "une méditation serrée sur les qualités premières de l'espace."[10] ("An intense meditation on the basic qualities of space," but note the word *serrée*, mirror image of Serres's own name.) In Serres's view, Foucault's language is geometrical, he studies madness in its linear, spatial aspect, hence the images of Samuel Butler's Utopia, Erewhon (Nowhere reversed), and Nemo (Nobody), the name the wily Odysseus gives, as the author of his misfortune, to the blinded Cyclops. Thus when his fellow giants ask Polyphemus who put out his eye so that they may avenge him, he is obliged to howl, "Nobody." Identity is given and denied in the same breath. Polyphemus counts his sheep but Odysseus passes out of the cave clinging to the underbelly of one of the animals.

This is Foucault's strategy. Can women appropriate it? Where do they find themselves in his work? Perhaps in the Infanta Margarita, the ostensible subject of *The Maids of Honor*, but really the object, as Foucault shows. Perhaps the place we should aspire to is outside the frame, the place Serres attributes to the archaeologist, that is, to Foucault himself. "His site is neither that of the transmitter nor the receiver," writes Serres, "but that of the interceptor, precisely that of the viewer or the painter of Las Meninas, who finds himself there, by surprise, thanks to a paradoxical cleft [interstice]."[11]

Let us take up that position, in order to gaze at the following three disparate images.

Las Meninas *(The Maids of Honor), by Diego de Silva Velázquez. The Infanta Margarita is the object of the painting according to Foucault; see his essay "Les Suivantes"* in Les Mots et les choses *(Paris: Gallimard, 1966).*

"Her world reduced to Odd Lot Trading." From Shopping Bag
Ladies: Homeless Women Speak About Their Lives *by Ann
Marie Rousseau. Copyright © 1981 by Ann Marie Rousseau. Used
with permission.*

*"Forty Seated Shoulders," by Magdalena Abakanowicz. Photo
courtesy of Mary Jane Jacob, Curator, Museum of Contemporary
Art, Chicago.*

My problem was my name but you can change your name anytime you want. My first name was Mary, my second was Rayna, but Mary made me have trouble. I hated it so I'm using Rayna for now and it's been awhile. My name should have been Shirley. If I was a boy I should have been Lou. See, we're given the wrong names and our names fix us [Rayna Landry].[12]

Perhaps we can let Foucault provide the commentary:

To think within the context of categories is to know the truth so that it can be distinguished from the false; to think "acategorically" is to confront a black stupidity and, in a flash, to distinguish oneself from it. Stupidity is contemplated; sight penetrates its domain and becomes fascinated; it carries one gently along and its action is mimed in the abandonment of oneself. . . . "It's all so senseless—life, women, death! How ridiculous this stupidity!" [*TP*, p. 189]

And let Roland Barthes add a gloss:

. . . stupidity is a hard and indivisible kernel, a *primitive:* no way of decomposing it *scientifically*. . . . What is it? A spectacle, an aesthetic fiction, perhaps a hallucination? Perhaps we want to put ourselves in the picture? It's lovely, it takes your breath away, it's strange . . .[13]

But let Molly Bloom have the last word: "and I said on the canal bank like a fool . . ."

Notes

1. Michel Foucault, *La Volonté de savoir* (Paris: Gallimard, 1976), volume 1 of a projected six-volume *Histoire de la sexualité;* translated by Robert Hurley as *The History of Sexuality, Vol. I: An Introduction* (New York: Pantheon, 1978). Subsequent references in the text are to the English translation, referred to as *HS*.
2. Friedrich Nietzsche, *On Truth and Lie in an Extra-Moral Sense*, in Walter Kaufmann, trans., *The Portable Nietzsche* (New York: Viking Press, 1954), p. 47.
3. Elizabeth Janeway, *Man's World, Woman's Place* (New York: Delta, 1971).
4. Michel Foucault, "Theatricum Philosophicum," in Donald F. Bouchard, ed., *Language, Counter-Memory, Practice: Selected Essays and Interviews* (Ithaca, N.Y.: Cornell University Press, 1977), p. 168. Subsequent references will be cited in the text as *TP*.
5. Michel Foucault, *Ceci n'est pas une pipe* (Montpellier: Fata Morgana, 1973); Richard Howard, trans., *October* (Spring 1976): 7–21, 10.
6. Virginia Woolf, *Three Guineas* (1938; rpt., New York: Harcourt, Brace, Jovanovich, 1966), p. 63.
7. Colette, *Mes Apprentissages* (Paris: Ferenczi et fils, 1936), trans. Helen Beauclerk, in *Earthly Paradise*, ed. Robert Phelps (New York: Farrar, Straus and Giroux, 1966), p. 92.
8. [Edwin A. Abbot], *Flatland: A Romance of Many Dimensions*, 2d revised ed. (1884; rpt., New York: Harper and Row, 1963), pp. 12, 13.

9. Jean de Simone, Journal presented in fulfillment of the requirements of Comparative Literature 230: "Women Artists and Their Discontents," The University of Wisconsin–Milwaukee, Semester 2, 1981.

10. Michel Serres, "D'Erewhon à l'antre du Cyclope," in *Hermes II: La Communication* (Paris: Editions de Minuit, 1968), p. 170. My translation.

11. Ibid., p. 200.

12. Ann Marie Rousseau, *Shopping Bag Ladies* (New York: Pilgrim Press, 1981), p. 41.

13. Roland Barthes, *Roland Barthes by Roland Barthes*, trans. Richard Howard (New York: Hill and Wang, 1977), p. 51.

Peggy Kamuf

Penelope at Work: Interruptions in *A Room of One's Own*

> . . . but always
> I waste away at the inward heart, longing for Odysseus.
> These men try to hasten the marriage. I weave my own wiles.
> The Odyssey, *XIX, 135–137*

As so often throughout our culture's poetic text, one encounters in *The Odyssey* moments of abyssal self-representation when the poem tries to occupy a place in two different and mutually exclusive spheres, when it slips between representing something and being the something represented. One such moment occurs in Book I, where it happens to coincide with the first direct representation of Penelope. In fact, Penelope enters the scene of narration in order to interrupt it. In the passage to which I refer, Telemachos and the suitors are gathered in front of the palace, where they are listening to "the famous singer . . . [who] sang of the Achaians' bitter homecoming / from Troy."[1] Penelope, who "heeded the magical song from her upper chamber," is drawn down the stairs and, in tears, begs the singer to choose another song. At this point, Telemachos takes the floor, reproaches his mother for her intervention and says to her:

> "Go therefore back in the house, and take up your own work,
> the loom and the distaff, and see to it that your handmaidens
> ply their work also; but the men must see to discussion,
> all men, but I most of all. For mine is the power in this household."
> Penelope went back inside the house, in amazement.
>
> [356–60]

Much later in the poem, at a crucial moment that prepares Odysseus's attack on the suitors, Telemachos again sends his mother out of the room, using almost the same terms but with one important difference. Instead of the poem or discussion, it is an instrument of force—Odysseus's famous bow—that Telemachos orders his mother to leave in men's hands.

> "Go therefore back into the house, and take up your own work,
> the loom and the distaff, and see to it that your handmaidens
> ply their work also. The men shall have the bow in their keeping,
> all men, but I most of all. For mine is the power in this household."
> Penelope went back inside the house, in amazement.
>
> [XXI, 350–54]

By means of this repetition, the poem establishes a connection between the art of storytelling and the practice of force. Both fall within a son's prerogative to exercise power in his household, the power to send women out of the room. If, however, a distribution of power and the sexes occurs here, it turns on the designation of woman's work as "the loom and the distaff," the instruments of weaving and spinning. Both of these tasks supply the poet with endless metaphoric possibilities in this tale of men whose fate, for example, is "spun with the thread at his birth" (VII, 198), where the storyteller can spin out a well-made tale and where cleverness weaves designs and deceptions. Thus, in a way that we have been taught to recognize,[2] the exclusion of the distaff from manly discussion is necessarily incomplete, since Penelope's work is set out as a kind of material support for the metaphorical field from which the poem draws its crafty designs and deceptive stories. But rhetorical repetition is not all that is working here to confound the distinction Telemachos would make. Power in the household is interrupted in quite another fashion by a woman's art.

Pressed by her household to choose a new husband, Penelope does not want to decide. Instead, she has given herself the tedious task of unweaving by night what she has woven during the day. It is not a terribly clever trick, nothing like saying "No man" to the Cyclops Polyphemos, although perhaps that is what her unweaving means. In any case, it is a homelier remedy in a tight spot, which works even though her suitors, unlike Odysseus's Polyphemos, are perfectly able to see the tissue of her lies. Like a spider, she watches them fly into the web she has stretched across the entrance to the room in which she sits weaving. It is the same room she enters at night when others suppose her in bed. Here, then, is Penelope's great secret, what no man can see, for no man imagines her anywhere but in bed. It is this secret passage out of the bedchamber that allows Penelope to promise her bed and yet always defer the terms of the promise: no clever play on words, but rather a spatial and temporal shift between the two centers of her woman's life preserves Penelope's indecision. The suitors remain strangers to a woman's work that is never done, the tedium of the interior. As a result, their manly discussion is mystified by an obvious trick.

A Room of One's Own, the published text of lectures delivered at Newnham and Girton Colleges in 1928, begins with the question of its own title: "But, you may say, we asked you to speak about women and fiction—what has that got to do with a room of own's own? I will try to explain."[3] Likewise, the title "Penelope at Work"—that is to say, the right to claim attention to whatever Penelope might have to say about Virginia Woolf—needs some explanation. Because authority here is a fiction, it can claim only the credit due the speculations of a common reader, in the sense that Woolf gives that notion in her two anthologies of critical essays, *The Common Reader*. I would add as well the other sense taken by the narrator of *A Room of One's Own*, when she sets aside a more systematic sounding of the depths, examining instead "only what chance has floated to [her] feet" (p. 78).

I invoke Penelope in order to give a name to what is at work in a text like *A Room of One's Own*, although the phrase "at work" already covers up in too purposeful a fashion the way in which such work entails as well its own undoing. I take Penelope as a shuttling figure in power's household, one whose movement between outside and inside, violence and poetry, the work of history and the unworking of fiction may allow us to frame one or two notions about the place of woman's art. This figure, moreover, may also serve to reformulate that other notion of woman's exclusion that always seems to arise whenever one takes up the question of power in stories and in histories. Finally, then, Penelope is the name I take in order to designate a conjunction of fiction in history in which a woman's text plots the place of its own undoing.

As already mentioned, *A Room of One's Own* opens with the question of its title. To provide an answer, the lecture's narrator introduces another fictional narrator (" 'I,' she writes, 'is only a convenient term for somebody who has no real being' " [p. 4]), who proceeds to recount a series of events interspersed with a chain of literary analyses. Asked to explain, in other words, the narrator promises an answer once she is through spinning out her story. But this narrative sets out from a doubling back, or a crossing out, in which a meaning, a sense of direction, gets lost.

Having finally fished up an idea for her promised lectures on women and fiction, the narrator has set off at a rapid pace across Cambridge's campus, little heeding where her feet are taking her. Where she might have been going, however, no one can tell, because she is instantly called back to an order of distinctions that her thought had put aside in its unruly eagerness:

> Instantly a man's figure rose to intercept me. Nor did I at first understand that the gesticulations of a curious-looking object, in a cut-away coat and evening shirt, were aimed at me. His face expressed horror and indignation. Instinct rather than reason came to my help; he was a Beadle; I was a woman. This was the turf; there was the path. Only the Fellows and Scholars are allowed here; the gravel is the place for me. As I regained the path the arms of the Beadle sank, his face assumed its usual repose, and though turf is better walking than gravel, no very great harm was done. . . . [However], what idea it had been that had sent me so audaciously trespassing I could not now remember. [p. 6]

This setback is itself soon forgotten and the narrator is led, through a series of rapid associations, to set her course for a certain college library where one might consult the manuscript of Milton's *Lycidas*. Once again, she is carried forward unconsciously, her bodily movement forgotten as one text leads to another until it is a question no longer about Milton but about a Thackeray novel that brings her to the door of the library. Once again, her unruly associations have transgressed a fundamental order, and the intertextual weaving is broken off when the narrator is recalled to the reality of her own unfitness in such a place:

> but here I was actually at the door which leads into the library itself. I must have opened it, for instantly there issued, like a guardian angel barring the way with a

flutter of black gown instead of white wings, a deprecating, silvery, kindly gentleman, who regretted in a low voice as he waved me back that ladies are only admitted to the library if accompanied by a Fellow of the College or furnished with a letter of introduction. [pp. 7–8]

In its initial movement, then, the text describes a zigzag, a repeated reversal of direction. From this angle, we may begin to see how *A Room of One's Own* frames the question of women and fiction within the field of an exclusion. What appears there is a contradiction like the one the narrator discerns in the following passage:

if woman had no existence save in the fiction written by men, one would imagine her a person of utmost importance. . . . But this is woman in fiction. In fact, as Professor Trevelyan points out [in his *History of England*], she was locked up, beaten and flung about the room. [pp. 44–45]

The zigzag produced by a reversal of sense is here more clearly coordinated with the contradiction of fiction by history. And this zigzag intersects as well with the question of the title: Is "a room of one's own," in other words, an image, a metaphor with which to call up the immaterial, the timeless, and the imaginary defeat of power, or is it rather that which supports the metaphor, the denotative foundation on which figurative space is constructed? A place in history that exists therefore in social, political, and economic contexts? Or a place that transcends these limits much in the way the narrator looks down upon the street activity from her study window? How does *A Room of One's Own*, in other words, negotiate this angle of contradiction?

The narrator defers these questions by posing another in their place, as if she had found another use for Penelope's trick of leaving one room for another, as if the promise she has made engages her to keep the passage open between these two spaces, to let them interfere with each other. Woolf's narrator, for example, cannot simply escape into the library from a ruder reality; once there, she is drawn back into the rudest of scenes where young women are "locked up, beaten and flung about the room." Here, then, is another locked room within the first. The second enclosure takes shape in the fully loaded bookshelves lining the walls. Having locked women out of the library, history still rages at her from within. The narrator runs into this locked door repeatedly in the British Museum; even at home, in her own library, the violent encounters continue. Again and again she is shown the door. Again and again anger flares as it did when she was politely told she could not enter the college library. "Never will I wake those echoes, never will I ask for that hospitality again, I vowed as I descended the steps in anger" (p. 8).

The narrator spins in the revolving door of the library. While anger pushes her out, something else pulls her back in. That something else has the force of forgetfulness—in its pull, one forgets one's place, one's self. In this back and forth motion, the narrator is strung out between an exclusion or negation of women and a forgetting of herself as woman. Here, then, may be as well one space of woman's writing, which always risks hardening into the negative outline of anger and thereby losing its chance for forgetfulness. This is the sense of the encounter with Professor von X., whom the narrator sketches as she reads his thesis, *The Mental, Moral and Physical Inferiority of the Female Sex*.

> Whatever the reason, the professor was made to look very angry and ugly in my sketch, as he wrote his great book. . . . Drawing pictures was an idle way of finishing an unprofitable morning's work. Yet it is in our idleness, in our dreams, that the submerged truth sometimes comes to the top. A very elementary exercise in psychology, not to be dignified by the name of psychoanalysis, showed me on looking at my notebook, that the sketch of the angry professor had been made in anger. Anger had snatched my pencil while I dreamt. [pp. 31–32]

In this moment, the narrator has a view not only of the ugly face of the historian but also of her own distorted features: "My cheeks had burnt. I had flushed with anger." Yet these interceptions that snatch the pencil from the hand and push thought off the path it was following always set up the possibility of a new direction in which to proceed. When the negations of history are made to turn on themselves, the door of the library spins, setting the narrator in motion once again.

> All that I had retrieved from that morning's work had been the one fact of anger. The professors—I lumped them together thus—were angry. But why, I asked myself, having returned the books, why, I repeated, standing under the colonnade among the pigeons and the prehistoric canoes, why are they angry? And, asking myself this question, I strolled off. . . . [p. 33]

Through these deflections that turn a discourse back on itself, *A Room of One's Own* defines a novel position in relation to the locked room of history. That is, since women's history cannot be studied in the library, it will have to be read into the scene of its own exclusion. It has to be invented—both discovered and made up. As it spins around its promise to decide on the place of woman's writing, this text *ravels* the crossed threads of history and fiction. It ravels—which is to say it both *un*tangles, makes something plain or clear, and *en*tangles, or confuses, something. An alternative definition of the transitive verb "to ravel" is (quoting from the decisive Oxford authority) "to unravel." Turning in the door of culture's most exclusive institution, Penelopeian work blurs the line between historical prerogatives and fictional pretensions, always deferring the promised end of its labor, unraveling clear historical patterns at its fictional border.

In order to specify further this figure of the self-raveling text, one may turn to three different moments in *A Room of One's Own* where interruption marks the scene of writing. First, however, let us take a rather large detour whose only logic may be that of one text interrupting and unraveling another. The digression is proposed in order to step beyond a limited notion of interruption and thus a limited reading of Woolf's text. It passes through the work of Michel Foucault, most particularly his *Will to Knowledge (La Volonté de savoir)*. It might be useful to break into *A Room of One's Own* with Foucault's history of sexuality so as to point up the zigzagging fault lines in Woolf's speculations about woman's writing. Although the fault lines are quite plainly there, they can be too easily overlooked when this text is taken as a model authority for a critical practice that is content to go on making nasty caricatures of Professor von X., the nameless author and authority of masculine privilege and feminine subjection. The fault line beneath this sketch is the notion of sexual differentiation as a historical production that, if it has produced a privileged masculine subject, cannot also be understood as originating in the subject it only produces. To the extent, however, that one accepts seeing "man" at the origin of his own privilege, then, one chooses paradoxically to believe the most manifest lie of "phallosophy": that of man giving birth to himself as an origin that transcends any difference from himself. It is with just such a notion of production that Professor Foucault's history, for example, may interrupt whatever sketch we might make of privileged masculine subjectivity.

To resume very quickly: Foucault elaborates his history over against a certain Freudian-Marxian tradition that has consistently distinguished sexuality from the power mechanisms that repress it. According to this common notion, which Foucault labels "the repressive hypothesis," power is structurally opposed to the anarchic energy of sexuality and functions to repress it, for example, by forcing conformity to the model of the monogamous heterosexual couple. The corollary to this hypothesis, therefore, is the value placed on sexual liberation as evidence of effective resistance to the bourgeois hegemony of power. Foucault, on the other hand, proposes that the repressive model of power is at best a limited and at worst a mystified one, insofar as it accounts only for negative relations and ignores the far more pervasive evidence of power's production of *positive*—that is, real—effects. He argues that, for at least two centuries in the West, power has maintained just such positive relations to sex and sexuality—sexuality, that is, is to a large extent produced by power—and these have progressively assumed a more important role as means for articulating power effects in the individual and society. All of which is why the various movements of sexual liberation need to be systematically reevaluated as instances also of the deployment of a will to knowledge, of power's articulating itself in the first-person confessional mode that also constitutes sexual identity. In an earlier work on disciplinary institutions *(Discipline and Punish)*, Foucault gives an even clearer distinction of power in modern Western society as articulated in the various sciences of the subject, through the increasingly refined and differentiated techniques of identifying and classifying the "I" of any discourse.

While one should hesitate to force Woolf's text into parallel with this analysis, one may at least accept seeing in it a background for a certain ambivalence. Woolf consistently sets the apparent political and social gains of a new women's consciousness over against the disturbing signs of an intensification of exclusive sexual identities, of sexually grounded subjectivity, and of subjectively grounded sexuality. What can emerge perhaps from the excursus into Foucault's history is another context within which to read *A Room of One's Own* as turning away from this historical preoccupation with the subject, closing the book on the "I." The gesture one can now read somewhat differently is that of the narrator when, near the end of her story and after leafing through the works of many women writers from Aphra Behn to her own contemporary Mary Carmichael, she takes one last book off the shelf. It is a novel by a certain Mr. A. (whose initial, like the Professor's *X*, seems to stand for the whole alphabet of possible proper names). Quickly, however, she replaces it on the shelf because

> after reading a chapter or two a shadow seemed to lie across the page. It was a straight dark bar, a shadow shaped something like the letter "I." One began dodging this way and that to catch a glimpse of the landscape behind it. Whether that was indeed a tree or a woman walking I was not quite sure. Back one was always hailed to the letter "I." One began to be tired of "I." [p. 103]

What our detour through the Foucauldian critique should allow us to see is that the power of this "straight dark bar" to obliterate everything it approaches is not a power derived from the identity of a masculine subject to which the "I" simply refers. Rather, the identification of subjects is already an effect of power's articulating itself on bodies, differentiating and ordering their intercourse.

Having noted this, however, what remains of Woolf's particular critique of the patriarchal subject's historical privilege? Have we not passed over this aspect in order better to assimilate Woolf's text into the broader critique of the humanistic subject which is Foucault's project? Is it simply insignificant that the latter's analysis never interrogates the hierarchical opposition of the sexes as an important link in the deployment of power, while that distinction repeatedly forces itself on Woolf's thought, interrupting it, causing it to lose direction? Is there not, in other words, a sense in which *The Will to Knowledge* itself occupies a privileged space that knows no interruption?

Consider, for example, what one may call the narrator of *The Will to Knowledge*, the "I" that assumes direction of the discourse's argument. Like the narrator of *A Room of One's Own*, this "I" is "only a convenient term for somebody who has no existence," it marks only a relative position in a discursive or textual network. Nonetheless, it is in a clearly different position. As we have seen, *A Room of One's Own* proceeds on the model of an interruption that forces the narration to deviate in some fashion, that intrudes with an effective, forceful objection to the momentary forgetting of a woman's identity. In *The Will to Knowledge*, on the other hand, it is the narration that defines other discursive procedures as "deviations" and, compared to Woolf's narration, itself proceeds virtually free from distraction, since no one ever gets in its way with anything but spurious objections. To cite just one instance, it anticipates the particular obstacle to its progress that the Lacanian theory of desire might pose, the theory, that is, of desire as constituted in and by, rather than against, the law. That theory, then, has already carried out a critique of ego psychology's repressive hypothesis, but its implications for a history of sexuality are opposed to those drawn by Foucault. One need not enter too far into the details of this debate in order to appreciate the discursive mode in which this objection is first formulated. Foucault writes:

> I can imagine that one would have the right to say to me: By referring constantly to the positive technologies of power, you are trying to pull off a bigger victory over both [Lacanian psychoanalysis and ego psychology]. You lump your adversaries together behind the figure of the weaker one, and by discussing only repression, you want to make us believe incorrectly that you have gotten rid of the problem of the law [which is constitutive of desire].[1]

While the "I" will eventually respond to this objection, notice how in this moment (but there are many such moments)[5] the discourse imagines another position from which to address itself as "you." Is it any wonder the narrator is never at a loss for a reply? These interruptions of the narrator's pursuit of the analysis may be frequent, but they are never serious, since no figure appears there who, like the Cambridge beadle, has the position and the power to wave the narrator off the turf or to demand to see his permit to enter the library.

It is in this sense, at least, that a discourse like Foucault's can still retain a place in the privileged domain of patriarchal thought, a train of thought that has been trained, precisely, to think without interruption. And in a very important sense the privileged space in question is The Room of One's Own. These capital letters will refer us to the original room, the room properly named, the room of the Cartesian subject, where *Ego sum* is struck as an emblem bearing a proper name, taking up space the limits of which can be delineated and, perhaps most importantly, where the subject becomes one—both singular and whole. Michel Foucault is among those who have forced entry into this room so as to see what is going on there. In an appendix to the second French edition of *Histoire de la folie (Madness and Civilization)*, he writes that it is "a peaceful retreat" to which Descartes's philosopher retires in order to transcribe the exercise of radical doubt. In that exercise, the subject of the meditation encounters an early "point of resistance" in the form of the actuality of the moment and place of meditation: the fact that he is in a certain room, sitting by a fire, before a piece of paper. These conditions—a warm body next to a fire, writing instruments—are then taken by Foucault as synecdoches of the whole system of actuality, which the subject cannot be thought to lack and still be posited as the subject of a reasonable discourse. In the appended essay to which I refer, "My Body, This Paper, This Fire," Foucault imagines that the meditating subject would have to reason as follows:

> If I begin to doubt the place where I am, the attention I am giving to this piece of paper, and of the fire's warmth which marks my present moment, how could I remain convinced of the reasonable nature of my enterprise? Will I not, by putting this actuality in doubt, make any reasonable meditation impossible and rob of all value my resolve to discover finally the truth?[6]

For Foucault, Descartes's place in the history of the Western episteme is so important because it situates the juncture of an exclusion—of unreason, of madness—with the seizure of material reality by the Subject of Reason. By means of that exclusion and that seizure, reality can be a quiet place in which to meditate on oneself.[7] However, when Foucault takes up the synecdochal figure "My Body, This Paper, This Fire" as the title of his essay, he does so in order to reassert the abrogated claims of madness, to reassert, that is, the points of resistance to the elaboration of a reasonable subject. In a certain sense, these points provide leverage on the subject's discourse and give access to intrusion into it.[8]

> It was as if someone had let fall a shade. . . . Something seemed lacking, something seemed different. And to answer that question, I had to think myself out of the room. [p. 11]

Let us place this scene of a certain kind of intrusion into reason's discourse beside another that is imagined by Woolf's narrator. One will recognize a few reasons for doing so: the actuality of a scholar's meditation, a resistance, an intrusion—all are in play here. The narrator in this passage is spinning out her image of the great man of letters, seen not as he labors in the overheated library of Cartesian discourse, but rather in an idle moment. In fact, he has left the actuality of the library for another room.

> He [e.g., Johnson, Goethe, Carlyle, Voltaire, or any other great man] would open the door of drawing-room or nursery, I thought, and find her among her children perhaps, or with a piece of embroidery on her knee—at any rate, the centre of some different order and system of life, and the contrast between this world and his own . . . would at once refresh and invigorate; and there would follow, even in the simplest talk, such a natural difference of opinion that the dried ideas in him would be fertilised anew; and the sight of her creating in a different medium from his own would so quicken his creative power that insensibly his sterile mind would begin to plot again, and he would find the phrase or the scene which was lacking when he put on his hat to visit her. [p. 90]

A man of letters, a scholar, leaves his place by the fire in that quiet room and opens the door to a drawing room or nursery. There, the weary philosopher's work is supplemented by a "different medium" and he is given to see "the scene which was lacking" from the drama taking shape behind the other closed door. Notice that Woolf's narrator is both making up and making up for this scene. It has no place in the history and the biographies of great men which one may consult. It is thus invented, but to take the place of what is missing in the scholar's medium. In other words, the encounter with a supplemental difference takes place as fiction in history. Or, rather, it takes place in a mode that has as yet no proper name. Woolf writes:

> It would be ambitious beyond my daring, I thought, looking about the shelves for books that were not there, to suggest to the students of those famous colleges that they should re-write history . . . but why should they not add a supplement to history? calling it, of course, by some inconspicuous name so that women might figure there without impropriety? [p. 47]

When it acts to restore a missing scene in history's self-narrative, the narrative of the great man, Woolf's text catches history at a loss for words, interrupted in its train of thought. What is restored here, then, is not simply some unrecorded moment in the history of power but an interval, a hiatus, where that discourse has been momentarily broken off.

In order to figure such an interval or interruption, Woolf's text creates a passage out of the library and into another room. Let us briefly compare this passage to the one located by Foucault in the Cartesian scene of meditation. The subject of that meditation reappears in Foucault's essay just as he depicted himself, sealed in his heated study. Now, we could say that Foucault, unlike Woolf, simply finds no reason to imagine the philosopher wandering about from room to room at a loss. No doubt one would have to acknowledge that such moments occur, but it is reasonable for the historian of discourse to exclude them. Indeed, if one did not exclude them but allowed such idle fantasies to intrude, then it could hardly be called history that one is writing. Notice how, when it is considered in this manner, the reasonable omission reassembles the elements of the Cartesian subject's exclusion of its own madness. In this sense, at least, it constructs history by figuring only this comfortably situated position of power.

To return to the scene as it is imagined by Woolf's narrator: surely the interruption figured there is too quickly, too easily recuperated to the benefit of the suspended work. The great man is just taking a little break. Woolf's text, however, also figures two other sorts of interruption that are not so neatly resumed within the continuous work of history. Both are described as eruptions into the space of woman's work.

The first frames the nineteenth-century middle-class woman who, if she wrote, "would have to write in the common sitting-room" (p. 69) as Jane Austen did and where, of course, "she was always interrupted" (p. 70). The narrator quotes this passage from James Austen-Leigh's memoir of his aunt Jane:

> How she was able to effect all this is surprising, for she had no separate study to repair to, and most of the work must have been done in the general sitting-room, subject to all kinds of casual interruptions. She was careful that her occupation should not be suspected by servants or any persons beyond her own family party. [p. 70]

To this the narrator adds: "Jane Austen hid her manuscripts or covered them with a piece of blotting-paper." Austen, in a recognizably Penelopeian fashion, undoes her work repeatedly so that it might continue.

Each interruption blots out evidence of a fictional work and replaces it with the cover of domestic tasks.[9] The homely fiction of domestic enclosure disguises the worldly fiction. That fiction is thus situated historically, materially. At the same time, however, a certain historical determination of woman's place is also seen to be conditioned by a fiction and based on a ruse that hides the contradictions of history.[10]

To understand some of the possible implications of this double hinging effect of interruption, what I am calling Penelopeian labor, one need only imagine that the weary scholar whom we earlier followed out of his study into a drawing room might have, without realizing it, walked in on someone like Miss Austen and found her "with a piece of embroidery on her knee—at any rate, the centre of *some different order* and system of life." The scholar's visit to this lady culminates in an inspiration which allows him to fill a gap in the discourse of reason, the discourse produced in a space of no difference, no interruption. By rewriting this familiar scene as we are suggesting, the phrase "some different order" comes to imply a difference not only from the order that governs the scholar's work, but as well a difference from itself insofar as that piece of embroidery just may hide the text unraveling the domestic scene. The inspiring vision of difference, that representation that always implies an identity, is acted out as a mask for this other difference from itself, the difference within identity. The scholar is able to draw inspiration for his task because he believes he has glimpsed a scene other than the scene of writing, has caught sight of someone different, doing something else. Yet, because there may be a hidden text in the picture, it is perhaps someone much more like himself whom he has interrupted. The man of letters—historian, biographer, novelist, playwright, or literary critic— has failed to see himself as already represented in the room he has entered; it is precisely this blindness to his own reflection that induces a credulous inspiration for his work. Is he not, like one of Penelope's suitors, fooled by his eagerness to find her keeping the promise of her embroidery? What the text may thus display beneath its embroidered cover is a self-delusion, and in the very place, at the very moment that the scholar imagines for himself a way to fill a gap in the self's narrative. If history records the subject's delusion about its own identity, then fictions like Austen's and Woolf's restore to history the moments that precipitate such delusions, moments when difference can just be glimpsed before it disappears beneath a reassuring cover of familiar design.

All of this, of course, is quite fanciful speculation. Indeed, the little fiction about Jane Austen may be even more farfetched than it appears, since at least one of Austen's recent biographers suspects that the whole description of the author hiding her manuscripts is apocryphal, at the very least an exaggeration. Despite her caution, however, this biographer cannot wholly avoid perpetuating the fiction, for she writes: "I think this story . . . must be the happy later *embroidery* of Austen's nieces."[11]

Nevertheless, the caution is well placed. Let us try to conclude on more solid ground by returning to the language of Woolf's text and yet another scene of interruption. The passage in question begins simply enough with the phrase "One goes into the room," followed by a dash, a punctuated hesitation. This pause is just long enough to raise a question about the identity of the "one" in the opening sentence. Then, having hesitated, the narrator goes on:

> but the resources of the English language would be much put to the stretch, and whole flights of words would need to wing their way illegitimately into existence before a woman could say what happens when she goes into a room. [p. 91]

This sentence marks the limit, or threshold, of any lecture on women and fiction. Unlike the ease with which one can imagine the scholar walking into the drawing room or nursery, a woman enters the room in an unfamiliar, yet-to-be-written, even illegitimate mode. Clearly, for Woolf, such forced entry into the language will not simply substitute a feminine "one" for a masculine. This becomes clear when, as the passage continues, Woolf shifts, without transition, from the question of the identity of the subject entering the domain of language to that of the many rooms one may enter.

> One goes into the room—but the resources of the English language would be much put to the stretch, and whole flights of words would need to wing their way illegitimately into existence before a woman could say what happens when she goes into a room. The rooms differ so completely, they are calm or thunderous; open on to the sea, or, on the contrary, give on to a prison yard; are hung with washing; or alive with opals and silks; are hard as horsehair or soft as feathers—one has only to go into any room in any street for the whole of that extremely complex force of femininity *to fly in one's face*. How should it be otherwise? For women have sat indoors all these millions of years, so that by this time the very walls are permeated by their creative force. [p. 91; emphasis added]

In effect, Woolf displaces the issue of the "one" who enters the room by figuring in rapid succession a series of rooms to be entered, surveyed, plotted, described. But less obviously intervening here in the question of one's identity is the insistence of a form of self-interruption. By substituting the passive "a woman's room is entered" for the active phrase "one enters the room," this passage creates a disturbance on both sides of the threshold of subjectivity. And when the place of the feminine subject is abandoned in view of the multiple places of the "complex force of femininity," then, retroactively and with a certain delay, it has become possible to begin to say what happens when a woman enters the room: in a word, femininity, already there, already at work, *flies in one's face.* We must try to hear this phrase—a figure of self-interruption—in both its possible senses at once: to become overwhelmingly obvious and to transgress flagrantly some law or rule. There is both a recognition and an infringement of the place of a creative subject that is no longer or not yet a "one." The feminine "subject" is here constituted through illegitimate intervention in the language: its "one-ness" resides already in the other's place(s), its unity derives retrospectively from an infraction that flies in the face of the grammatical order of subject and predicate.

Far more radically than first imagined, *A Room of One's Own* can offer refuge to no "one," for the history, no less than the fiction, accumulated there leaves the door open to intrusion. As we began by suggesting, Penelope's clever labor is figured by and reiterates the cleverness of Odysseus. The stories of their different exploits together assemble the elements for a meaningful reunion. In that fictional moment that closes the circle of the poem, when the ruse of power rejoins the ruse of no power, it has become impossible and thus irrelevant to know who is interrupting whom, whose task is suspended and whose continues, or which room is being entered and which left behind. Interpreted as a space of interruption, *A Room of One's Own* cannot give title to the room it names in its title. No "one" figures there who is not already many and no ownership guarantees there an undivided property. Instead, the title promises a place of intermittent work, a book that, like a woman's thought, a woman's body, is frequently broken in upon. And broken off. We can leave the last word to the narrator who advises the audience at her lecture that

> the book has somehow to be adapted to the body, and at a venture one would say that women's books should be shorter, more concentrated than those of men, and framed so that they do not need long hours of steady uninterrupted work. For interruptions there will always be. [p. 81]

Notes

1. Translated by Richmond Lattimore (New York: Harper, 1957), 325–27; other references are noted in parentheses.

Peggy Kamuf

2. By, for example, J. Hillis Miller in "Ariachne's Broken Woof," *Georgia Review* 30 (Spring 1977).
3. Virginia Woolf, *A Room of One's Own* (New York: Harcourt, Brace and World, 1929), p. 3; future references are noted in parentheses in the text.
4. Michel Foucault, *La Volonté de savoir* (Paris: Gallimard, 1976), p. 108; my translation.
5. Perhaps the most striking example of the technique is the final section of *L'Archéologie du savoir* (Paris: Gallimard, 1969), where the discourse, in effect, interviews itself and answers all the questions it can think of.
6. Michel Foucault, *Histoire de la folie à l'âge classique* (Paris: Gallimard, 1972), pp. 595–96. For a critique of Foucault's reading of Descartes, see Jacques Derrida, "Cogito et histoire de la folie," in *L'Ecriture et la différence* (Paris: Seuil, 1967).
7. See Susan Bordo, "The Cartesian Masculinization of Thought" (*Signs* 11, 3) for another, significantly different account of "masculinization" as an effect of separation.
8. However, as Foucault writes in *La Volonté de savoir*, points of resistance "by definition . . . can only exist in the strategic field of power relations" (p. 126). Jean Baudrillard has pointed out that resistance has a rather unexplained status in Foucault's discourse; see *Oublier Foucault* (Paris: Galilée, 1977), pp. 50ff.
9. On how this "cover story" may be functioning thematically in Austen's novels, see Sandra Gilbert and Susan Gubar, *The Madwoman in the Attic* (New Haven, Conn.: Yale University Press, 1979), pp. 153ff.
10. Woolf's tampering with the distinction between fiction and history should also be read as an effect of their mutual implication in each other. For an excellent study of this question, see Suzanne Gearhart, *The Open Boundary of History and Fiction: A Critical Approach to the French Enlightenment* (Princeton, N.J.: Princeton University Press, 1984).
11. Jane Aiken Hodge, *Only a Novel: The Double Life of Jane Austen* (New York: Coward, McCann & Geoghegan, 1972), p. 133; emphasis added.

The Uses of Foucault for
Feminist Praxis

III

Winifred Woodhull

Sexuality, Power, and the Question of Rape

French philosopher Michel Foucault's work on sexuality and power converges in interesting and potentially productive ways with feminist theory, social analysis, and practice as they have evolved in the 1970s. At the most general level, of course, Left feminists share with Foucault the conviction that Marxist theories of oppression cannot themselves adequately account for the genesis, mechanisms, and effects of power. Women have insisted on the need to acknowledge the relative autonomy and apparent universality of patriarchal domination, but also on the need to analyze the specific form this domination takes in a particular society at a given historical moment. They have claimed that an analysis of women's oppression challenges the traditional distinctions between the public and the private, the political and the personal.

Similarly, Foucault has suggested that power, far from emanating solely or even predominantly from relations at the economic base and being localized in the state apparatus, is diffused throughout the social body. In the first volume of *The History of Sexuality*, he postulates "the omnipresence of power"

> not because it has the privilege of consolidating everything under its invincible unity, but because it is produced from one moment to the next, at every point, or rather in every relation from one point to another. Power is everywhere, not because it embraces everything, but because it comes from everywhere.[1]

In the same work he shows that sexuality is indeed a domain saturated with power, produced through the complex interaction of multiple discursive and institutional practices ranging from the confession and the dissemination of a pedagogy of sexuality in the seventeenth century to the medicalization and psychiatrization of sexuality in the nineteenth and twentieth centuries. Foucault's analysis of power as a process that produces particular forms of sexuality and implants them in the body confirms and throws new light on the feminist contention that sexuality and sexual relations are social constructs. Though these constructs have functioned historically to engender and reinforce women's subjugation, they are nonetheless subject to liberatory change.

The relational character of power posited by Foucault shifts the emphasis from power's repressive function—its capacity to say "no"—to its productive function. So though power produces instances of sexuality that reshape, constrain, and oppress human beings, it can also be said to generate new forms of pleasure and new positions from which to resist. Women cannot effectively resist, however, by attempting to spell out or live out a supposedly authentic sexuality. For as Foucault has argued, power, far from silencing sexuality, has tirelessly coaxed and forced its articulation, making of it the truth of our being that knowledge must try to discover. He maintains that to designate sexuality as the locus of our freedom—as if it stood outside and against power—is to fall victim to a ruse of power. To fix upon giving voice to sexuality, or to our supposed "identity" as gendered beings, as the path to liberation is to ignore our own history, for such articulations have been integral to power's functioning from the seventeenth century to the present day. Moreover, to grant priority to sexual experience as an exercise of freedom is to allow ourselves to be contained by very limited forms of pleasure. According to Foucault, the preferred strategy is to "desexualize" sexuality by multiplying and diffusing pleasures, in order to cancel the now-obsolete understanding of it as a circumscribed domain fundamentally opposed to power and the law.[2]

There is a striking congruence between these formulations of Foucault's and recent developments within the women's movement. Women have not limited the challenge to male domination to questions traditionally recognized as falling within the realm of sexuality, but have instead shown how sexuality is bound up with economic and political structures, language and philosophy, the world of work and the world of play. On the level of their concrete relationships, feminists have built a community in which it is possible to affirm all kinds of activity—paid labor, political organizing, intellectual exchange, artistic production, consciousness raising, socializing in their own bars and restaurants, intense friendships and love, as well as sex—as significant and pleasurable forms of bonding among women. Adrienne Rich's suggestion that this "range . . . of woman-identified experience" be called a "lesbian continuum"[3] converges with Foucault's call for desexualization of the categories "woman" and "homosexual." Similarly, Lillian Faderman's book *Surpassing the Love of Men*[4] has been applauded by Foucault as an instance of critical desexualization, although lesbians have objected, with reason, that Faderman's study obscures the important sexual component of contemporary lesbian relationships. Rich's concept of "lesbian existence," which refers to "both the fact of the historical presence of lesbians and our continuing creation of the meaning of that existence," must accompany the notion of the lesbian continuum, since lesbians' lives, and the specific character of their oppression, do differ qualitatively from heterosexual women's experience and challenge the prevailing view of heterosexuality as a "choice."[5]

The desexualization strategy adopted by many feminists and promoted by Foucault is perhaps most problematic when brought to bear on the issue of rape. Foucault has spoken in favor of desexualizing rape by decriminalizing it, making rape a civil offense akin to any other form of physical attack, such as a punch in the face, an offense punishable by a fine.[6] The approach he proposes seems to be informed by his own analysis of sexuality as obstinately tied to, and mistakenly understood as being fundamentally opposed to, the Law (capital *L*, with all its Lacanian psychoanalytic resonances). From his formulations in *The History of Sex-*

uality, it is reasonable to infer that in Foucault's view decriminalization might undermine the supposed "prestige" of rape as a grand transgression.

French feminist Monique Plaza has taken Foucault to task for this suggestion, pointing out that he fails to consider the very real power differences between women and men, and that rape is in many ways a mere extension of what are culturally defined as "normal" heterosexual relations.[7] As Plaza argues, Foucault's desexualization strategy is inappropriate in the realm of rape law since the immediate effects of decriminalization are focused on women in such a potentially violent way.

Foucault is not alone, however, in viewing the desexualization of rape as a productive form of resistance. Although they do not propose decriminalization, many American feminists insist on the importance of desexualizing rape by defining it as a crime of power, not of sex. According to this view, rape should be seen as a logical outcome of political, economic, and social processes that generate and foster men's domination over women in every cultural domain. The refusal to link the crime to sex comes in response to the reactionary claim that rape is the inevitable result of a supposedly innate male aggressivity coupled with an uncontrollable sexual need. However, the feminist counterargument ultimately rests on a notion of power divorced from sex, as if sex preexisted the social, from which power is said to derive. In so doing, it falls prey to the ruse of power cited by Foucault, namely, the designation of "sex" as a biological or ontological given whose function is to guarantee that sexuality appear to have its origin outside of and prior to power. To accept this theoretical alibi is thus unwittingly to comply with the very power one aims to elude.

One finds striking evidence of this unintentional compliance in Susan Brownmiller's *Against Our Will: Men, Women, and Rape,* where the complex social processes that produce rape are ultimately reduced to the anatomical difference between the sexes. In her preface, Brownmiller maintains that

> Man's structural capacity to rape and woman's corresponding structural vulnerability are as basic to the physiology of both our sexes as the primal act of sex itself. Had it not been for this accident of biology, an accommodation requiring the locking together of two separate parts, penis and vagina, there would be neither copulation nor rape as we know it. . . . We cannot work around the fact that in terms of human anatomy the possibility of forcible intercourse incontrovertibly exists. *This single factor may have been sufficient to have caused the creation of a male ideology of rape.*[8] [Emphasis added.]

So while sex is said to be "primal" and thus, implicitly, to precede power relations of any kind, the structural features of male and female anatomy are nonetheless considered to be marked by an equally "basic" asymmetry, which makes the male powerful and the female powerless. At the same time that it implicitly idealizes sex as the secret of our identity, then, Brownmiller's argument inadvertently presents women as primordially disempowered—and thus confirms the very assumption her book sets out to invalidate. The political cost of adopting such a position is scarcely balanced by the dubious attribution of moral superiority to women, who, unlike men, do not carry a built-in weapon.

These problems with Brownmiller's analysis point to the need to investigate the cultural codes that inform human sexuality in order to understand the role they play in engendering and consolidating the power relations of a given society. If we are seriously to come to terms with rape, we must explain how the vagina comes to be coded—and experienced—as a place of emptiness and vulnerability, the penis as a weapon, and intercourse as violation, rather than naturalize these processes through references to "basic" physiology.[9] Instead of sidestepping the problem of sex's relation to power by divorcing one from the other in our minds, we need to analyze the social mechanisms, including language and conceptual structures, that bind the two together in our culture. Socialization theory is inadequate to this task, since it assumes an already constituted, if empty, individual subject who is "filled up" with cultural values once s/he enters the world; it locates sex neatly on the side of the individual, power on the side of society.[10] Psychoanalytic theory, on the other hand, allows us to apprehend the processes through which the gendered subject, and indeed individuality itself, are socially generated. However, a psychoanalytic account of women's experience must be grounded in an analysis of patriarchy as it takes shape in relation to a particular mode of production. Foucault's theory of sexuality as an instance of power points the way toward an account so grounded, even as it casts suspicion on psychoanalytic practice as the last avatar of a power apparatus that produced sexuality and its supposed secrets.

The urgency of analyzing the complex relations between sexuality and power is underscored by the fact that rape, and the fear of rape, are experienced by women sexually, not just as domination. As the testimonies in Diana Russell's *The Politics of Rape*[11] show, women who have been raped recall not only the pain inflicted and the terror of being beaten or killed, but their sense of disgust at being forced to become the "impure" woman for the rapist. Ms. X: "When I realized he was gone, I wanted to pour Lysol all over me. I wanted to be cleansed. . . . Sometimes I would get very depressed. I'd think, I'm never going to get this out of my head. When is this garbage going to get out of my head?" (pp. 19, 23). Ms. Cohen: "I didn't have any more sexual escapades after that time. I was horrified by the whole thing. . . . This thing had happened to me, and I couldn't tell anybody. I had to maintain my innocence and virginity" (p. 30). Ms. Stewart: "After each rape I felt dirty and disgusting . . . I was aware of pain and dirtiness in my body" (pp. 47, 48). The experience of rape as a *sexual* assault is inevitable in a culture where many forces converge to define women as essentially sexual beings. Because women do not merely apprehend this definition as something alien imposed from the outside, but live it concretely, sexuality, like power, is central to the experience of rape.

An analysis of sexuality's relation to power is no less crucial to an assessment of the difficulties women encounter in appealing to legal rights in the fight against rape. In the course of a typical rape trial it becomes clear that women are regarded as criminals and are punished accordingly—albeit not by legal means—merely for presuming to circulate in public without men's protection, or for daring to articulate what it means for them to be in control of their bodies, in this case, by deciding where, when, with whom, and under what circumstances they will participate in a sexual act. The disjuncture between the rape victim's grounds for appealing to the legal system—including the violation of her right to liberty and self-determination—and the court's response underscores a basic feature of the bourgeois social order, namely, that it rests on static concepts abstracted from the social relations prevailing at a particular moment in history. The general applicability it claims for its laws is simply false, in this case because the subject whose rights are protected, ostensibly regardless of sex, is in fact male. The fundamental challenge to the social relations of production and reproduction necessary in the struggle against rape cannot ultimately come, then, from demands for rights in legal battles, yet neither can these claims be renounced as long as women are forced to choose between problematic "protection" and no protection at all.

The contradictory character of women's relations to power at the level of the state apparatus is highlighted also in the activities of many feminist groups formed in response to rape and sexual harassment. These groups try both to increase public awareness of rape as a chronic, widespread, *political* problem and to get legislatures, judges, and police forces to take steps to eliminate it. Most often, this means urging that (1) existing laws against rape be enforced and that the offenders, rather than the victims, be put on trial (with respect to one's sexual history, for example); (2) stricter laws be enacted requiring harsher and more systematic punishment of sexual assault, with the probable result that men from racial and ethnic minorities, especially blacks, will be prosecuted and given severe sentences in numbers that exceed the proportion of rapes committed by those groups, particularly if their victims are white; and (3) more safety be assured in city streets and public buildings, which in effect means more male police and security guards.

Women, then, are forced to call for more general repression in order to secure for themselves a modicum of safety in public space. The "protective" measures taken do little or nothing to prevent the rape of women inside the home, whether by husbands or lovers, acquaintances or intruders. Moreover, because the law, the courts, and the police are male dominated, women are obliged to call for male protection in the face of male brutality, a situation that calls to mind Mae West's ironic query: "Every man I meet wants to protect me. Can't figure out what from."[12]

Thus women's appeals to the state for protection of their rights, while necessary, nonetheless force them to rely on men for their safety. They also incorrectly assume that what is at issue is simply making the law of the land prevail equally for everyone. What we must recognize, however, is that the very coherence of the bourgeois state depends upon an illusory legal equality masking not only economic inequality and class domination but also the general social and sexual subordination of women. Furthermore, because it reserves for itself the capacity to define its channels of access, the state effectively reproduces its exclusive power in every request, however critical, made of it. Women's demands for protection from the crime of rape can therefore come only from the position of the supposedly genderless subject recognized by the state, a position that cancels the specificity of their concrete situation as women.

If rape is indeed the most desperate and brutal form that social interaction takes for women in a society where men speak their desire for them, it is easy to see how "taking control of our bodies" became a watchword and a central effort in the women's movement. As Rosalind Petchesky has shown, the concept of having control over one's body has its roots in the bourgeois liberal tradition and the "natural rights" of individuals, including the Leveller idea of "property in one's person."[13] Insofar as it is tied to the ideology of individualism—and to capital's exploitation of the "right to self-determination" in its disruption of oppositional collectivities, for instance in union busting—this concept stands in contradiction to a socialist feminist analysis of women's collective oppression and the joint struggle necessary to overcome it. Nonetheless, the notion of the free individual remains crucial to a defense of women's autonomy under the current social order and to feminist struggles for revolutionary change. In addition to the significant gains made by feminists since the eighteenth century in the name of individual rights and legal equality, we should consider the concept's importance in Marxist theory. The Marxist notion of individuals' concrete and specific *needs*, as opposed to their abstract and impersonal *rights*, emphasizes an understanding of the subject as a subject in history, one whose sensual experience is the measure of social liberation. This idea is critical for women because it allows the possibility of articulating subjective needs and desires in terms that are class- and gender-specific.

However, as suggested above, psychoanalysis has compromised the adequacy of the concept of the individual to account for the historical subject. It has shown that the individual subject as a gendered and unified entity is at once produced by a complex interplay of social, discursive, somatic, and psychic forces, and is unstable, that is, traversed by unconscious impulses, drives, and the contradictions of social life under capitalism, which continually undermine its simple unity. From this perspective, it is hardly possible to posit the relation of the subject to its body, or to other bodies, as unproblematic. Nor can one claim unequivocally, for example, that the principle of bodily self-determination is founded on the transhistorical "fact" of our biological status as discrete individuals. On the contrary, feminist arguments against rape, and analyses of rape culture, can seriously challenge the prevailing social relations only if they take into account an understanding of the historically produced gendered subject, not only where social interaction is concerned, but with regard to the subject's relation to the body as well. To fight in the name of bodily self-determination, as the concept is traditionally understood, is to deny the specificity of female experience by containing it within a category of the bourgeois legal code, which, as we have seen, denies women their very existence. However, if the individual's experience of and relation to the body and other bodies is seen as culturally produced *at every level*, feminists can work more effectively to generate new concepts that permit a recognition of that experience as one that is in struggle and whose destructive aspects can be altered.

By investigating the interplay between sexuality and power, feminist theory can indicate new avenues of opposition to rape and other forms of male domination. Already, however, various women's organizations are challenging the present economy of that interplay. Rape crisis centers, for instance, insofar as they are run exclusively by women, help to consolidate a women's community that can overcome individual isolation and ineffectiveness in the fight to stop rape. They become a space where women debate and act on questions immediately and gravely affecting them, such as how to respond supportively to a woman who has been raped and feels she has lost control of her life, and whether and how to prosecute the rapist. The centers are places where women offer each other aid and comfort, interacting in ways that are not mediated by men in the usual fashion. This mode of interaction in turn provides a model for critical reflection on rape, rooted in women's common experience of oppression and collective struggle against it. Despite the obvious reactive dimension to the effort, rape crisis centers do advance women's struggles for control of their bodies.

Similarly, women's ride services, whose aim is rape prevention, establish a degree of control by rejecting the notion that women must either stay home or depend on the company of "protective" men when going out at night. The women who run and use these services are acting on the recognition that rape is used to justify the regulation of women's movement and, worse, that it is tolerated as a means to obstruct their circulation in public without men. Generally, the services are available at low cost, so that even women with limited financial means can move about more safely.

There are of course serious limitations involved, not the least of which are the paucity of ride services and the difficulty of staffing them, since the labor is often unpaid. Women going out at night are still dependent on others for their mobility, and are still badly served by "public" transportation. But in a situation where they are accompanied by other women who share a political consciousness of rape, a form of resistance is created and incorporated into a daily life routine that is otherwise fundamentally hostile. However marginal it may be, this resistance challenges women's forced dependence on men and their separation from each other.

At the practical level, women who organize a ride service or rape crisis center critically formulate both their experience and their desire to alter it in particular ways. Whatever credence the organizers and clients may give to the bourgeois legal system and the "right to self-determination," the dynamics of their interaction are such that it is necessarily a collective rather than an individual subject, and a gendered rather than a supposedly gender-free subject, whose interests are being articulated *against* a state apparatus that claims to represent the individual regardless of sex. It is this sort of challenge to the principles and practices of the current social order that feminist reflection on sexuality and power can help to shape, broaden, and strengthen, with a view toward eliminating the subjection of women and, with it, the crime of rape.

Notes

1. Michel Foucault, *The History of Sexuality*, vol. 1, trans. Robert Hurley (New York: Pantheon, 1978), p. 93.
2. See "The Confession of the Flesh," an interview with Foucault, in *Power/Knowledge: Selected Interviews and Other Writings, 1972–1977*, ed. Colin Gordon (New York: Pantheon, 1980), pp. 194–228.
3. Adrienne Rich, "Compulsory Heterosexuality and Lesbian Existence," *Signs* 4 (1980): 648.
4. Lillian Faderman, *Surpassing the Love of Men: Romantic Friendships and Love between Women from the Renaissance to the Present* (New York: William Morrow, 1981).
5. Rich, "Compulsory Heterosexuality and Lesbian Existence," 648.
6. Foucault introduces a debate on rape published by the Change Collective in *La Folie encerclée* (Paris: October 1977).
7. Monique Plaza, "Our Costs and Their Benefits," *m/f* 4 (1980): 28–39.
8. Susan Brownmiller, *Against Our Will: Men, Women, and Rape* (New York: Bantam Books, 1975), p. 4.
9. The recently translated work of French theorists Luce Irigaray and Hélène Cixous, for example, links an analysis of the male libidinal economy both to conceptual structures in the Western philosophical tradition and to social relations.
10. Socialization and sex-role theory informs several feminist studies of rape, such as Brownmiller's, cited above, Susan Griffin's *Rape: The Power of Consciousness* (New York: Harper and Row, 1979), Diana Russell's *The Politics of Rape* (New York: Stein and Day, 1975), and Andra Medea and Kathleen Thompson's *Against Rape* (New York: Farrar, Straus & Giroux, 1974). For a discussion of the limits of socialization theory that draws on Foucault's work, see Parveen Adams and Jeff Minson, "The 'Subject' of Feminism," *m/f* 2 (1978): 43–61.
11. Russell, *The Politics of Rape*.
12. Cited by Griffin in *Rape: The Power of Consciousness*, p. 9.
13. Rosalind Petchesky, "Reproductive Freedom: Beyond a Woman's Right to Choose," papers from "The Second Sex—Thirty Years Later," New York Institute for the Humanities, Sept. 27–29, 1979, pp. 91–98.

Jana Sawicki

Identity Politics and Sexual Freedom: Foucault and Feminism

At a time when attention to differences among women is at the forefront of feminist discussion, differences concerning sexual behavior and politics have produced particularly heated debates within feminism. The sexuality debates that have been raging for over four years now have increasingly led to a polarization of American feminists into two camps, radical and libertarian.[1] Some have stayed above the fray, watching with impatience and skepticism, believing that the debates are a red herring or a self-indulgent diversion from more important struggles. Others, myself among them, have watched with interest. Not a prurient interest, but one sparked by the conviction that the debates have exposed certain lacunae in feminist theory.

In particular, they have brought to light inadequacies in current feminist conceptions of power and freedom, and confusion (even "crisis") over what constitutes membership in the "feminist community." Yet the debates have been productive insofar as they have redirected feminist attention to two important questions. What is (or ought to be) the relationship of feminism to struggles for sexual liberation, that is, to sexual-identity politics? What are the implications of the differences among women for building a unified feminist theory and practice?

In a recent issue of *Signs*, Ann Ferguson has attempted to move debate forward by offering a constructive critique of the concepts of freedom, power, and sexuality that underlie the positions of both camps.[2] She is part of an emerging third camp that rejects the division between radical and libertarian feminists as exhaustive. I too want to contribute to the movement beyond polarized debate, specifically by further developing the theoretical and practical implications of a more adequate "sexual politics" in the recent work of Michel Foucault. Although Foucault is sometimes described as a libertarian himself, I hope to show how his analysis of power and sexuality can provide the basis for a sexual politics that steers between the Scylla of a moralistic dogmatism and the Charybdis of a libertarian pluralism in which anything goes.[3]

Sexual Freedom and Sexual Repression

Ann Ferguson offers a useful sketch of the two paradigms of sexual freedom that inform the sexuality debates:

Radical Feminists:

Sexual freedom requires the sexual equality of partners and their equal respect for one another as both subject and body. It also requires the elimination of all patriarchal institutions (e.g., the pornography industry, the patriarchal family, prostitution, and compulsory heterosexuality) and sexual practices (sadomasochism, cruising, adult/child and butch/femme relationships) in which sexual objectification occurs.[4]

Libertarian Feminists:

Sexual freedom requires oppositional practices, that is, transgressing socially respectable categories of sexuality and refusing to draw the line on what counts as politically correct sexuality.[5]

What I find remarkable about these definitions, and the many particular positions from which they are abstracted, is what they have in common. As we shall see, both involve repressive models of power. Moreover, both locate power in a key institution or group of individuals. Indeed, a more careful look reveals two distinct versions of repression, which I will refer to as the traditional repressive hypothesis and the social constructionist repressive hypothesis.

The Traditional Repressive Hypothesis

Feminist commentators have frequently addressed the naturalist and biological determinist tendency in radical feminist theory.[6] Such tendencies are particularly evident in their attribution of male dominance to male biology and their identification of femininity with women's biological role in procreation.[7] Thus, they appeal to a form of essentialism in which "male sexuality" is associated with violence, lust, objectification, and a preoccupation with orgasm, and "female sexuality" with nurturance, reciprocity, intimacy, and an emphasis on nongenital pleasure. Accordingly, sexual freedom is construed negatively, as freedom from male-dominated institutions whose elements are crystallized in pornography, particularly its s/m varieties. In patriarchal societies like our own female sexuality can presumably flourish only in isolated and marginal contexts, such as egalitarian lesbian relationships. In short, a natural and inherently good female sexuality is portrayed as repressed by a male sexuality based on coercion and violence against women. Sexual freedom requires the restraint of male sexuality as we know it, or its elimination altogether.

Some libertarians have also appealed to the notion of a repressed, natural, and innocent sexuality.[8] They borrow this model from the sexual liberationist instinct/control paradigm rooted in Freudian psychology and found in the writings of more recent sexologists from Reich and Marcuse to Masters and Johnson. In this view, the basic difference between male and female sexuality is that the latter is more repressed. For example, while all libertarian feminists acknowledge sexism in pornography, they regard the release of female sexual energy as more important than the restraint of male sexuality. Therefore, they resist drawing lines between safe and dangerous, politically correct and incorrect sex. The primary obstacle to sexual freedom, according to this view, is the existence of normative hierarchies of sexual expression that inhibit the release of an inherently liberatory (or benign) sexual energy. Again, as in the radical feminists' accounts, we find a negative view of freedom, that is, freedom is freedom from repressive norms.

The difficulties with the traditional repressive hypothesis and its concomitant versions of sexual freedom have often been pointed out. In the first place, it is ahistorical, that is, it fails to address the social and historical construction of sexual desire and behavior and the dialectical character of the relationship between biology and culture.[9] Moreover, insofar as radical feminists universalize "male" and "female" sexuality, they fail to account for sexual diversity across divisions of race, class, age, and the like. Libertarians fall into the same ahistoricity, naturalism, and essentialism by default when they accuse radicals of a "female" sex prudishness and fail to explore the ways in which desires are constructed in the context of patriarchal and capitalist social relations. Finally, both groups fail to identify a positive model of sexual freedom in the present. Many radicals are asking us to wait until male-controlled sexuality has been overthrown; libertarians offer an inadequate account of the dangers that accompany female sexual exploration in a sexist society.

The Social Constructionist Repressive Hypothesis

Not all radical and libertarian feminists operate with the instinct/control model of sexual repression presented above. To be sure, the feminist sexuality debates have reflected the influence of recent work in the history of sexuality that rejects the idea of an autonomous sexual drive.[10] Members of both camps speak of the social construction of desire.[11]

Ironically, essentialist tendencies that plague naturalistic accounts of sexual repression sometimes reappear in social constructionism. One obvious difference in the latter is the recognition that desire can be transformed. Nevertheless, as philosopher Sandra Bartky has pointed out, feminists lack an adequate "politics of personal transformation."[12] How one goes about altering one's desires when they appear to conflict with "feminist" political or moral principles is not obvious. Nor is the extent to which such desires can be consciously altered at all clear. What should be clear in any social constructionist account of sexual desire is that the naturalistic recourse to an innocent or malevolent desire is inadequate. So, too, is a retreat into liberal arguments about the sanctity of private life. (Indeed, one of the strengths of radical feminism has been its consistent rejection of such strategies.) These strategies fail to analyze the degree to which sexuality is both a target of oppression and an arena of political struggle with liberatory potential.

Radical feminists who acknowledge that desire is socially constructed still operate with a model of power as centralized in male institutions and as possessed by men. Hence, they regard male control of the modes of reproduction as the most fundamental form of oppression and call for women to seize control of the material base of patriarchy in order to effect revolution. An adaptation of this model to the issue of sexual freedom is found in the following statement by Karen Rian in her article "Sadomasochism and the Social Construction of Desire":

> Since our sexuality has been constructed for the most part through social structures over which we have had no control, we all "consent" to sexual desires and activities which are alienating to at least some degree. However, there is a vast difference between consent and self-determination. The latter includes the former, but in addition entails *control over the social structures which shape our lives*, including our sexual desires and relationships. . . . Sexual liberation involves the freedom to re-define and reconstruct our sexuality, which in turn reshapes our sexual desires.[13]

What is undesirable about Rian's understanding of sexual freedom is its sex-negativity and totalistic view of power. According to Rian, sexual self-determination is possible only if women control the social structures that shape their lives—in other words, after the feminist revolution. This is a utopian conception of freedom that has nihilistic consequences for the present. Here radical change consists in the complete negation of present sexual relations. The ambiguity and multiplicity of current sexual practices are effectively denied and social transformation detemporalized.[14]

Furthermore, although Rian herself acknowledges that *all* of us are sexually alienated to some degree, other radical feminists have tended to focus exclusively on the construction of female desire, particularly the desires of females whose sexual behaviors are regarded as more suspect, for example, lesbian sadomasochists and butch/femme couples. The result is an overemphasis on the victimization of women and a portrayal of them as passive containers of male sexual ideology. The picture of history that emerges in this view reflects little struggle and leads to little hope of radical social transformation. Nor does this picture of female containment by male domination offer an account of deviance from the male-defined norms. How are "feminist" sexual practices possible in male-dominated society? Finally, the process through which *male desire* has been constructed remains unanalyzed. We are left to surmise that an unalienated and monolithic male desire is actually reflected in the current system. Again, the argument rests on covert essentialist premises.

A more promising direction for future thinking about sexuality, feminism, power, and freedom within the social constructionist framework may be developed from the writings of radical social theorist and historian

Michel Foucault. Foucault offers an analysis of sexuality and power that, in the words of Foucauldian feminist Gayle Rubin, "recognizes repressive phenomena without resorting to the language of libido."[15] Foucault does not deny that there is sexual repression, but rather shifts attention to a larger set of productive power relations operating throughout the social body that constitute us as the subjects of modern sexual experience.

It is by now well known that, according to Foucault, power has not operated primarily by denying sexual expression but by creating the forms that modern sexuality takes. In the *History of Sexuality* he describes a process through which sexuality in the twentieth century comes to be understood as a key to self-understanding and human liberation. Through this deployment of sexuality, sex becomes a target for intervention into family life by medical, psychiatric, and governmental experts whose discourses and practices create the divisions healthy/ill, normal/perverse, and legal/criminal and carry an authoritative status enabling them to be used as effective means of social control. However, Foucault's interests do not lie only in analyzing the power of experts. More importantly, he examines the maintenance of social control through a marginalization and medicalization of "deviancy," which diverts attention from tolerated "abnormalities" within "normal" social intercourse. (One might analyze marital rape or white-collar crime along these lines.) Rather than treat the history of sexuality as a history of the imposing or lifting of restrictions on sexual expression, Foucault describes how power has produced our ways of understanding and taking up sexual practices, and how these discourses later become the primary positions in struggles concerning sexuality, thereby eliding the reality of other experiences and practices. Thus, Foucault rejects Reich's science-based sexual liberationist claim that saying yes to sex is saying no to power. This is not an endorsement of s/m (as one radical feminist has charged), but rather the claim that relaxing restraints on sexual expression is not inherently liberatory. Foucault wants to shift our attention away from a preoccupation with "repression" as the central concept for analyzing the relationship between sex and power.[16]

In effect, Foucault claims that individuals have been repressed *through* sexuality, particularly through the production of discourses in the human sciences and the practices associated with them, but also in our own everyday practices. "Repression" refers to efforts to control socially constructed desires. In fact, Foucault claims that deviancy is controlled and norms are established through the very process of identifying deviant activity as such, then observing it, further classifying it, and monitoring and "treating" it. Hence, as some gays and lesbians achieve a modicum of acceptance in the contemporary U.S., new norms have been established within these groups through the identification of practices that are deviant relative to theirs. We have here another example of what Foucault refers to as the "deployment of sexuality." Accordingly, he recommends that we "de-sexualize" the contemporary political domain and has endorsed feminist strategies which do just that. For example, when questioned about strategies for sexual liberation, Foucault replied:

> What I want to make apparent is precisely that the object "sexuality" is in reality an instrument formed long ago, and one which has constituted a centuries-long apparatus of subjection. The real strength of the women's movement is not that of having laid claim to the specificity of their sexuality and the rights pertaining to it, but that they have actually departed from the discourse conducted within the apparatuses of sexuality . . . a veritable de-sexualization, a displacement effected in relation to the sexual centering of the problem, formulating the demand for forms of culture, discourse, language . . . which are no longer part of that rigid assignation and pinning down to their sex. . . ."[17]

Thus, when feminists expand the domain of sexuality to include such issues as abortion and reproduction, they engage in a de-sexualization of their struggles and move away from gender-based identity politics. In contrast, homosexual liberation movements have been (understandably) "caught at the level of demands for the right to their sexuality."[18]

At this point it might seem that Foucault's work would provide an unlikely source of support for radical sexual liberationism. Foucault's comments on de-sexualizing political struggle do seem to put into question the viability of sexual struggles centered on individuals' attachments to their sexual identities—homosexual, sadomasochist, fetishist, and so forth. In other words, Foucault does sometimes speak as though the domain of sexuality were already colonized beyond redemption.

It is essential to clarify the nature of Foucault's misgivings concerning liberation struggles rooted in identity politics in order to avoid misunderstanding. In effect he has described a form of domination that operates by categorizing individuals and attaching them to their identities, a form of power that locates the truth of the individual in his or her sexuality. Hence, it is not surprising that he would be skeptical about a strategy for liberation founded on the very discourses he has attempted to debunk, the discourses of medicine and psychiatry that emerged in the nineteenth century. They located identity within the psyche or body of the individual, conceiving of the latter as a fixed and unified entity. Gays and lesbians today still appeal to this notion of identity when they describe their own sexualities as "orientations" (a matter of how they were born) rather than "preferences." In contrast to this static and individualistic model of identity is one that views personal identity as constituted by the myriad of social relationships and practices in which the individual is engaged. Because these relationships are sometimes contradictory and often unstable, the identity that emerges is fragmented and dynamic. Thus, for example, in a racist and homophobic society, a black lesbian experiences the conflicting aspects of her identity in terms of conflicts over loyalties and interests relative to the black and lesbian communities. In the same way, lesbian feminists involved in butch/femme role playing experience conflicting loyalties.

In this view of the self, the relationship between the individual and society is not pictured as one of social determination—complete socialization. Socialization, rather, emerges as a theoretical project that is never fully realized in practice. Therefore, social constructionism need not imply social determinism. Foucault's certainly does not.

In the above account of the construction of personal identity, the notion of the individual's interests also becomes problematic. As Ann Ferguson aptly states:

> In a situation where various important aspects of one's identity in ongoing social practices lead one to define contrary interests in relation to different groups, an individual cannot simply accept the social practices, and the interests defined through them, as given.[19]

In such a relational view of personal identity, one's interests are a function of one's place in the social field at a particular time, not given. They are constantly open to change and contestation.

Indeed, individuals experiencing such conflicts are in an especially good position to understand the desirable features of coalition politics. Coalitions provide an opportunity for individuals who experience some of the privileges of dominant groups to redefine how they differ from individuals in subordinate groups. Moreover, those in subordinate groups can come to appreciate how it is possible for someone who is dominant in some, but not all, respects to share their interests.[20]

An understanding of sexual liberation based on this latter notion of identity, one that is a product of social relations and conflicts, requires more than the demand for a right to one's sexuality, for, on this model, one's "sexuality" is a matter of socially and historically specific practices and relationships that are contingent and dynamic, and thus a matter of political struggle. In such a model of identity, freedom is not something following from a notion of one's true nature or essence as "human being," "woman," or "proletarian," but rather our capacity to choose the forms of experience through which we constitute ourselves.[21]

Foucault's skepticism concerning struggles for sexual liberation must be understood in the light of his rejection of totalizing theories that prescribe universal strategies for human liberation on the basis of essentialist sciences of sexuality, the economy, or the "libidinal economy." Essentialist humanisms obscure the irreducible plurality of habits, practices, experiences, and desires within the many different sexual subcultures. Foucault wants to avoid the dominating features of the universalism implicit in such humanisms and the elision of difference to which they lead. According to Foucault, there are many sides to political struggles for social transformation. Indeed, as we have seen, struggle goes on within and between subjects.

Thus, while Foucault's analysis of sexual identity is not sufficient to reject radical sexual politics, neither should it be the basis for rejecting coalitions with sex radicals. Following the example of Foucault's analysis of the history of the power to punish in *Discipline and Punish*, Gayle Rubin has recommended that we displace the categories of thought about sexuality from "the more traditional ones of sin, disease, neurosis, pathology . . . [etc.]" (those that Foucault has described as part of the deployment of sexuality) to "populations, neighborhoods, settlement patterns, migration, urban conflict, epidemiology, and police technology."[22] Thus, she hopes to provide detailed analyses of the relationships between "stigmatized erotic populations and the social forces which regulate them," thereby bringing into focus the particular forms of oppression that sex radicals face.[23]

Furthermore, Foucault himself provides justification for continuing to struggle at the level of sexual politics when he acknowledges that discourse is ambiguous. His most recent remarks about discourse, power, and resistance make it clear that there is no final word concerning the political status of sexual struggles—even those based on sexual identity. Foucault defines discourse as a form of power that circulates in the social field and can attach to strategies of domination as well as to those of resistance. Neither wholly a source of domination nor of resistance, sexuality is also neither outside power nor wholly circumscribed by it. Instead, it is itself an arena of struggle. There are no inherently liberatory or repressive sexual practices, for any practice is co-optable and any is capable of becoming a source of resistance. After all, if relations of power are dispersed and fragmented throughout the social field, so must resistance to power be. Thus, evaluating the political status of sexual practices should be a matter of historical and social investigation, not a priori theoretical pronouncement.

Finally, according to this analysis of power and resistance, freedom lies in our capacity to discover the historical links between certain modes of self-understanding and modes of domination, and to resist the ways in which we have already been classified and identified by dominant discourses. This means discovering new ways of understanding ourselves and each other, refusing to accept the dominant culture's characterizations of our practices and desires, and redefining them from within resistant cultures.

Lesbian feminists have certainly been effective at such reconceiving. But their new self-understandings are not immune to co-optation within dominant power relations. For example, lesbian feminists could be tempted to capitulate to more conservative forces by disavowing their affiliation with other oppressed sexual minorities rather than engaging in efforts to further articulate their connections with the sexual fringe. One way to achieve the latter would be to engage in a process of collective consciousness raising. This would require that we continue to provide detailed historical analyses of the ways in which sexuality has become a pivotal target in strategies of domination. The purpose of such consciousness raising would not be to tell us who we are, but rather to free us from certain ways of understanding ourselves, that is, to tell us who we do not have to be and to tell us how we came to think of ourselves in the ways that we do.

Beyond Dogmatism and Liberal Pluralism

There are several advantages to this Foucauldian analysis of power and freedom. In the first place, like radical feminist theory, it politicizes the personal domain and thereby avoids the liberal trap of conceiving of our personal desires and relationships as outside power. But unlike radical feminist theory, it does not locate power in a monolithic structure or central institution such as pornography or compulsory heterosexuality. This should be desirable to radical feminists who learned from their experiences with Leftists in the 1960s how oppressive the economic reductionism of gender issues could be. At that time personal politics were not only given a low priority, but were treated as self-indulgent and bourgeois. The recent radical feminist position on sexual freedom, which requires that women control the modes of reproduction before they can determine their sexuality, parallels early Marxist skepticism about radical transformation in the personal domain until after the revolution.

A second advantage of this analysis is that it enables us to think of difference as a resource rather than a threat. In another essay I have developed more fully the idea of a "politics of difference."[24] In such a politics one is not always attempting to overcome difference. Neither does one regard difference as an obstacle to effective resistance. Difference can be a resource insofar as it enables us to multiply the sources of resistance to the myriad of relations of domination that circulate through the social field. If there is no central locus of power, then neither is there a central locus of resistance. Moreover, if we redefine our differences, discover new ways of understanding ourselves and each other, then our differences are less likely to be used against us. In short, a politics that is designed to avoid dogmatism in our categories and politics as well as the silencing of difference to which such dogmatism can lead is a welcome alternative to polarized debate. Dialogue between women with different sexual preferences can be opened, not with the aim of eliminating these differences, but rather learning from them and discovering the basis for coalition building. Of course, this means discovering what we have in common as well; we need not universalize difference, either. In this view our basis for common struggle is a democratic and provisional one, subject to re-creation and renegotiation.[25]

Only if feminists democratize their struggles by giving equal respect to the claims of other oppressed minorities will they avoid what Richard Sennett once described as "destructive Gemeinschaft."[26] Destructive gemeinschaft refers to the destructive sense of community in which conflict is experienced as an "all or nothing contest for personal legitimacy," that is, for the right to have one's feelings.[27] Individuals involved in such conflicts sometimes become preoccupied more with bolstering their own identities than with their political goals. Such identity politics can be self-defeating insofar as it often leads to internal struggles over who really belongs to the community. I fear that Sennett aptly characterizes the current situation within a part of the feminist movement when he remarks: "Powerlessness comes from the very attempts to define a collective identity instead of defining the common interests of a diverse group of people."[28] At its best, feminism has been very effective at realizing methods for sharing feelings in order to foster shared political commitment. We need to return to this model of consciousness raising in order to learn from our differences and utilize them to enrich our politics. In addition, if we recognize that identities are historically constituted, then we can accept their contingency. We might even be prepared for the dissolution of feminism or lesbianism as we understand them in the future and thus not attach ourselves to our identities so rigidly. I am not suggesting that we can will them away, but rather that we might be more effective if we became less concerned with preserving them or imposing them on others and more concerned with eliminating injustices wherever they arise. Furthermore, the differences among women could be productive insofar as they stimulated a wide variety of visions for the future.

A final advantage of Foucault's mode of analysis is that it politicizes theory as well. He often highlighted the oppressive practical consequences of humanistic revolutionary or liberal political theories. Again, Gayle Rubin follows his example when she points to the limits of her own totalistic analysis of the "sex/gender system" as developed in her landmark essay, "The Traffic in Women."[29] There she treated gender and sexual desire as systematically connected. In her most recent work she provides a methodological framework for exploring other structures, other power relations in which sexuality is enmeshed. In other words, she no longer believes that sexuality is wholly a product of the gender system and thinks it is a mistake to view feminism as capable of providing the ultimate and total account of social oppression.

Foucault also stressed the specificity and autonomy of the many modes of oppression in modern society. He emphasized the fragmented and open-ended character of the social field. Therefore, he was skeptical about the possibility and desirability of grand theory. Rather than offer one himself, he subjected modern theories in psychology and criminology, as well as Marxist and liberal political theories, to historical reflection in an effort to render them problematic in the present by focusing on the ways in which they have been linked to domination and oppression. Given his skepticism about grand theory, and his emphasis on the heterogeneity and fragmentation of the social field, he is led to a theoretical pluralism of sorts. For if difference is distorted and obscured in totalistic theories, the obvious path for resistance to take is to provide alternative mappings of specific regions of the social field. In other words, theoretical pluralism makes possible the expansion of social ontology, a redefinition and redescription of experience from the perspectives of those who are more often simply objects of theory. Feminists have begun to provide new maps. Sexually oppressed minorities can provide others.

Of course, on the basis of specific theoretical analyses one can make generalizations, identify links between forms of oppression, and locate patterns of domination. Thus, one can evaluate the relative practical values and dangers of particular tactics of resistance. But this represents a very different understanding of the role of theory from that promulgated by Freudian, Marxist, and feminist humanists. Foucault's theories do not tell us what to do, but rather how some of our ways of thinking and doing are historically linked to particular forms of power and social control; his theories serve less to explain than to criticize and raise questions. His histories of theories are designed to reveal their contingency and thereby free us from them.

To be sure, there is an element of pessimism in all of this. In the first place, the call for theoretical and practical pluralism is based on the implicit assumption that a power-free society is an abstraction and struggle a ubiquitous feature of history. Those engaged in struggle can expect the changes they bring about to take on a different face over time. Discourses and institutions are ambiguous and may be used for different ends. Second, and correlatively, a Foucauldian sexual politics does not aspire to control history or to bring about global transformation all at once. There is no single vision of life "after the revolution." Yet, one need not have an idea of utopia to recognize and struggle against injustices in the present. And if there is a vision of the future implicit in this approach, it is one of a democratic and heterogeneous society.

The history of sexual politics over the past 150 years has provided enough examples of theoretical and strategic inadequacy to make a theoretical and practical pluralism reasonable. This need not be a pluralism in which anything goes. In fact, it would be more appropriately described as a "pluralism in which nothing goes," that is, one in which everything is potentially dangerous.[30] In one of the last interviews before his untimely death, Foucault remarked: "My point is not that everything is bad, but that everything is dangerous. . . ."[31] Foucault's own reluctance to be explicit about his ethical and political positions is attributable not to nihilism, relativism, or political irresponsibility, but rather to his sense of the dangers of political programs based on grand theory.

Thus, turning to Foucault in our efforts to analyze the recent debates between radical and libertarian feminists does not answer the question "what should be done"; but if we reflect seriously on the lessons of the sexuality debates, a few conclusions concerning what could be avoided do emerge. Foucault's analyses of power and sexuality put into question the viability of using essentialist notions of sexual identity as a basis for building a feminist theory and politics. Moreover, they have highlighted the importance of keeping open the question "which desires are liberating." Indeed, they raise doubts about the possibility or desirability of ever giving a final answer to this question. Finally, they point to the need to subject our feminist categories and concepts to critical historical analysis in a continual effort to expose their limitations and highlight their specificity. Perhaps the least dangerous way to discover whether and how specific practices are enslaving or liberating us is not to silence and exclude differences, but rather to use them to diversify and renegotiate the arena of radical political struggle.

Notes

1. See Alice Echols, "The Taming of the Id: Feminist Sexual Politics," in *Pleasure and Danger: Exploring Female Sexuality*, ed. Carole S. Vance (Boston: Routledge and Kegan Paul, 1984), pp. 50–72. Echols distinguishes "cultural feminism" from early radical feminism and associates the former with the positions here attributed to "radical feminists."

2. See Ann Ferguson, "Sex War: The Debate Between Radical and Libertarian Feminists," *Signs* 10, no. 1 (1984): 106–12.

3. This is a goal that many radical feminists have affirmed. See *Against Sadomasochism: A Radical Feminist Analysis*, ed. Robin Ruth Linden, et al. (East Palo Alto, Calif.: Frog in the Well Press, 1982).

4. Ferguson, "Sex War," 108.

5. Ibid., 109.

6. See, for example, Alison Jaggar, *Feminist Politics and Human Nature* (Totowa, N.J.: Rowman & Allanheld, 1983), pp. 106 ff.

7. See, for example, Mary Daly, quoted in *Off Our Backs*, May 1979; Adrienne Rich, *Of Woman Born* (New York: W. W. Norton, 1976); Susan Griffin, *Woman and Nature: The Roaring Inside Her* (New York: Harper and Row, 1978). Note that some radicals (e.g., Andrea Dworkin) are explicitly opposed to biological determinism.

8. Pat Califia has referred to sexual desire as "impeccably honest." ("Among Us, Against Us—The New Puritans," *The Advocate*, April 17, 1980, p. 14.) Curiously enough, one radical feminist has accused libertarians of appealing to the biological superiority of the female. See Sally Roesch Wagner, "Pornography and the Sexual Revolution: The Backlash of Sadomasochism," in Linden, *Against Sadomasochism*, pp. 34ff.

9. On the "dialectical" relationship between biology and culture, see Alison Jaggar, "Human Biology in Feminist Theory: Sexual Equality Reconsidered," in *Beyond Domination*, ed. Carol C. Gould (Totowa, N.J.: Rowman & Allanheld, 1984), pp. 21–42.

10. See, for example, Robert Padgug, "Sexual Matters: On Conceptualizing Sexuality in History," *Radical History Review* 20 (Spring/Summer 1979): 3–24; Bert Hansen, "The Historical Construction of Homosexuality," *Radical History Review* 20 (Spring/Summer 1979): 66–75; Jeffrey Weeks, *Coming Out: Homosexual Politics in Britain from the Nineteenth Century to the Present* (London: Quartet Books, 1977); and Michel Foucault, *The History of Sexuality, Volume I: An Introduction*, trans. Robert Hurley (New York: Pantheon, 1978).

11. For examples, see the essays by Sally Roesch Wagner ("Pornography and the Sexual Revolution: The Backlash of Sadomasochism") and Karen Rian ("Sadomasochism and the Social Construction of Desire") in Linden, *Against Sadomasochism*. See also Gayle Rubin, "Thinking Sex: Notes for a Radical Theory of the Politics of Sexuality," in Vance, *Pleasure and Danger: Exploring Female Sexuality*, pp. 267–319.

12. Sandra Lee Bartky, "Feminine Masochism and the Politics of Personal Transformations," *Hypatia* 7, no. 5 (1984): 323–34.

13. Rian, "Social Construction," pp. 45–50, esp. p. 49; emphasis added.

14. Iris Young provides an interesting analysis of the detemporalization of change in her provocative paper "The Ideal of Community and the Politics of Difference," *Social Theory and Practice* 12, no. 5 (Spring 1986): 1–26, esp. p. 17.

15. Rubin, "Thinking Sex," p. 277.

16. Judy Butler, "Lesbian S&M: The Politics of Dis-Illusion," in Linden, *Against Sadomasochism*, pp. 169–74, esp. p. 169.

17. Michel Foucault, *Power/Knowledge: Selected Interviews and Other Writings, 1972–1977*, ed. Colin Gordon (New York: Pantheon, 1980), pp. 219–20.

18. Ibid., p. 220.

19. Ann Ferguson, "Public Patriarchy and How to Fight It: A Tri-Systems Theory," unpublished manuscript, Department of Philosophy, University of Massachusetts, Amherst, Mass., pp. 13–14.

20. See Ferguson, "Public Patriarchy," for an extended discussion of coalition politics.

21. See John Rajchman, "Ethics After Foucault," *Social Text* 13/14 (Winter/Spring 1986): 165–83, esp. p. 167, for a similar discussion of Foucault's notion of freedom.

22. Rubin, "Thinking Sex," p. 277.

23. Ibid.

24. See Jana Sawicki, "Foucault and Feminism: Toward a Politics of Difference," *Hypatia* 1, no. 2. (Fall 1986): 1–13.

25. Cf. Ernesto Laclau and Chantal Mouffe, *Hegemony & Socialist Strategy: Towards a Radical Democratic Politics*, trans. Winston Moore and Paul Cammack (London: Verso Press, 1985), pp. 188ff.

26. See Richard Sennett, "Destructive Gemeinschaft," in *The Philosophy of Sex and Love*, ed. Alan Soble (Totawa, N.J.: Rowman and Allanheld, 1980), pp. 291–321.

27. Ibid., p. 311.

28. Ibid., p. 312.

29. See Gayle Rubin, "The Traffic in Women: Notes on the 'Political Economy' of Sex," in *Toward an Anthropology of Women*, ed. Rayna R. Reiter (New York: Monthly Review Press, 1975), pp. 157–210.

30. I owe this phrase to Vicky Spelman.

31. Michel Foucault, "Afterword," in Hubert Dreyfus and Paul Rabinow, *Michel Foucault: Beyond Structuralism and Hermeneutics*, 2nd ed. (Chicago: University of Chicago Press, 1983), p. 232.

Irene Diamond and Lee Quinby

American Feminism and the Language of Control

Modern feminism is often said to be an outgrowth of liberalism, in particular of its ideal of individual self-determination. And indeed this is one of the reasons why historically Marxists and socialists have often dismissed women's movements as bourgeois and more reformist than revolutionary. Nevertheless, in America, during the first women's movement beginning in the 1830s, women drew on the language of rights as a way of illuminating problems and mobilizing political energies. During the second wave women used the language of rights and individual autonomy to expand their access to virtually all public institutions, as well as to question those areas of life that appeared to be the most private and immutable—from who could do housework to who could initiate sex. In short, since the modern idea of rights for women was first raised in the seventeenth century, liberal ideas have been central in overturning restrictions on women as individuals.

Yet as a number of different feminist theorists have pointed out, the language of rights is at the same time problematic and may even undercut efforts to establish a less violent and more humane world.[1] Access to men's rights to make war is perhaps the most vivid instance that rights in and of themselves cannot transform the world. Because this discourse obscures the webs of connection that sustain human existence, the goal of creating our common life and shared responsibilities becomes ever more difficult to achieve the more we focus on individual self-determination.

Our concern in this essay is how contemporary feminism's use of the language of rights intersected with, and in effect amplified, a discourse that is also problematic—the language of control of the body and sexuality. For this wave of feminists Margaret Sanger's plea in the early twentieth century that a woman's right to own and control her body was the fundamental route to freedom resonated in a way that it had not for her contemporaries. In fact, for today's feminism the right to control one's body and sexuality has come to be seen as the most radical demand women can make. It is argued that if such control were to be realized, women, indeed all of human society, would experience the most profound revolution ever.

This language has been a powerful mobilizing tool because it seems to speak on the one hand to women's desire for sexual pleasure and on the other hand to women's fears regarding abuse by men. But where did this language come from? What vision is it imbued with? Does it still serve as a challenge to masculinist ideology or has it become a principle of regulation within that form of domination? Though many questions have been raised about feminist discourse on the female body, on the whole there has been little questioning of how and why the language of control and sexuality came to dominate feminist discourse. Our goal here is first to raise some questions about the genealogy of such language and about how it has framed the development of feminist issues. We will then turn to some of the discourses within feminism that offer alternatives to the language of control.

In considering how the language of control became so fundamental to feminist discourse, it is perhaps relevant to note the emergence of feminism out of liberalism and its shared borders with Marxism as a theory of society and revolution. Despite important philosophical differences between Marxism and liberalism regarding human sociality, both ideologies partake of the Enlightenment's uncritical acceptance of science and reason as the sole means for discovering truth and knowledge. It is thus ironic that Marxism, which purports to challenge the value system of the dominant class, has nonetheless readily adopted that class's notion of scientific control. While most contemporary radical feminists self-consciously reject Marxism (although socialist feminists and Marxist feminists still labor to effect a unified synthesis), because both of these streams emerged from the Left it is understandable why so much of modern feminism has emulated Marxism with the analogue of seizing control of reproduction.

To challenge that analogue, as we wish to do, is not to blanketly condemn all scientific thinking, for the scientific tradition is a complex one and is not thoroughly infused with the impulse to dominate nature.[2] It is likely that the development of scientific consciousness facilitated contemporary feminism's challenge to biological determinism even while it also contributed to it. Moreover, this wave of feminists, in contrast to the first wave, has been able to conceive of men as potential nurturers, a shift in perspective that is potentially profoundly transformatory. But we jump ahead.

Among the interrelated problems inherent in the language of control, one of the most important is an ethical one: the language of control slips too readily into a language of domination, for it conceals the way in which an autonomous self is created at the expense of the Other. Another problem is that this language presumes a centering of power that may no longer exist in contemporary society: we are asked to seize power when power is no longer held by a clearly identifiable and coherent group. Finally, as many artists, philosophers, and scientists have recognized, our physical-cultural world is largely an indeterminant one. Crediting the human mind with the ability to control such a world ignores a point of wisdom summed up centuries ago by Euripides: "A knowing mind that ignores its own limits / has a very short span."[3]

Problems surrounding the language of the body and sexuality are perhaps more difficult to describe because of the pervasive current belief that the truth of one's self is to be found in one's sexuality. Feminism, which broke from the New Left in declaring that "the sexual revolution is not our revolution," has on the whole not developed a strategy or vision to supplant the idea that sexuality is in itself the means to liberation. To better appreciate the problems surrounding sexuality as the means to liberation, we need to consider the confluence of science, sex, and power that marks our society.

The work of Michel Foucault is especially helpful in this regard, particularly the analytics of power that he puts forth in *The History of Sexuality*, vol. 1, and the interviews and lectures in the collection entitled *Power/Knowledge*. Sexuality is, according to Foucault, a historical phenomenon, emerging in the seventeenth and eighteenth centuries. To understand what enables him to make such a claim, we must first look to his description of the nature of scientific discourse, which had as its precursor the Christian confession. For centuries, he argues, the confession governed the production of the true discourse of flesh. Today our society has, to quote Foucault, "pursued the task of producing true discourses concerning sex, and this by adapting—not without difficulty—the ancient procedure of confession to the rules of scientific discourse."[4] Science, in its pursuit of truth, seeks to render the invisible visible. Upon the demise of the metaphysical universe, sex emerged as one of the last invisible realms to be conquered.

Foucault offers an analysis of how power infuses and induces a "deployment of sexuality" in a scientized society. He argues that power is no longer merely vested in the sovereign's "right of seizure" but is now also a "power bent on generating forces, making them grow, and ordering them" ("rather than one dedicated to impeding them, making them submit, or destroying them").[5] This new form of power he sometimes calls "disciplinary power" and sometimes "bio-power." Historically, this disciplinary power did not simply replace sovereignty, but rather intersected with it. The continuation of the juridical discourse of sovereignty permitted the concealment of new microcenters of power, which operate through the production, regulation, surveillance, and labeling of human activities. These processes, he argues, lead to a *"society of normalization,"* a society governed less by legal rights than by the authority of the human sciences.[6]

In the nineteenth century, as this normalizing process gained ascendancy, the developing disciplines of medicine, education, and psychology focused their investigatory concerns on the body and on the secret it was said to harbor: sex. This confluence of science, sex, and power produced and continues to produce an intensified focus on sexuality as the instrument of truth. Sex, writes Foucault, "is the most speculative, most ideal, and most internal element in a deployment of sexuality organized by power in its grip on bodies and their materiality, their forces, energies, sensations, and pleasures."[7] Thus the body is experienced exclusively in terms of sex, creating what might be called the "sexuated body," a body situated in, satiated with, and standardized by sex. Paradoxically, in a society that sees sexual intimacy as the realm for the deepest expression of individuality, even so-called diverse innovations in sexual practices have been processed for us. Furthermore, this narrowing of bodily pleasure to sexual pleasure also has the consequence of ignoring other pleasures and of valorizing privatized pleasure at the expense of community and communion.

Although Foucault's analytics of power provides an astute revision of how power operates in contemporary societies, he does not particularly illuminate the effects of a society of normalization on the lives of women. We speak here of the routinization of battery, sexual exploitation, harassment, and sexual abuse in contemporary society. These are perhaps the darkest by-products of what Foucault has called the "technologies of sex."[8] Such technologies include everything from the "pornographization" of magazines, cable T.V., and video games to the manufactured need for body spas to home parties for the sale of sexual novelties to the proliferation of cosmetic counters loaded down with flavored body creams, vaginal deodorants, and nipple rouges to the dispersal of contraceptive devices for instant sex to sex manuals that cater to perfecting myriad sexual practices. Investigating the operations of these technologies leads us to a better understanding of the emergence of contemporary feminism. Feminism was clearly born in reaction to these technologies, as evidenced by the initial demonstrations against the objectification of women's bodies. Yet feminism is also implicated in them: perhaps the clearest example is the early popularity of the sexologists Masters and Johnson, whose works have also been the gospels of *Playboy*.[9]

The discourse around reproductive rights, which has become the central issue for many feminists today, and in particular the call for abortion on demand, provide cases in point. Linda Gordon and Allen Hunter have claimed, for example, that abortion is the "leading point of political contest in the area of both women's liberation and sexual freedom."[10] This claim, which not only narrows feminist concerns but also reinforces heterosexism insofar as it implies that women have sex only with men, can best be understood as an integral part of the accelerated deployment of sexuality in this century. Although we strongly uphold the importance of legal access to abortion, we want to point out that many feminists argue for reproductive rights in the language of control and sexuality characteristic of a technology of sex.

Such a technology poses problems for feminism because it first obscures the connective tissues that sustain us and then excises complex decisions from an ethical context. The net effect of this technological approach is, quite literally, a desensitization to human experience. Indeed, one of the consequences of the contemporary struggle for reproductive rights is a desensitization to abortion itself. As Wendy Brown astutely observes in an essay on the paradox of arguing for reproductive freedom on the basis of privacy, "Most proabortion groups defensively argue that abortion is a private, technical act so banal that were it not for the hysteria of the Moral Majority no one besides a pregnant woman and her doctor would think twice about it."[11] Carol Joffe perceptively describes how abortion counselors themselves respond to this tendency to treat abortion reductively. According to Joffe, the counselors "did not want their clients to perform only abortions. . . . Abortion seemed most manageable to these workers when they could experience it as part of a larger mosaic of human activity."[12] This move on the part of the counselors to contextualize their work suggests that the very word "reproduction" denies the sensuous, emotional, and evocative features of the activities it purports to name. In short, recognizing the pervasiveness of this capitalistic, scientific term, so devoid of the ambiguities and richness of human experience, forces us to confront feminism's involvement in the deployment of sexuality.

Perhaps the most obvious example of such feminist involvement is the assumption that sexuality exists outside of and untainted by power. To claim, as Gordon and Hunter have, for instance, that "we can be in principle unequivocally pro-sex because sex itself is a human activity that has its own worth and which can be separated from those oppressive power relations that invade it" is to ignore both the historicity of sexuality and the interplay between power and sexuality.[13] Heeding Foucault's analysis of how power operates in a society of normalization enables feminists to deal with such complex issues as teenage sexuality, sex education, and media enticement. Preliminary investigations suggest that feminists need not automatically rush to the defense of all sex-education programs. Indeed, a more helpful approach may be gender education in the context of social and political inequalities rather than the continuation of technologized service-delivery programs.[14]

Another form of feminist involvement in the deployment of sexuality is the tacit acceptance of sexuality as identity and as the means to truth and liberation, a stance that occurs in both heterosexual and lesbian feminist discourse. Contemporary research indicates that viewing sexual practice as synonymous with core identity is a relatively recent phenomenon. This research suggests that the late nineteenth century was a crucial turning point in the process that converted practice into identity. The emergence of homosexual identity is one of the better-known examples of this process. Foucault notes that, prior to the nineteenth century, "sodomy was a category of forbidden acts; their perpetrator was nothing more than the juridical subject of them," but that, during the nineteenth century, the "homosexual became a personage, a past, a case history, and a childhood, in addition to being a type of life, a life form, and a morphology, with an indiscrete anatomy and possibly a mysterious physiology."[15] As homosexuality became a classification, so too did heterosexuality, albeit one with the privileges accruing to prescribed "normality." Lesbian feminist arguments against viewing homosexuality as deviant have been particularly important in challenging heterosexist assumptions, but, ironically, they have often done so through positing homosexuality as innate. The consequence is to normalize homosexual identity rather than to provoke a rethinking of our society's reduction of sexual practice to one identity. In other words, to claim that lesbianism—or any sexual identity—is in itself a challenge to prevailing power relations is to accept the terms of the enterprise one seeks to defeat.

Feminist debates about lesbianism pivot on variations of this identity/practice matter. On the one hand is the argument that in order to be a true feminist one must practice same-gender sex. On the other hand is the argument that feminist identity is not contingent on same-gender sex but does hinge on legal and social support of lesbian practices. At times these debates have been so intense that they have threatened feminist political action. Attempting to reconcile these sometimes polarized points of view, Adrienne Rich offers the concept of a "lesbian continuum." She attempts to desexualize lesbianism by including along the continuum nurturant relations among females of all ages and races, while also endorsing those women who bond with other women through their sexual practices. Despite her profound insights into the ways in which the institution of heterosexuality operates and her eloquence in affirming that nurturance has been a vital force in the lives of women, she nonetheless reinforces the deployment of sexuality in a telling way. At the most basic level, although she recognizes the clinical nature of the term lesbian, she still retains this sexuated and scientized word. Thus her term "lesbian continuum" remains at cross-purposes. In addition, her argument that "lesbian experience comprises both the breaking of a taboo and the rejection of a compulsory way of life"[16] obscures the extent to which the breaking of taboos is itself an integral part of the incitement to sexuality."[17]

In recent years, a small but vociferous group of feminists has made the breaking of taboos the foundation on which feminism should be built.[18] Insisting on the inherently radical nature of being pro-sex, groups such as SAMOIS assert that sadomasochism can be one of the most liberating forms of sexual practice. Their writings are imbued with an extreme form of the sexual-scientific imperative toward mastery. And while they are perceptive in discerning essentialist attitudes within lesbian feminism, their own works display two forms of essentialist thinking. For example, Gayle Rubin writes that "sex is fundamentally okay until proven bad," thereby ignoring the historical and cultural construction that she otherwise espouses, and in particular disregarding the patriarchal construction of sexuality that is our legacy.[19] Pat Califia speaks of recalling "a private world of dominance, submission, punishment and pain" since "the age of two," thus implying that people are born into sadomasochism.[20] In short, these writers have unreflectively accepted the idea of practice as identity. Typically, proponents of sadomasochism invoke the rhetoric of free, autonomous individualism, characterizing sadomasochism as a consensual activity. Although a number of other feminists have commented on the illusory nature of sexual consent within the context of a male-dominant society,[21] our analysis here suggests that the debate over consent raises a false issue. Given the current mechanisms of normalization in our society, sexual consent is often a function of disciplinary power, and the highly ritualized directives for engaging in sadomasochistic practices testify to just how prescriptive these activities are.

In this discussion of reproductive rights, the identity/practice issue, and sadomasochism, we have attempted to show some of the problematic aspects of anchoring feminist discourse in the demand for "control over our bodies." Our analysis thus makes us wary of the direction Catharine MacKinnon takes in her attempt to unify feminism via sexuality and its control.[22] MacKinnon perceptively notes that much contemporary feminist writing and practice has in fact been centered on sexuality. Yet potential dangers emerge precisely where she promotes formalization. More specifically, her notion of producing a feminist political theory exclusively from an analysis of sexuality may render women even more vulnerable to the deployment of sexuality. She argues, for example, that sexuality is "that which is most one's own, yet most taken away."[23] To accept this is to promulgate the larger culture's belief that sex is the measure of identity and the instrument of truth. Not surprisingly, this view of sexuality leads her directly into the language of control, an emphasis bolstered by her reliance on Marxist categories.[24] But, ironically, unlike the Marxist impulse to seize control for the purpose of achieving nonalienated labor, MacKinnon appears to be calling for control for its own sake—there is barely a hint of nonalienated sexuality in her agenda for theory. We suspect that any theory bent solely on exposing the brutalities of social relations will be blinded to life's rich and varied textures and will necessarily produce a weak vision by ignoring existing practices and discourses that resist and provide alternatives to oppressive power relations.[25]

The question of vision has always been important to political and social theory. In our critique of current discourse on the body it may appear that we have fallen into a form of legalism in our emphasis on legal rights. Given the contemporary political context, legal rights cannot be ignored, but we want to suggest that significant political change does not rest here. Indeed, as we suggested earlier in this essay, the language of rights, which is the one our legal system is derived from, is deeply insufficient. The events of the last decade make it all too clear that any program or stance based on notions of equality and rights that are abstracted from the immediate context of women's lives often falls short of giving women a greater say in their lives and can even bring harm. Within the courts, for example, no-fault divorce has too often been translated into no-obligation for the male spouse, and sex "neutrality" in custody determinations has been used to ignore years of primary parenting by women. Our own approach to theory, methodology, and the relationship between theory and political practice attempts to foreground the importance of context. It seeks to be, in effect, a contextual feminism.

By contextual feminism, we mean theory that is grounded in the conflicts *and* joys of women's lives, as well as political strategies that are responsive to visions—without forgetting that such visions are enacted in the lives of actual women rather than utopian heroines. Contextual feminism, then, does not aspire to construct a theory of women's oppression solely around our bodies or any other totalizing principle. Moreover, as this essay indicates, a contextual approach underscores the importance of the ways language functions to create us as subjects.

Once we become attuned to how discourse within the technology of sexuality manufactures and conceals disciplinary power, we can begin to inquire into existing discourses infused with alternative concepts of selfhood and ethical relations. Foucault's analytics of power reminds us that we are not totally encapsulated by the prevailing discourse. "Discourses," he writes, "are not once and for all subservient to power or raised up against it, any more than silences are. We must make allowance for the complex and unstable process whereby discourse can be both an instrument and an effect of power, but also a hindrance; a stumbling block, a point of resistance and a starting point for an opening strategy."[26] Thus it is important to continue to expose and reveal those languages that center on mastery and monolithic identity, as well as to seek languages that evoke a fuller range of our senses, emotions, intellect, and imagination.

Some alternatives already exist within a century and a half of feminist writing and activism and in the strengths and richness of the women's experiences that contemporary feminist scholars are naming and giving voice to. Early in the American feminist tradition Margaret Fuller recognized the dangers of untrammeled intellect, calling on American women to infuse public institutions with sentiment.[27] Jane Addams's turn-of-the-century struggles against the ravages of industrialization virtually embody public nurturance. In one of her lesser-known works, *The Spirit of Youth and the City*, she emerges as an early critic of the technologies of sex:

> It is nothing short of cruelty to over-stimulate [the adolescent's] senses as does the modern city. . . . Most improbable tales hold the attention of the youth of the city night after night, and feed his starved imagination as nothing else succeeds in doing. . . . Sexual susceptibility is thus evoked without a corresponding stir of the higher imagination. . . . Sex impulse then becomes merely a dumb and powerful instinct without in the least awakening the imagination or the heart, nor does it overflow into neighboring fields of consciousness.[28]

Although these earlier feminists tend to assume a philosophical essentialism that is problematic, they nevertheless provide important challenges to the language of control. And, more recently, some second-wave feminists have found ways to foster alternatives to the discourse of mastery of control and still avoid essentialism. Carol Gilligan's research on women's moral development, for instance, reveals that women tend to use a language of morality that differs from that sanctioned by the dominant ideology; in this "different voice," "identity is defined in a context of relationship and judged by a standard of responsibility and care." According to Gilligan, because this alternative morality takes interrelatedness as a given, it arrives at "an understanding of life that reflects the limits of autonomy and control."[29]

The alternative morality that Gilligan points to is not as unified as she sometimes implies. Indeed, its strength lies in its diversity of voices willing to pool their resources of difference in order to combat the totalizing impulses of masculinist morality. As Gloria Anzaldúa writes in *This Bridge Called My Back* regarding the ethical responsibilities of these different voices of resistance:

> We have come to realize that we are not alone in our struggles nor separate nor autonomous but that we—white black straight queer female male—are connected

and interdependent. We are each accountable for what is happening down the street, south of the border or across the sea. . . . We are learning to depend more and more on our own sources for survival, learning not to let the weight of this burden, the bridge, break our backs. Haven't we always borne jugs of water, children, poverty? Why not learn to bear baskets of hope, love, self-nourishment and to step lightly?[30]

Thus this alternative morality carries with it an alternative politics, one that can cross national borders as readily as domination does.

Ecofeminists raise our awareness of the connections between the well-being of our bodies and the well-being of the earth. They note, for example, how the "advances" of embryo transfer, which divide our bodies into smaller and smaller parts, are heralded as the cure for the infertility produced by IUDs and toxic contamination of the planet. In place of current scientific theories and practices imbued with questionable notions of certainty, objectivity, and domination, ecofeminist discourse emphasizes indeterminancy, interconnectedness, and nurturance. As Susan Griffin observes of the views expressed in the ecofeminist collection *Reclaim the Earth:*

If there is one idea that can be said to link together all that is said and reported here, this idea is also a feeling. It is a grief over the fate of the earth, that contains within it a joyful hope that we might reclaim this earth. Does this one idea answer all our questions? It is not meant to. It is meant to make us ask more questions. And it is not necessary that we agree on every point, for what we have in common is not small.[31]

Whereas today bodies, skills, and pleasures are on the whole linguistically sexuated and scientized, discourses of caring and nurturance have the potential to challenge disciplinary power's claims to control. As Griffin suggests, self-reflexivity inheres in these emerging discourses. These languages which foster connectedness and the sharing of responsibilities can help us to ask what we might become. This mode of choosing and questioning holds the possibility of paths out of the impasse feminism has reached in its involvement with the languages of rights and control of the body. We anticipate some feminist disquietude about lending further support to languages of nurturance, for over the last few centuries in particular, nurturance has been seen as innately female and has reinforced historical patterns of excluding women from public activities. But the contemporary situation has opened up new possibilities, reminding us of our capacity to envision alternative conceptions. Feminist explorations of the historical contexts of women's experiences reveal that nurturance is not part of some unchanging female essence. Rather, nurturance is imbued in modes of being and thinking that evolve from women's different activities in the sustenance and preservation of life. In this age threatened by carcinogic air and water, genetic engineering, and nuclear annihilation, inventing nurturant conceptions of bodies, skills, and pleasures is no less than vital.

While scientific mastery has led us toward the abyss of ecological destruction, the cultivation of nurturance would attend to ecological needs; instead of the demand for the right to control our bodies, it would support practices that treat our bodies and the planet with care, concern, and lightness; instead of the perfection of our technical skills, it would cherish and encourage the diversity and richness of human cultures; instead of sexuated pleasures, it would foster such pleasures as intimacy, citizenry, cooperation, community, and communion. Through its respect for the varied contexts of women's lives and its appreciation of the multiplicity of human pleasures, a feminist cultivation of self-reflexivity and caring could encourage political renewal and transformation.

Notes

This essay draws from our discussion in "The Feminist Sexuality Debates," *Signs* 10 (Fall 1984): 119–25.

1. See, for example, Wendy Brown, "Reproductive Freedom and the Right to Privacy: A Paradox for Feminists," and Mary Lyndon Shanley, "Afterword: Feminism and Families in a Liberal Polity," in *Families, Politics and Public Policy: A Feminist Dialogue on Women and the State*, ed. Irene Diamond (New York: Longman, 1983), pp. 317–21.
2. See, for example, Evelyn Fox Keller, "Feminism and Science," *Signs* 7 (Spring 1982): 589–602, and Keller, *A Feeling for the Organism: The Life and Work of Barbara McClintock* (New York: W. H. Freeman, 1983).
3. As stated by the Chorus in Euripides, *The Bacchae*, trans. Michael Cacoyannis (New York: New American Library, 1982), p. 23.
4. Michel Foucault, *The History of Sexuality, Volume I: An Introduction*, trans. Robert Hurley (New York: Pantheon, 1978), pp. 67–68.
5. Ibid., p. 136.
6. Michel Foucault, *Power/Knowledge, Selected Interviews and Other Writings, 1972–1977*, ed. Colin Gordon (New York: Pantheon, 1980), p. 107.
7. Foucault, *History of Sexuality*, p. 155.
8. Monique Plaza astutely points to Foucault's stopping short of his own investigation of the deployment of sexuality in regard to rape. Plaza, "Our Damages and Their Compensation, Rape: The Will Not to Know of Michel Foucault," *Feminist Issues* 1 (Summer 1981): 25–35. While sexual abuse of women has existed in societies without these technologies, our hypothesis is that these technologies exacerbate abuse.
9. For a critique of Masters and Johnson's technologized approach to sexual relations, see Patricia Y. Miller and Martha R. Fowlkes, "Social and Behavioral Constructions

of Female Sexuality," *Signs* 4 (Summer 1980): 788–89. Miller and Fowlkes observe of Masters and Johnson: "They have earned for women the right to have equal time and space with men on the sexual production line."

10. Linda Gordon and Allen Hunter, "Sex, Family and the New Right: Anti-feminism as a Political Force," *Radical America* 11 (November 1977–February 1978): 20.

11. Brown, "Reproductive Freedom," 332.

12. Carole Joffe, "The Abortion Struggle in American Politics," *Dissent* 28 (Summer 1981): 270.

13. Gordon and Hunter, "Sex, Family and New Right," 19.

14. For the concept of gender education, see Anne Harper, "Teenage Sexuality and Public Policy: An Agenda for Gender Education," in Diamond, *Families, Politics and Public Policy*, pp. 220–35.

15. Foucault, *History of Sexuality*, pp. 42–43; Jeffrey Weeks, *Sex, Politics and Society* (New York: Longman Press, 1981), chap. 6; Robert A. Padgug, "Sexual Matters: On Conceptualizing Sexuality in History," *Radical History Review* 20 (Spring/Summer 1979): 3–24; and Ellen Ross and Rayna Rapp, "Sex and Society: A Research Note from Social History and Anthropology," *Comparative Studies in Society and History* 23 (Summer 1981): 51–73.

16. Adrienne Rich, "Compulsory Heterosexuality and Lesbian Existence," *Signs* 4 (Summer 1980): 649.

17. Foucault observes that "the task of discovering this difficult truth of sex was finally turned into an invitation to eliminate taboos and break free of what binds us." *History of Sexuality*, p. 80.

18. For example, Pat Califia asserts that "S/M eroticism focuses on whatever feelings or actions are forbidden, and searches for a way to obtain pleasure from the forbidden. It is the quintessence of non-reproductive sex." "Feminism and Sado-masochism," *CoEvolution Quarterly* 33 (Spring 1982): 37 (reprinted from *Heresies*).

19. Gayle Rubin in a discussion with Deidre English and Amber Hollibaugh, "Talking Sex: A Conversation on Sexuality and Feminism," *Socialist Review* 11 (July–August 1981): 43.

20. Califia, "Feminism and Sadomasochism," 33–35. In contrast to Califia's essentialist assumptions concerning sadomasochism, see Foucault's remarks on the current proliferation of homosexual S&M practices in "Sexual Choice, Sexual Act. An Interview with Michel Foucault," James O'Higgins, interviewer, *Salmagundi* 58–59 (Fall 1982–Winter 1983): 19–21. Also see the report on the Barnard College conference, "Toward a Politics of Sexuality," *Off Our Backs* 12, no. 6 (June 1982).

21. See, for example, critiques in *Off Our Backs* (cited in n. 20) and, in a British socialist-feminist journal, Lal Coveney, "Sado-Masochism," *Scarlet Women* 13 (July 1981): Part II on Sexuality.

22. MacKinnon claims that "sexuality is the linchpin of gender inequality," in "Feminism, Marxism, Method, and the State: An Agenda for Theory," *Signs* 7 (Spring 1982): 533. We question the fruitfulness of single-origin, single-explanation theory and concur with Michelle Zimbalist Rosaldo's cautions in "The Use and Abuse of Anthropology: Reflections on Feminism and Cross-Cultural Understanding," *Signs* 5, no. 3 (Spring 1980): 389–417.

23. MacKinnon, "Feminism, Marxism, Method, and State," p. 515.

24. Following a Marxist parallel, MacKinnon asserts that "heterosexuality is sexuality's structure, gender and family its congealed forms, sex roles its qualities generalized to social persons, reproduction a consequence, and control its issue"; ibid., p. 516.

25. Foucault's writings also seem to suffer in this respect. While he attempts to offer an alternative in Ars Erotica, the distinctions between Ars Erotica and the deployment of sexuality remain problematic at best.

26. Foucault, *History of Sexuality*, pp. 100–101.
27. Margaret Fuller, *Woman in the Nineteenth Century* (1845; rpt. New York: W. W. Norton, 1971).
28. As quoted by James Dougherty in "Jane Addams: Culture and Imagination," *Yale Review* 71 (April 1982): 367–68.
29. Carol Gilligan, *In a Different Voice* (Cambridge, Mass.: Harvard University Press, 1982), p. 172.
30. Gloria Anzaldúa, "Foreword to the Second Edition," *This Bridge Called My Back: Writings by Radical Women of Color*, ed. Cherrie Moraga and Gloria Anzaldúa (New York: Kitchen Table: Women of Color Press, 1983), pp. iv–v.
31. Susan Griffin, "Preface," in *Reclaim the Earth*, ed. Léonie Caldecott and Stephanie Leland (London: Women's Press, 1983), p. 4.

Sharon Welch

The Truth of Liberation Theology: "Particulars of a Relative Sublime"

A feminist theology of liberation is part of an epistemic shift, a redefinition of the truth of Christian faith. The truth of Christian faith is at stake not in terms of its coherence with ontological structures and their potential modification, but in life-and-death struggles, in daily operations of power/knowledge. It is in this arena of the determination of the character of daily life that the truth of Christian faith, both its method and referent, must be determined. The battle against nihilism and oppression is not primarily conceptual but practical. The focus, therefore, of a liberating faith and of theology is not primarily the analysis of human being and its possibilities but the creation of redeemed communities.

My feminist theology of liberation emerges from the tension I experience between skepticism and resistance to oppression and domination. The skeptical moment is rooted in my awareness of the power and peril of discourse, my encounter with the transitory nature of "the order of things," and my acknowledgment of the effects of truth resident within forms of discourse—the continued operation of power as intrinsic to all discourse, including my own.

Entanglement in power and particularity is not a condition to be avoided, but one to be understood. This becomes ironically clear as I realize that the very possibility of critique and of resistance is rooted not in a universal sense of justice, but in concrete, varied, tenuous experiences of resistance and liberation, that is, in my participation in different forms of power/knowledge.

The seemingly positivistic work of genealogy—the critique of apparatuses of power/knowledge—occurs within a nonpositivistic framework. Such a critique is possible because of a prior commitment to the oppressed, a prior belonging to another apparatus. Even in critique, then, the task of genealogy is constructive, for the critique of dominant systems and the disclosure of suppressed systems is part of an insurrection of subjugated knowledges.

In this work there is the disclosure of what might be called "proleptic universals," alternate visions of society, humanity, institutional structures, orders of knowing, that are then brought into play. While it may be unsettling to think only within these categories, it is not an endeavor without precedents. Richard Rorty describes this concept of truth in *Philosophy and the Mirror of Nature*. Rorty argues that it is possible to think if the claim to know essences is relinquished. He describes the philosophers who have made such claims.

> These peripheral, pragmatic philosophers are skeptical primarily *about systematic philosophy*, about the whole project of universal commensuration. . . . They [Heidegger, Wittgenstein, Dewey] hammer away at the holistic point that words take their meanings from other words rather than by virtue of their representative character, and the corollary that vocabularies acquire their privileges from the men [*sic*] who use them rather than from their transparency to the real.[1]

The wisdom found in these philosophers is a wisdom of conversation, an offering of another set of descriptive vocabularies without making the arrogant claim of disclosing the definitive commensurating vocabulary. Rorty finds this wisdom in the work of the edifying, as distinct from the systematic, philosophers.

Edifying philosophers want to keep space open for that sense of wonder which poets can sometimes cause—wonder that there is something new under the sun, something which is *not* an accurate representation of what was already there, something which (at least for the moment) cannot be explained and can barely be described.[2]

The Primacy of the Particular

Wallace Stevens is another writer whose thought avoids universals and names, rather, the particular *as* particular.[3] In his poem "On the Road Home" he expresses the plenitude of particularity and the wealth of insight possible as one forgoes the search for absolutes and accepts and acknowledges the particular as such.

It was when I said,
"There is no such thing as the truth,"
That the grapes seemed fatter.
The fox ran out of his hole.

You . . . You said,
"There are many truths,
But they are not parts of a truth."
Then the tree, at night, began to change,
smoking through green and smoking blue.
We were two figures in a wood.
We said we stood alone.

It was when I said,
"Words are not forms of a single word.
In the sum of the parts, there are only the parts.
The world must be measured by eye";

It was when you said,
"The idols have seen lots of poverty,
Snakes and gold and lice,
But not the truth";

It was at that time, that the silence was largest
And longest, the night was roundest,
The fragrance of the autumn warmest,
Closest and strongest.[4]

I do not wish to leave a false impression by quoting this piece. Despite the lyrical quality of Stevens's poetry, it is not easy to maintain this mode of thought. Rorty claims that it can be maintained, that more traditional philosophers should avoid the "bad taste" of asking edifying philosophers to be ontological or systematic.[5] Rorty's gentility is misleading. A Foucauldian perspective lays bare the agony of this refusal. It is not easy to avoid the solace of universals. This is done only at great cost. To remain "edifying," to use Rorty's deceptively benign phrase, is a great risk.

Wallace Stevens expresses the pain as well as the promise of this choice. It does not always result in an experience of the plenitude of particularity. In "Chaos in Motion and Not in Motion" he speaks of the possible loss of all meaning following this refusal.

> Oh, that this lashing wind was something more
> Than the spirit of Ludwig Richter . . .
>
> . . . .
>
> People fall out of windows, trees tumble down,
> Summer is changed to winter, the young grow old,
>
> The air is full of children, statues, roofs
> And snow. The theatre is spinning round,
>
> Colliding with deaf-mute churches and optical trains.
> The most massive sopranos are singing songs of scales.
>
> And Ludwig Richter, turbulent Schlemihl,
> Has lost the whole in which he was contained,
>
> Knows desire without an object of desire,
> All mind and violence and nothing felt.
>
> He knows he has nothing more to think about,
> Like the wind that lashes everything at once.[6]

The risk of chaos outside the safe boundaries of systematic, conventional thought is like the "earthquake phenomenon" described by Mary Daly, the loss of meaning that occurs in the process of creating meanings outside of patriarchy.

> Crones spinning closer and closer to the Center of our Centering Selves sometimes speak to each other of a certain experience which I shall call "the earthquake phenomenon." . . . A Crone may be moving swiftly over some ground and find/feel to her horror that it gapes open before her; there is a chasm at her feet. She must focus very quickly in order to strike a new balance. She holds fast until the horror passes, converting the necessary efforts of resistance into increasing assertion of her energy and discovery of latent power.[7]

Daly finds it possible to affirm the particular after the earthquake. This affirmation is not so unequivocal in Stevens. Some of his later poetry (for example, "The Motive for Metaphor") has a tone of self-loathing; he seems to be suspicious of the disavowal of the absolute.[8]

A resolutely particularistic style of thought does not represent merely the effort of brash minds to uncover the truth unencumbered by the weight of tradition. The passages from Daly and Stevens remind us that to reject the past and its forms of knowledge, to refuse to be at home in them any longer, is not a carefree attempt to live *de novo*. It is a painful refusal of what has been experienced as false security. This refusal is necessitated by an awareness that my work may well be, to quote Wallace Stevens, "disillusion as the last illusion."[9]

Strategic versus Theoretical Critique

The costliness of the endeavor to choose strategic over theoretical critique must be recognized in order to understand two things: the constant tendency to elide the reality of discourse and the importance of the refusal of that elision. I find it difficult to avoid returning to a former episteme in which faith means some sort of certainty. There are times when I return to absolutes. Yet I still maintain that for Christianity to remain critical, it must retain a skeptical edge. Without this edge, Christianity becomes oppressive. Without it, Christian affirmations lose their reference to concrete situations, a reference that arises from a self-conscious recognition of the inextricable fusion of power/knowledge. To acknowledge with Foucault that truth is not the "child of freedom" but of power/knowledge, that theory and practice cannot be separated in actuality but only cautiously and reservedly in reflection, is to always remain tentative in one's affirmations, suspicious even of one's feelings of certainty, recognizing that these feelings are only the concomitant of participating in a well-established episteme, or, as Rorty puts it, in normal discourse.

The courage to act and to think within an uncertain framework is not easily achieved. It may be that this is what is meant by faith. Faith is not a belief "in spite of," or a belief that I can act in a particular way without sufficient evidence. It is a stance of being, an acceptance of risk and openness, an affirmation of both the importance of human life (its dimension of ultimate significance) and the refusal to collapse that ultimacy into a static given, identifying it as definitively achieved in some concrete medium of its manifestation.

To engage in genealogy may itself be an act of faith, an expression of a willingness to live out conversion to the other as something that matters. To be critical of personal positions, to realize that they are partial, is also an act of faith, an acceptance of finitude and a refusal to cling to what may be transitory determinations of justice, freedom, and solidarity.

Faith impels genealogy as it evokes conversion to the other. It also evokes critique as it challenges self-security. Faith does not bring certainty to liberation thought, though it may produce the motivating tension for critical thought and the ability to live within that tension.

The Critical Dialectic of Resistance

Granted that some tension with skepticism may be necessary for those of us who are oppressors and are aware of the power and tenacity of repressive apparatuses of power/knowledge, how does the tension between skepticism and commitment actually enable resistance to oppression? Does not resistance require some understanding of truth, even if it is only a prior definition of freedom? On what other basis does one resist than the awareness that something in human nature is being violated?

These questions are fair, but they imply a separation between theory and practice that is inadequate for critical theory. There is in resistance the operation of concepts of human nature, of some sort of theory. This theory is not the result of abstract speculation, however, but is grounded in concrete practice. To speak of liberation is to speak out of the experience of being oppressed, of resisting, and of being liberated. To speak of liberation is to make a particular type of statement, one not applicable to human being as such but to human being as it exists under conditions of oppression. It is the social and political equivalent of the traditional Christian language of sin and redemption. Those are not ontological categories but speak of modifications of human existence through the distortion of sin and release from that distortion. Resistance comes out of the experience of redemption, out of the practice of liberation from oppression, or from the experience of an alternate type of sociality that did not require structures of oppression. Knowledge that the criticized structures are not necessary emerges within the act of resistance.

Does the fact of resistance mean that the structure for which I (and others) work is an accurate reflection of human essence? To make such a statement is to claim too much. The weight of my critique lies not in its certain locus in an ontological structure but in its locus in a particular form of existence. My critique is not based on theoretical determinations of what should be the case but momentary experiences of what is the case.

My critique is grounded in actual insurrections, in the struggle between competing determinations of the nature of human sociality. I am able to work for freedom from sexism not because of a theoretical determination of the essence of human nature, an essence that is distorted by sexist structures, but because I have experienced a nonsexist type of existence. That actuality gives a theoretical analysis of patriarchy its plausibility. Recognizing the primacy of the historical leads to an acceptance of both the fragility and efficacy of this concrete, particular basis for resistance. To attempt to give these particular instances of liberation a "theoretical coronation" is both unnecessary and dangerously illusory.[10]

Emphasis on the fragility and efficacy of a practical basis for resistance emerges from my experience in the women's movement. I am acutely aware of both the power of sisterhood, of concrete instances in which I and other women have been freed from sexism, and the tenuousness and rarity of that particular form of human sociality. It would be an act of the greatest folly for me to criticize sexism on the grounds of such universally recognized values as equality, the nature of moral persons, or any other determination of what characterizes the human, and thus women, as such.

I can only explain this reticence by turning to autobiography. I have always been a token. Although access to universalizing discourse, to participation in the work of philosophy and theology, is withheld from most women, I was encouraged to study those disciplines. The steady procession of my intellectual female friends turning to traditional pursuits seemed only to confirm the cultural stereotype of women as less rational and less aggressive than men. As a result, I defined myself as different from most members of my sex; I defined myself primarily in universal rather than gender-specific categories.

My blithe pursuit of universal structures (of course open to study by anyone with the requisite desire and ability) might have continued indefinitely. It was, however, interrupted by a rude reminder of the reality of the primacy of definition by gender. I confronted discrimination as a woman in my first job after college. This shattered any illusions I had about merit being a matter of pure achievement. I became aware that emphasis on universal human rights and the dignity of all persons obscured some people's sensitivity to the abrogation of those rights and that dignity on the basis of sex. I was faced with the paradox of seeing men who were fully committed to such universals as freedom and equality and yet were thoroughly sexist.

In light of this brief history, let me try to explain more clearly the irony I find in an oppressed person criticizing oppression in the name of universal values or ontological structures. The privilege to undergo the type of education that allows one to understand and use ontological categories and refer to universal values is a privilege denied many women in the present and most women in the past. It is a privilege denied those who are poor. Universal discourse is the discourse of the privileged. My inclusion in this community of discourse was not due to something intrinsic in the ideas and values themselves. These ideas did not immediately lead their proponents to advocate the full equality and humanity of all people, as is painfully evident in the struggle for the equal rights of black men and of women of all races in a society supposedly dedicated to the concept that "all men [*sic*] are created equal."

To use the very categories that masked my oppression in order to denounce it seems absurd. Better to refer to the particular events, the breakthroughs in practice that have challenged men's dominance: the emergence of the women's movement and its influence on women attempting to understand the forces that blocked them and the possibilities being opened to them. My critique of sexism is grounded in my experience of women who are excellent ministers in a denomination that did not ordain women, women who refuse definitions of themselves as sexual objects, women whose learning and political organizing broke patriarchal, individualistic, competitive models in the creation of communities that were cooperative and supportive.

To acknowledge and to accept this particular basis for resistance and critique is frightening. It is tempting to seek solace in the realm of universal values and in certain determinations of the nature of human being. But such refuge is an illusion. It is a denial that the ability to be aware of universal categories is accidental and fortuitous. Born twenty years ago or one hundred years ago (maybe even ten years in the future), such concerns might not be mine; they were not the concerns of most women in the past. I am aware of the oddity of my participation in the academy. Academic participation has not been the birthright of intellectual women. The inclusion of women in the worlds of academia, politics, and business may be a brief anomaly. Our gains could be as easily erased as were the gains of women in the Roman Empire, the gains of women in the first decades of the Christian movement, and the moves women made toward equality in England and the United States at the beginning of this century. Decisions that women participate in universal structures of human being will not protect or enable that participation. This change is a matter of changes in practices and in institutions, changes in not just knowledge but changes in apparatuses of power/knowledge. The primary challenge of liberation is not to construct the correct theory but the struggle to achieve freedom in history.

Universal Accountability and the Integrity
of the Particular

Given such a locus in the particular, how can a liberation theologian claim that other systems of power/knowledge are oppressive? Can a feminist theology of liberation be anything other than provincial? If my definition of freedom is based on the experience of liberation from sexism, how can I address other forms of domination, such as racism and capitalism? Concerns such as these seem to indicate the value of universally applicable definitions of freedom and justice.

Affirmations of the worth of all persons, concepts of universal human dignity, are not totally oppressive. They are liberating when they express a concern for the well-being of all people, when they lead us to care about justice for other groups of people, when they move us beyond a concern for our small social world. These ideas are not, however, liberating in their attempt to articulate that which is universal. Their liberating function lies in the concern they express for other people. This concern is, ironically, distorted by the very concepts that express it. To work for human rights, but to base our definition of those rights solely on the experience of one race, gender, or class, is itself oppressive.

The ambiguity intrinsic to a universal basis for resistance to injustice can be mitigated if the concern is expressed in terms of universal accountability rather than in terms of what is universally true about human being. Universal accountability may lead people to examine the impact of their social and economic systems on the lives of other people. It is an expression of concern for other races and classes, for the lives of all those who are adversely affected by our political and economic systems. An affirmation of universal accountability means that we Americans must reevaluate our patterns of consumption; we are responsible to the rest of the world for our exploitation of scarce resources, for our use of them to support a life-style of relative affluence while millions die of starvation and millions live in the most abject poverty.

The idea of universal accountability leads quite naturally to another ideal, that of the integrity of the particular. While we may be accountable to all people for the economic and environmental costs of our way of life, the solution to the world's environmental problems, the solution to the problems of world hunger, is not necessarily the creation of a world government or the creation of standardized, uniform agricultural systems and systems of economic distribution. While we are responsible to each other, our responsibility may be met in innumerable ways. It is arrogant to assume that only the highly technological culture of the West can offer responsible, sustainable, equitable models of social organization.

What sort of social critique is possible for one guided by the two ideas of universal accountability and the integrity of the particular? I have found that protest against oppression is most effective and can best preclude a slide into oppressive discourse when it forswears the simple application of universal definitions of justice and freedom to other situations. A provisional definition of these terms—justice and freedom—is a component of resistance and critique. These preliminary definitions arise, however, not from speculation, but from practice, from an experience of freedom and justice in unique situations. Rootedness in the practical gives the definitions both their power and their limitations. They are inevitably limited by their formation in historically peculiar situations of oppression and liberation.

Given a particular experience of freedom and justice, how is it possible to criticize something like the torture of political prisoners in Chile? I should begin with my own experientially based definition of freedom and justice and then determine where the Chilean system contradicts those values. I should also look for resistance within the Chilean social system. Such resistance indicates that the system that seems oppressive has not completely established itself as definitive of humanity. If there is resistance, I should try to understand its basis—the experience of liberation or redemption that undergirds it—and seek to further its expression.

But what role is there for critique if there are no subjugated knowledges actively resisting a given system? If there is no resistance does that mean that the alternate ideals of freedom are provincial and not applicable? If oppression is so complete that there are no glimmers of resistance, I have to acknowledge that in this situation humanity as I know it has been obliterated. It is important to work against the extension of that form of humanity, but I must not deny its efficacy and power.

This may seem like giving up too soon. Is there not some power and purpose in denouncing oppression as invalid in essence albeit effective in practice? When a system of domination is weak, there may be some value in such a proclamation. Statements of condemnation may be valuable, especially if there is a history of a connection between such statements and political action. Neither of these qualifications pertains in the United States. Militarism, for example, is so strong in the United States that political demonstrations against the nuclear arms race can be tolerated throughout the country and even inside the Pentagon.[11] Advanced capitalism, racism, and sexism are equally resilient. The ability of these systems of domination to withstand critique is enhanced by the failure of church bodies, political parties, and scholarly associations to translate rhetoric into action. In the United States we could conclude that the statement is the opiate of the people.

Universal denunciations of systems of oppression are a dangerous evasion of the relationship of power/knowledge, of the fragility of discourse. It is illusory to deny the reality of the defeat of a particular project of human being. To denounce the arms race, for example, as unjust is merely a declarative act. It does not actually challenge that structure and may even function as a dangerous illusion that in the denunciation something has been accomplished. Such statements may be evasions of the difficult strategic task, the determination of how people might create structures of justice. To challenge the truth of oppression is not to point to its intellectual or conceptual frailties, but to expose its frailties of practice, to disclose and nurture alternate forms of human community that challenge it on the level of daily operations of power/knowledge. To challenge oppression effectively is to point to its failure to determine the nature of human existence and to seek to extend the sphere of influence of alternate structures.

What are the advantages of such an apparently circumscribed form of resistance? It is both more effective and less tyrannical than other forms of resistance. Instead of assuming that universally valid goals can be ascertained from a particular situation, the present experience of liberation can mark the beginning of a definition of and struggle for further liberation. The temptation to define others' hopes for liberation must be avoided. The cultural genocide of an imperialistic Christianity is not accidental, but is grounded in such an arrogant approach to liberation. It is oppressive to "free" people if their own history and culture do not serve as the primary sources of the definition of their freedom.

In the struggle for liberation, the understanding of the nature of freedom that is held by the oppressors who wish to renounce their oppression of others must change. If such change does not occur, it is unlikely that the struggle for freedom is noncoercive. Instead, the error of Habermas is perpetuated: the assumption that an elite can effectively ascertain the contours of oppression and liberation and offer this theoretical work to the oppressed as a *fait accompli*.

The first advantage of the specific over the universal intellectual in resistance is that a thoroughly self-critical position avoids both the horrors of psychoanalysis, with its imposition of a binding "freedom" on women, and the tragedy of the suppression of dissent in some socialist systems. The oppressed must be heard by the oppressors as they name their own oppression and liberation. To deny those voices is to perpetuate oppression, even if it is done in the name of a universal concept of freedom.

Specific analyses emphasizing the strategic and the practical have a second advantage over more traditional theoretical critiques. The struggle against oppression gains power by drawing on people's heritage and experience, not merely on abstractions from their experience. A concept of freedom is most effective as it is rooted in the imagination of the people to be freed, if it does indeed speak to something in their experience and their history. The aim of a feminist theology of liberation is to seek the ground for resistance not on the level of the universal but on the level of the particular and the historical. This makes possible the recognition of unique or divergent forms of resistance and freedom.

Another advantage of the specific, strategic approach is its lack of naïveté, its recognition that oppressive definitions of humanity do have effects of truth—they have shaped human existence. This is a way of acknowledging what Doris Lessing refers to as the twist and damage wrought by the mass murders of the twentieth century. It is to acknowledge with Mary Daly the "patriarchal demons" that do influence how we think and know and act, that continue to emerge and imprison us when we least expect it.[12] This approach reflects the awareness that liberation is not merely a matter of will and thought, but of practice and power, a matter of the transformation of systems of language and behavior that imprison us, a matter of the destruction of webs of oppression whose extent we only dimly ascertain.[13] To acknowledge this is to struggle at the level of the effects of truth of apparatuses of power/knowledge.

Intrinsic Relativism of a Feminist Theology of Liberation

A feminist theology of liberation is intrinsically relative and thus maintains an ambiguous position. It has two contradictory strands: on the one hand, a relativist limitation of truth-claims and a qualified nihilism, an acceptance that might does shape reality, if not make right. On the other hand, nihilism and relativism are held in tension with a strong normative claim, an attempt to identify values and structures that can transform society and end oppression. Both strands are necessary. The tension between the two constitutes genuinely liberative theology and critical theory.

How can such a skeptical stance be reconciled with faith? Traditional understandings of faith imply just the opposite stance. There is no skepticism or nihilism in faith, because those who are faithful are certain that nihilism is false, that there is a structure of meaning in which human existence participates. I concur that faith is opposed to a capitulation to nihilism, but I understand the contribution of genealogical work to be the clarification of the extent to which all truth is embedded in relations of power. It follows that we engage in a struggle with nihilism, not assume that its failure is in any sense guaranteed.

I realize that this skeptical attitude and the corresponding renunciation of universals is not found in the work of most liberation theologians. Yet I find such a renunciation required by my situation, which is that of a commitment to struggle against oppression by one who is an oppressor by reason of race and nationality. Without this skepticism and modesty, "liberation" can become another form of oppression: the imposition by an elite of a particular understanding of freedom.

There is another reason for skepticism, one also grounded in the historicity of discourse. When we address the modification of actual structures of human existence, it matters greatly if those modifications are not achieved. The discourse of liberation has no realm of consolation other than the historical. Hopes for redemption have failed in the past (as shown by the many holocausts of history) and may fail in the future. Nuclear holocaust and the destruction of the human species would mean the failure of Christianity and its promise of redemption. The economic and moral costs of the arms race themselves represent the failure of Christianity to establish conditions of justice.

As a Christian theologian, I feel compelled to take seriously the failure of Christianity. I evade this failure if I speak of the absolute truth of Christian faith as something that transcends its actualization in history. It is a perversion of a faith that claims to be concerned with the historical to locate its truth in an ahistorical realm, one unsullied by actual events in history.

It is important to note that this is not an "eschatological reservation." Skepticism is required, not because of the inevitable disparity between events in history and a transcendent ideal, but because of the fragility and unpredictability of the historical process itself: the possibility of the failure of a genuinely liberative ideal, or the oppressive impact of an ideal that is ostensibly liberating.

Skepticism about the truth of Christianity is not new. Ernst Bloch quotes a passage in which Marx and Engels claim that the failure of Christianity to transform history is evidence of its falsity:

> They would preach the kingdom of love in opposition to a rotten actuality and hatred . . . but when experience shows that this love has not been effective in 1800 years, has not changed social relationships and has not been able to build its kingdom, then it clearly follows that this love which has been unable to overcome hatred does not offer the dynamic power needed for social reforms. This love is consumed in sentimental assertions which cannot remove any actual conditions; it merely acts as a soporific on those whom it feeds with its sentimental mash.[14]

This rhetoric is harsh, but the history to which it refers is as brutal as the critique. Christianity has failed. To acknowledge this failure and yet to remember and name the few instances of liberation that have occurred in communities of faith is to discover the relativism intrinsic to Christian faith.

My acknowledgment that the failures of Christian faith are as real as its successes has led me to a commitment to social change colored by skepticism and relativism. I have two overlapping reasons for my position. First, skepticism is required by the inescapable limitation and peril of discourse. Preventing the imposition of particular structures on other cultures, preventing the foreclosure of discourse or its limitation to an elite, requires a consciousness of the relativity of even a liberating Christianity's point of view, a suspicion as to the adequacy of its ability to determine the meaning of justice and freedom, and a willingness to have such ideas modified through dialogue and through evaluation in light of their effects of truth.

This skepticism leads me to a relativistic definition of humanity. I can claim with no hesitation that the actions of Hitler are manifestations of inhumanity, but I cannot be at all sure that my own understanding of humanity is not limited by the acceptance of some unseen form of oppression. Just as slavery and the treatment of women were for centuries not even recognized by sensitive theologians and people of faith as oppressive, it is possible that my thought and actions share in the perpetuation of as yet unrecognized forms of oppression. To be truly liberative, my feminist theology of liberation must not regard itself as the definitive exposition of the structure of freedom and justice, but must remain open to critiques like those of Foucault, critiques that reveal the dominations constitutive of even ostensibly humanizing procedures and reforms.

A second reason for relativism and skepticism is the need to remain consistently within one strand of the Jewish and Christian traditions, a strand that emphasizes that faith is not primarily declarative but revolutionary. The faith of the prophets and elements of the gospels proclaim an active process of redemption. These faiths motivate reform and action, not compliance with some already existing state of affairs. The direction of verification for this faith is practical. Knowledge that this faith is true comes only as it is effective, as it fulfills in action what it promises in hope: the blind see, the lame walk, the prisoners are loosed from their chains.

Outside of the actualization in history of these hopes for liberation, I do not know if they are ontologically or historically possible. There is always an element of risk in faith, an attempt to live on the basis of a wager that my hopes do indeed reflect an order of possibility. I can never know decisively that I am correct in my assessment. The history of Christian faith, its checkered past as both supporter of oppression and matrix of resistance, prevents a triumphal ecclesiology or christology, prevents an affirmation that sin has been conquered either in Jesus or through the church. There is more of the crucifixion than the resurrection in the history of the church.

I find it impossible to hold the universals of faith, the hope of universal solidarity, the hope for the total elimination of oppression, in any but a tensive and equivocal manner. My use of the universal concepts of freedom, justice, and solidarity is a tensive use for two reasons, one positive, one negative. The positive reason is that I simply cannot know the contours of a free society within an oppressive framework. I acknowledge the power of oppressive concepts of freedom and humanity, oppressive concepts both of the method of ascertaining "true statements" and of the continued internal operation of oppression in my attempts to define liberation and solidarity. Not only are my insights particular and finite, they are also tainted by sin, by the power of oppression. My struggle with oppression is ongoing and must not be forestalled by the hasty attempt to identify universal structures of human existence.

There is a second, more negative reason for the tensive application of universals: the application could be wrong, and this at any of three levels.

1. Efforts to create free, just communities could fail. Oppressive definitions of truth, of human nature, could win in practice, could have the overriding effect of truth. I cannot deny the victory of oppression in individual lives and social groups, in the type of human being created by sexism, the prison, the Gulag, the brutalities of war. In all these instances, what liberation theologians identify as oppressive is victorious. Lives have been irrevocably shaped by oppressive structures. No amount of resistance can bring back the lives lost in the Nazi holocaust. What I regard as humane is defeated daily in the torture of the women and men of Latin America.

2. A second possible source of error in the application of universals

is the too hasty imposition of commensuration, the refusal to listen to other descriptions of human existence, the assumption that I already have the definitive understanding in outline if not in full construction. To hold to truth as conversation rather than as reflection of essence is to live out an openness to continued change and modification, and is to relinquish the hope for an end to the conversation through the achievement of a complete understanding of liberation and justice. An awareness of the difficulty of the embodiment of structures of freedom and an openness to the likelihood of encountering alternate descriptions of solidarity and liberation require that I bring the definitions ascertained through my own experiences of liberation into dialogue with other interpretations, without assuming that the dialogue is to be one-sided, a "dialogue" of persuasion of the other.

3. Finally, the most pressing reason for the maintenance of a tensive use of the ideals of freedom and solidarity is a tendency in liberation faith itself that impels me toward nihilism. This is the recognition of the possibility that my own experience of liberation within some particular forms of ecclesia is nothing but a fluke. That is, liberation and redemption do not reflect something that can be universalized, but reflect contingent configurations of human existence. The barbarism of the twentieth century—the continued ravages of sexism, the threat of nuclear war, mass famine, the atrocities of Auschwitz, Vietnam, and El Salvador—may illustrate either the contingent or necessary limits of human morality.

Liberation Faith and Nihilism

The fear that liberation may be either structurally or contingently impossible is internally required by a liberating faith. Soelle and Metz speak of the dangerous memory of liberation faith as the refusal to forget the suffering of others in the past and in the present. Liberation faith is conversion to the other, the resistance to oppression, the attempt to live as though the lives of others matter. The paradox of this faith is that as resistance to oppression increases, as I begin to reflect on the dangerous memory of human suffering, it becomes more difficult to imagine a compensation for that suffering, even if similar suffering is eradicated in the future. The weight of past and present suffering is such that it seems irredeemable.

There is in liberation faith, with its conversion to the other, a sense of tragedy and loss. The loss of so many lives in history cannot be easily reconciled. To honestly live and believe as universal the imperative of love and freedom is to hope that suffering can be ended, to hope that all lives without liberation in history were not meaningless—but it is to work for this hope without the guarantee that such meaning is possible.

The human species may be fatally flawed. If there is anything universal about human nature, it may be our incapacity for community and justice. Christian faith and revolutionary struggles would then be only futile efforts to prevent the inevitable—the self-destruction of a tragically cruel and shortsighted form of life. Momentary actualizations of peace, justice, and freedom could be mere aberrations in the experience of a people incapable of survival. History, especially the record of the complicity of the Christian church with injustice, offers us little evidence to the contrary. I speak here as both an oppressor and a victim of oppression, well aware that patriarchy, militarism, and exploitation have characterized most of human history. Visions of equality, peace, and universal prosperity have, in the main, remained dreams and not realities.

This struggle with nihilism is not methodological, but is grounded in particular experiences within the peace movement and within Third World solidarity groups. The more I work to end the arms race, the less confidence I have that the dominant episteme can be vanquished. The more aware I become of the logic of war, of our dependence on a system of militarized sovereign states as a means of international order, and of the pervasiveness of patriarchy and its reliance on violence, the more fragile the contrasting episteme appears. I honestly do not know if the power of patriarchy and militarism can be broken before there is either a full-scale nuclear war or the unforgivable use of a single nuclear weapon.

To respond to the threat of nuclear war with protestations in the name of universal ideals such as the dignity of the human or the importance of freedom seems tragically absurd. To hold the values of the Enlightenment requires the condemnation of a society shaped by those values. The ideal of the rule of reason, of equality, and of justice has served as a screen for the irrationality of a technological society, the inequalities of a capitalistic world economy, and the injustice of a particular system of lawfulness threatening mass murder and global annihilation.

The twentieth century is the denouement of the Enlightenment and of Western ideals of civilization. We stand on the brink of extinction through nuclear holocaust or ecological disaster, a species whose greatest achievement in the last century has been the perfection of the art of genocide. From the first bombings of civilian targets by the fascists in the Spanish Civil War, through Hitler's death camps and the genocidal warfare of the United States against the people of Vietnam, to the United States' flirtation with limited nuclear war, the "age of reason" has distinguished itself by its folly and cruelty. To speak of Christian ideals of love for the neighbor being in any sense true, or of the benefits of the rule of reason in an age gone mad in its acceptance and justification of oppression and exploitation, is an unspeakable outrage.

I find, therefore, in liberation faith an intrinsic correlation with doubt and a deepening awareness of the tragic dimensions of life. For as conversion to the other grows, as I experience more intensely the power of the dangerous memory of human suffering, doubt as to the possibility of reconciliation also rises. The elevation of the significance of particular human lives also makes it more difficult to imagine any way in which the dead can be redeemed or liberated. Even to speak of life after death is to use the language of hope and imagination, not the language of certainty, not the language of a realized or directly experienced form of reconciliation. If not directly ideological, a refusal of the weight and finality of history, this belief in an "afterlife" is at best an expression of hope that the dangerous memory of human suffering will somehow be reconciled.

The awareness of tragedy contains another ground for nihilism. At the heart of liberation faith, at the moments of actualization of its imperative of solidarity with the other, I have found a chasm that threatens to swallow both the possibility of hope and the realization of solidarity.

To explain this threat, I turn again to autobiography. I have done educational and political work against United States support of the government of El Salvador. My motive came from empathy with the poor of El Salvador and from an assessment of the cause of their suffering that placed responsibility for the torture and murder of thousands of people with the military and with an ineffective government unable either to control the military or to plan and implement adequate land reform.

My participation in a solidarity group was fairly straightforward and unproblematic until I saw a film about the revolution in El Salvador. Watching pictures of the police and the military dragging people into the streets, beating and terrorizing them, hearing descriptions of tortured and mutilated bodies, feeling a fraction of the horror of that situation, shattered all my worlds of meaning. My ideals of universal solidarity faded in face of a suffering too great to name. My sanity was my insensitivity; my humanity was my inability not to care.

Can these two, the imperatives of sanity and of humanity, be reconciled? I do not know. I have not been able to reconcile them. I do not find many indications that our society embodies an adequate reconciliation. People are dying now, and our sane lack of caring is an intrinsic part of their deaths.[15] Just as we have become inured to the human costs of our economic system, of our government's support of "friendly" authoritarian regimes, so we continue to blithely or callously or ignorantly benefit from those systems, failing to demand, in the name of the people, their radical transformation.

Awareness of human suffering, an awareness that impels me and others to work for revolution, carries with it the danger of madness and the frightening conclusion that even if we win now, even if injustice is eradicated, something irretrievable has been lost. Christian hope is a shallow and callous lie if it fails to be silenced or at least chastised by the voices of all those who suffer and die without relief.

I do not think that my sorrow is the result of inordinate guilt. I do not intend the focus of this description to be on myself as responsible for all evils. Nor is this guilt in another sense, an attempt to respond to an abstract imperative to love the other. I am speaking rather of a painful tension in liberation faith. Inasmuch as I have been freed by ecclesia, by sisterhood, so does my concern for others increase. My concern is not the fruit of obligation or guilt, but the gift of freedom and the superabundance of human love. My horror is due to the threat of insanity and despair that accompanies this life-giving gift.

Might we have here the theological equivalent of the mad philosopher? Foucault speaks suggestively of the madness of the philosopher:

> the experience of the philosopher who finds, not outside his [sic] language (the result of an external accident or imaginary exercise), but at the inner core of its possibilities, the transgressions of his [sic] philosophical being.[16]

I am speaking of the mad theologian, the liberation theologian who finds unspeakable and unbearable anguish to be the child of life-giving compassion and solidarity.

The recognition of the partial victory over oppression in the lives of the dead, the fear of its complete victory, and the struggle with nihilism motivates the paradoxical affirmation of a feminist theology of liberation. I am pulled back from self-indulgent ennui and despair only as I remain in community with those who are oppressed and are struggling against that oppression. To live in community with women helping other women and children recover from the trauma of rape, incest, and wife abuse, with men working against rape by identifying and challenging the equation of sexuality and violence in male socialization, with women and men trying to create communities of nonviolence in a violent world reminds me that suffering is real, that it must be addressed even if one is not certain of its causes or aware of the best means of healing its damage. To remember the reality of oppression in the lives of people and to value those lives is to be saved from the luxury of hopelessness.

A Poetics of Revolution

The type of theology I have described affirms with Bloch "that learned hope is the signpost for this age—not just hope, but hope and the knowledge to take the way to it."[17] Within this theological perspective, my struggle with nihilism and with alternate views of human destiny and capabilities is practical. This theology emerges from the struggle to create, not merely to proclaim, a human community that embodies freedom. The verification of this struggle is not conceptual, but practical: the successful process of enlightenment and emancipation, a process that is open and self-critical. This theology emerges from an effort to live on the edge, accepting both the power and the peril of discourse, engaging in a battle for truth with a conscious preference for the oppressed.

A feminist theology of liberation understands Christianity as a perspective that is not already true but that becomes true where human beings are freed. Feminist theology is located in the horizon of the memory of the many times and places where Christian faith and hopes are not actualized and the Christian definition of the nature of human being is defaced or obliterated. Given this horizon, the search for the verification of Christian faith is a practical one. The primary evidence of the truth of Christianity is its successful actualization. The primary threat to it, the basic denial of its truth, is the actualization of structures that subvert solidarity, that destroy human dignity, that take human lives.

The truth of faith is not found in theoretical certainty about the eventual necessary victory within history of the Christian project. The truth of faith is found rather in struggle or in a certain way of determining the true, a way that enhances and creates solidarity and full participation in the making of culture and society. Within a feminist theology of liberation, faith is not the denial of risk, but living within the fragile balance of absolute commitment and infinite suspicion.

To live for a particular definition of human being without a guarantee of its historical possibility is not an easy task. The particular ideal of a feminist theology of liberation compounds the risk. The ideal of solidarity is dangerous. Solidarity may be impossible: full empathy with the suffering of all people would surely lead to insanity, to the collapse of all conventional structures of meaning. I do not even know what the results would be if a person or community acknowledged with total seriousness the suffering of those people within their immediate field of vision.

My skepticism is caused not only by an awareness of the difficulties of social and political transformation and of the possibility of failure; it is also rooted in the extreme contingency and probable arbitrariness of my own projects. My concept of solidarity has unknown determinants; its ramifications are unpredictable; it is tenuous and fragile. And yet, my commitment to solidarity leads to as active a struggle for its implementation as if I were certain of its future success and inherent possibility.

A feminist theology of liberation operates within a paradoxical tension, making transcultural claims and normative judgments, yet always remaining open to challenge and modification, trying to avoid any sort of moral imperialism or triumphalism. The value of Christian faith may be that it gives us the ability to live with that tension. If the life of faith is one of absolute commitment and infinite suspicion, the ground of commitment is neither rationalistic nor authoritarian. It is possible to avoid both the intellectual certainty of rational explanation and the mysterious certainty of an authoritative revelation and faith.

A feminist theology of liberation can perhaps best be understood as a poetics of revolution. Just as poetry can sacrifice meaning to explanation, so theology in its search for the clarity and precision of absolutes is certain to lose the meaning of revolution: the rich profusion of possibilities, the vision of new worlds to be attained. In its critique and in its vision, a feminist theology of liberation should remain concrete and open to further analyses and refinements. It is a discourse that is imbued with the particular tragedy of human existence—the dangerous memory of despair, barrenness, suffering—and with the particular moments of liberation—the equally dangerous memory of historical actualizations of freedom and community.

Notes

1. Richard Rorty, *Philosophy and the Mirror of Nature* (Princeton, N.J.: Princeton University Press, 1979), p. 368.
2. Ibid., p. 370.
3. The phrase quoted in the title of this essay is from Wallace Stevens's "Sail of Ulysses," in *The Palm at the End of the Mind*, ed. Holly Stevens (New York: Random House, Vintage Books, 1972), p. 392.
4. Stevens, *Palm*, pp. 164–65.

5. Rorty, *Philosophy*, p. 372.
6. Stevens, *Palm*, p. 278.
7. Mary Daly, *Gyn/Ecology: The Metaethics of Radical Feminism* (Boston: Beacon Press, 1978), pp. 409–10.
8. Stevens, *Palm*, p. 240.
9. "Inescapable romance, inescapable choice / Of dreams, disillusion as the last illusion, / Reality as a thing seen by the mind." Stevens, "An Ordinary Evening in New Haven," in *Palm*, p. 333.
10. Michel Foucault, *Power/Knowledge: Selected Interviews and Other Writings, 1972–1977*, ed. Colin Gordon (New York: Pantheon, 1980), p. 88.
11. This was borne out at a series of demonstrations sponsored by Jonah House held at and within the Pentagon in 1980.
12. Daly, *Gyn/Ecology*, pp. 29–31.
13. The metaphor "webs of oppression" was developed in an unpublished paper by Joel Martin (spring 1983).
14. Karl Marx and Friedrich Engels, "Circular Letter Against Kriege, May 11, 1846," in Ernst Bloch, *On Karl Marx* (New York, Herder and Herder, 1971), p. 87.
15. I am alluding to Doris Lessing's depiction of the human costs of World War II: "Forty-odd million human beings had been murdered, deliberately or from carelessness, from lack of imagination; these people had been killed yesterday, in the last dozen years, they were dying now, as she stood under the tree, and these deaths were marked on her soul." Doris Lessing, "Landlocked," in *Children of Violence* (New York: Simon and Schuster, 1964), p. 463.
16. Michel Foucault, *Language, Counter-Memory, Practice: Selected Essays and Interviews*, ed. Donald F. Bouchard (Ithaca, N.Y.: Cornell University Press, 1977), p. 44.
17. Ernst Bloch, *Man On His Own: Essays in the Philosophy of Religion* (New York: Herder and Herder, 1970), p. 91.

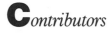Contributors

FRANCES BARTKOWSKI is an assistant professor at Carnegie-Mellon University, where she teaches Literary and Cultural Theory in the English Department. She is the author of *Feminist Utopias* and has published articles on French feminist and literary theory.

SANDRA LEE BARTKY is a professor of Philosophy at the University of Illinois at Chicago, where her fields of specialization include existentialism and phenomenology, critical theory, Marxism, and philosophy of feminism. She is also a member of the Women's Studies Program at Illinois, which she helped to establish, as well as president of the Radical Philosophy Association (Central Division), a founding member of the Society for Women in Philosophy, and an associate editor of *Hypatia*.

SUSAN BORDO is an associate professor of Philosophy at Le Moyne College. She is co editor (with Alison Jaggar) of *Gender/Body/Knowledge: Feminist Reconstructions of Being and Knowing* and author of *The Flight to Objectivity: Essays on Cartesianism and Culture*. Her current work, *Food, Fashion and Power: The Body and the Reproduction of Gender*, is forthcoming from the University of California Press.

IRENE DIAMOND is currently an associate professor of Political Science at the University of Oregon. She is the author of *Sex Roles in the State House* and editor of *Families and Public Policy: A Feminist Dialogue on Women and the State*.

KATHLEEN B. JONES is an associate professor of Women's Studies at San Diego State University, where her area of specialization is contemporary feminist political theory. She is contributing author and co-editor of *The Political Interests of Gender* and has published articles in *NOMOS*, *Women and Politics*, *Fiction International*, and other journals. She is currently completing a book entitled *Authority, Democracy, and the Citizenship of Women*.

PEGGY KAMUF is a professor of French at Miami University. She is the author of *Fictions of Feminine Desire: Disclosures of Heloise* and has just completed *Signature Pieces: On the Institution of Authorship*, forthcoming from Cornell University Press.

MARY LYDON is an associate professor of French at the University of Wisconsin at Madison. She is the author of *Perpetuum Mobile: A Study of the Novels and Aesthetics of Michel Butor* and editor of *Visible Language: Freud's Imprint* (*Visible Language* 4, no. 3). Her essays, which adopt a psychoanalytic and feminist view, have appeared in *Yale French Studies*, *SubStance*, and other journals.

BIDDY MARTIN is an assistant professor of German Literature and Women's Studies at Cornell University, where she teaches nineteenth- and twentieth-century German literature and feminist theory. She has published articles on German women's literature and feminist theory in many journals and is currently completing a book on Lou Andreas-Salome.

MEAGHAN MORRIS is a former lecturer in semiotics and a film critic in Australia; she now writes full-time. She has co-edited two collections, *Language, Sexuality and Subversion* and *Michel Foucault: Power, Truth, Strategy*, and is the author of a collection of essays in feminist criticism, forthcoming from Verso.

LEE QUINBY is an assistant professor of English and American Studies at Hobart and William Smith Colleges. Her work has appeared in such journals as *Signs* and *The American Historical Review*. She is currently completing a book on American moral-aesthetic writing.

JANA SAWICKI is a feminist philosopher and associate professor at the University of Maine. She has written extensively on the strengths and limits of Foucauldian feminism, particularly as it applies to issues concerning sexuality and technology. She is currently a Visiting Scholar at M.I.T. and is at work on a book on Foucault and feminism.

SHARON WELCH is an associate professor of Theology and Theology and Society at Harvard Divinity School. She is the author of *Communities of Resistance and Solidarity: A Feminist Theology of Liberation* and *A Feminist Ethic of Risk*.

WINIFRED WOODHULL is an assistant professor of French at Carleton College. She has published essays on modern French fiction, feminism, and the politics of mass culture.

elect Bibliography

These suggestions for further reading make no claim to be comprehensive. We hope they will be helpful to readers interested in pursuing the topics and issues raised in this collection.

I. Books by Foucault

The Archaeology of Knowledge. Trans. A. M. Sheridan Smith. New York: Harper Colophon, 1972.

Madness and Civilization: A History of Insanity in the Age of Reason. Trans. R. Howard. New York: Vintage/Random House, 1973.

The Order of Things: An Archaeology of the Human Sciences. New York: Vintage/Random House, 1973.

The Birth of the Clinic: An Archaeology of Medical Perception. Trans. A. M. Sheridan Smith. New York: Vintage/Random House, 1975.

Discipline and Punish: The Birth of the Prison. Trans. Alan Sheridan. New York: Vintage/Random House, 1979.

The History of Sexuality, Volume I: An Introduction. Trans. Robert Hurley. New York: Vintage/Random House, 1980.

The Use of Pleasure, Volume 2 of The History of Sexuality. Trans. Robert Hurley. New York: Pantheon, 1985.

The Care of the Self, Volume 3 of The History of Sexuality. Trans. Robert Hurley. New York: Pantheon, 1986.

In Collaboration

I, Pierre Riviere, Having Slaughtered My Mother, My Sister and My Brother . . . A Case of Parricide in the 19th Century. Trans. F. Jellinek. New York: Pantheon, 1975.

Herculine Barbin: Being the Recently Discovered Memoirs of a Nineteenth Century French Hermaphrodite. Trans. Richard McDougall. New York: Pantheon, 1980.

II. Collections and Interviews

Language, Counter-Memory, Practice: Selected Essays and Interviews. Ed. Donald F. Bouchard. Ithaca, N.Y.: Cornell University Press, 1977.

Michel Foucault: Power, Truth, Strategy. Ed. Meaghan Morris and Paul Patton. Sydney: Feral Publications, 1979.

Power/Knowledge: Selected Interviews and Other Writings, 1972–1977. Ed. Colin Gordon. New York: Pantheon, 1980.

The Foucault Reader. Ed. Paul Rabinow. New York: Pantheon, 1984.

"Power and Sex: An Interview." *Telos* 32 (Summer 1977): 152–61.

"Politics and the Study of Discourse." *Ideology and Consciousness* 3 (1978): 7–26.

"A Conversation with Michel Foucault." *Christopher Street*, no. 64 (May 1982): 36–41.

"Sexual Choice, Sexual Act: An Interview." *Salmagundi* 58–59 (Fall 1982–Winter 1983): 10–24.

"Final Interview; Michel Foucault." *Raritan Review* 5 (Summer 1985): 1–13.

III. Works on Foucault

Balbus, Isaac. "Disciplining Women: Michel Foucault and the Power of Feminist Discourse." *Praxis International* 5 (4 January 1986): 466–83.

Butler, Judith. "Variations on Sex and Gender: Beauvoir, Wittig, and Foucault." *Praxis International* 5 (4 January 1986): 505–16.

Dreyfus, Hubert L., and Paul Rabinow. *Michel Foucault: Beyond Structuralism and Hermeneutics*. 2nd ed. With an Afterword and Interview with Michel Foucault. Chicago: University of Chicago Press, 1983.

Ferguson, Kathy E. *The Feminist Critique of Bureaucracy*. Philadelphia: Temple University Press, 1984.

Fraser, Nancy. "Foucault's Body-Languages: A Post-Humanist Political Rhetoric?" *Salmagundi* 61 (Fall 1983): 55–70.

———. "Foucault on Modern Power: Empirical Insights and Normative Confusions." *Praxis International* 1 (October 1981): 272–87.

———. "Michel Foucault: A 'Young Conservative'?" *Ethics* 96 (October 1985): 165–84.

Hoy, David Couzens, ed. *Foucault: A Critical Reader*. New York: Basil Blackwell, 1986.

Kurzweil, Edith. "Michel Foucault's History of Sexuality as Interpreted by Feminists and Marxists." *Social Research* 53 (Winter 1986): 647–63.

Lemert, Charles C., and Garth Gillan. *Michel Foucault: Social Theory and Transgression*. New York: Columbia University Press, 1982.

Merquior, J. G. *Foucault*. Berkeley: University of California Press, 1987.

Ostrander, Greg. "Foucault's Disappearing Body." *Body Digest, Canadian Journal of Political and Social Theory/Revue Canadienne de théorie politique et sociale* 11 (1987): 120–33.

Poster, Mark. *Foucault, Marxism and History*. Cambridge: Polity Press, 1984.

Rajchman, John. "Ethics After Foucault." *Social Text* 13/14 (Winter/Spring 1986): 165–83.

———. *Michel Foucault: The Freedom of Philosophy*. New York: Columbia University Press, 1985.

Schor, Naomi. "Dreaming Dissymmetry: Barthes, Foucault, and Sexual Difference." In *Men in Feminism*, eds. Alice Jardine and Paul Smith. New York: Methuen, 1987.

Sheridan, Alan. *Michel Foucault: The Will to Truth*. New York: Tavistock Publications, 1980.

Smart, Barry. *Michel Foucault*. New York: Tavistock Publications, 1985.

White, Stephen K. "Foucault's Challenge to Critical Theory." *American Political Science Review* 80 (June 1986): 419–32.

Index

Abakanowicz, Magdalena, 145
Abbot, Edwin A., 142
Abortion politics, 26, 197–98
Academia; and scholar as subject, 159; women's role in, 140–42, 214
Actuality, 158–59
Addams, Jane, 104, 202
Against Our Will: Men, Women, and Rape (Brownmiller), 170–71
Agoraphobia, 111, 115
Althusser, Louis, 27, 31
Amazon Odyssey (Atkinson), 40
Anatomy, political, 62
The Anatomy of Melancholy (Burton), 106
Anorexia nervosa, xviii, 87–117; and androgyny, 95, 114n63; and body-building, 98–99; and bulimia, 113n43, 114n60; causes of, 111n9; in commercials, 108–9; and control, 96–100; as cultural obsession, 65; definition, 110n2; and dream of immortality, 100; and flapper image, 108–9, 117; and gender associations, 101–9; as historically related to Platonic and Augustinian doctrine, 94–95; and image of women as voracious, 105–7, 108; increase of in low-income groups, 111n11, n13; and intellectuality, 98, 101; and motherhood, 115n–116n78; and

nineteenth-century hysteria, 103–4, 106–7; and obsession with hunger, 93–94; as protest, 105; and self, 94, 101; and sex abuse, 113n42; synchronicity with other cultural forms, 90
Antigone (Sophocles), 126
Anti-Oedipus (Deleuze and Guattari), 46
Anzaldúa, Gloria, 202–3
Archaeology, xvii; of knowledge, 49–50, 51. *See also* Genealogy
The Archaeology of Knowledge (Foucault), xvii, 50
Arendt, Hannah, 126, 128, 129, 132n11
Artemidorus, 53
Atkinson, Ti-Grace, 40
Augustine, 92, 93
Austen, Jane 160–62
Austen-Leigh, James, 160
Austerity, image of, 52, 55
Authenticity. *See* Truth
Authority, xv xvi, xviii, 43; as androcentric, 122; as augmentation, 126–28, 131; vs. compassion, 120–21, 128–30; definition, 119–20; in Demeter-Persephone myth, 127; development of in society, 79–80; and discipline, 75; and discourse, xv–xvi, 120–21, 129–31; exclusion of